Edwin Martin Stone

History of Beverly, Civil and Ecclesiastical: From Its Settlement in 1630 to 1842

Edwin Martin Stone

History of Beverly, Civil and Ecclesiastical: From Its Settlement in 1630 to 1842

Reprint of the original, first published in 1843.

1st Edition 2024 | ISBN: 978-3-38511-277-3

Verlag (Publisher): Outlook Verlag GmbH, Zeilweg 44, 60439 Frankfurt, Deutschland
Vertretungsberechtigt (Authorized to represent): E. Roepke, Zeilweg 44, 60439 Frankfurt, Deutschland
Druck (Print): Books on Demand GmbH, In de Tarpen 42, 22848 Norderstedt, Deutschland

HISTORY OF BEVERLY,

CIVIL AND ECCLESIASTICAL,

FROM ITS SETTLEMENT IN 1630 TO 1842.

BY EDWIN M. STONE.

BOSTON:
JAMES MUNROE AND COMPANY.
1843.

DUTTON AND WENTWORTH'S

Printing-House.

PREFACE

It is gratifying to perceive that the interest of late awakened in town histories is increasing. Until each town in the Commonwealth shall have had its historian, the most accurate history of Massachusetts will remain to be written. It is to be regretted that the work, in which for six months I have been constantly engaged, had not been undertaken at an earlier period. Had it been written at the commencement of the present century, many most interesting incidents, recorded only in the memory of aged inhabitants, would have been preserved, which are now irrecoverably lost.

In the preparation of this volume, I have made a thorough examination of the town records, the State archives, the collections of several historical societies, and a large number of private papers, amounting in all to nearly twenty thousand manuscript pages. Much information has also been obtained from individuals who were contemporaries of the Revolution, and from others whose antiquarian research has been minute and successful. My other principal authorities are Hutchinson's and Hubbard's Histories, Felt's Annals of Salem, and the Massachusetts Historical Society's Collections. But with all my care, it is possible some resource has remained undiscovered, though it is confidently believed no material documentary fact has been overlooked.

A considerable number of the following pages will be found under the ecclesiastical head. For the sake of unity, this portion

of the history has been separated from that belonging more strictly to the civil department: and with which, until the formation of
the second parish in 1713, it was blended. In preparing the
ecclesiastical history, I have had access to the parish and church
records of the several religious societies. From these I have
drawn such matter only as seemed proper to a work of this character, and with that I have interwoven materials placed at my
command by members of the different congregations.

It was a part of my original design to furnish genealogical
tables of all the families represented by the signers of the petition
for the first church, in 1666; but a few days of laborious investigation convinced me that such a plan was impracticable, and I
have confined a detailed genealogy to the principal founders of
the town.

To Hon. Robert Rantoul, whose long connexion with the public affairs of the town, together with much investigation, has
made him familiar with its early history, I am greatly indebted,
both for the free use of his manuscript lectures on Beverly, delivered before the lyceum in 1830, '31 and '32, and for other very
valuable assistance.

To Rev. Christopher T. Thayer, also, I am obligated for various interesting materials, and other important service, as well as
for a generous interest taken in the enterprize from its commencement. My acknowledgments are likewise due to Hon. George
Bancroft and Rev. Joseph B. Felt, of Boston, Samuel F. Haven,
Esq., librarian of the American Antiquarian Society, at Worcester, and to many gentlemen of this town, who have kindly aided
my inquiries.

E. M. S.

BEVERLY, 1842.

HISTORY OF BEVERLY.

TOPOGRAPHY.

BEVERLY, in Essex county, Massachusetts, is in north latitude 42° 36′, and longitude 70° 53′, west of London. It is situated on Massachusetts Bay, 16 $\frac{92}{100}$ miles from Boston,* and 20 from Newburyport. The bordering towns are Salem, Danvers, Wenham and Manchester. It is about 20 miles distant from the extreme point of Cape Ann, and 45 miles from the point of Cape Cod. Its greatest length in a direct line from the brick factory at Frost Fishbrook, the boundary towards Danvers on the west, to Chubb's Creek, the boundary towards Manchester on the east, is about 6$\frac{2}{3}$ miles; and its greatest width, from Tuck's Point, opposite Salem, on the south, to Wenham line on the north, is about 3$\frac{1}{2}$ miles. Its average length is about 5$\frac{2}{3}$ miles, and its width about 2$\frac{2}{3}$.

The soil of Beverly is yellow loam and gravel, mixed with veins of clay and sand. Clay suitable

---

* This distance is measured from the City Hall, in Boston, by the Salem Turnpike, to the First Parish meeting-house.

1

for coarse pottery and bricks, is found in many parts
of the town, and the coarse sand from West's and
other beaches, affords considerable employment to
vessels in which it is transported to Boston for sale.
From the beach between Paul's Head and Curtis
Woodberry's Point, black sand, for the supply of
stationers' shops, has been obtained in considerable
quantities. Being somewhat impure, from mixture
of other sand, it is separated by the use of magnets
which strongly attract the black. Several quarries
furnish an abundance of granite for cellar and sea
walls, fences, &c.; but, owing to its hardness and
darker color when hammered, it is less valued for
buildings than the stone obtained at Rockport. Green
felspar has been found embedded in other stone. In
1824, some fine specimens were obtained from an
excavation made in the lot of land adjoining the
southerly side of the common, which were distributed
among most of the public mineralogical collections in
this country.

The surface of Beverly is hilly. There is much
rocky and unproductive land, yielding poor pasturage; but there is also a good portion of valuable and
fertile soil, adapted to the production of English hay,
Indian corn, rye, oats, barley, potatoes, and various
kinds of vegetables and fruits. Much of the soil is
also adapted to the growth of wheat; but the uncer-
tainty of the crop, resulting from mildew, will probably prevent any general attention to its culture.

The principal wood is pine, oak, walnut, white
maple, birch and hemlock. There is also some elm,
cherry, butternut, red larch, balm of Gilead, sassa-
fras, red and white cedar, with many varieties of
smaller growth. It is supposed that there is more

wood standing now within the limits of the town, than there was thirty or forty years ago, an increased attention having been given to its growth and preservation. Many of the low meadows abound in peat, which, at present, is less used for fuel than it will be when the importation of wood from Maine, the great wood lot for all the sea-ports of Massachusetts, becomes more expensive.

Of shrubs, many of which are valuable for their medicinal properties, may be mentioned the thorn, two kinds of dog-wood, fever-bush, alder, high blueberry, whortleberry, savin, barberry, sweet fern, elder, bayberry, and laurel. The mountain laurel, which is here very abundant, is one of the most elegant shrubs. Its leaves are glossy and evergreen; and its flowers, which appear in June, grow in beautiful clusters, varying in their complexion from white to rose. There is also a dwarf laurel familiarly known as *lamb kill*, bearing clusters of delicate rose-colored flowers; but being common it attracts little admiration. The barberry bush bears a sensitive flower, which, if touched on the inside, immediately closes.

Beverly is by no means destitute of interest to the votaries of Flora. Of the flowers and flowering shrubs in the vicinity of Boston, catalogued by Bigelow, a very large number have been identified in this town by those skilled in botany; and probably many more may be found which have not fallen in the way of desultory observation. Besides those already named, the Side-Saddle flower, the Cardinal flower, so highly prized in Europe, the Swamp Pink, the bulbous Arethusa, the side-flowering Scullcap, recommended as a specific for hydrophobia, the modest Violet family, the Ladies' Slipper, the Marsh Marigold,

the Canadian Rhodora, the Crane's-bill and Solomon's
Seal, the sweet-scented Water Lily, the Autumnal
and veiny-leaved Hawkweed, the Buckbean and wild
Primrose, the scarlet Pimpernel, the Eglantine, and
many others, are here found in great profusion, beau-
tifying nature, and impregnating the atmosphere with
a delicious fragrance, themselves

> "But bright thoughts syllabled to shape and hue,
> The tongue that erst was spoken by the elves,
> When tenderness as yet within the world was new."

The fields and woods furnish the whole tribe of useful "roots and herbs," decoctions of which, when
seasonably administered, are often a sufficient substitute for more formidable medical prescriptions.

Beverly is well watered by springs and brooks,
though it cannot boast of any considerable streams.
Bass or Naumkeag river, takes its rise near the western boundary of the first parish, and after running in
a south-westerly course about a mile and a half, unites
at Ellingwood's Point with Porter's river. These waters form Beverly harbor. The noticeable brooks
are, Alewife brook, emptying into Ipswich river,—
one near the East Farms school-house, which carries
a saw-mill a part of the year,—and those running
under Hart's and Thissel's bridges, each of which
formerly supported a grist mill. Near Frost Fish
brook, and adjacent to the bridge in Conant street,
the late William Burley, during the last war, erected a brick factory for manufacturing cotton cloth;
but a deficiency of water, combined with other circumstances, induced an abandonment of the project.

The most considerable pond within the limits of
Beverly, is Beaver pond, situated about two hundred

rods south of Wenham line, and about half a mile east of Brimble Hill. It is a beautiful sheet of water, covering about 20 acres, and affords Perch, Yellow Shiners, Eels, Pickerel, and a shell-fish resembling the Muscle of the seashore. Another small sheet of water, called Round pond, is in the second parish, near the "Baker Tavern," and a few rods east of the road to Newburyport. It covers, perhaps, half an acre, and its circular margin is deeply fringed with high blueberry and other shrubs. It is said to be very deep, and no fish are known to exist there. It is probable that, at a remote period, the water covered the entire swamp in the midst of which it lies concealed, and which now sustains a large growth of wood.

The only mineral spring known in Beverly, is situated near the western foot of Snake Hill. From its chalybeate impregnation, it is called Iron Mine Spring. Iron ore is found near this spring, and for a time was worked, but not with sufficient profit to warrant a continuance of the business. The water has been used medicinally, but its effect has not been sufficiently powerful to attract much the attention of invalids.

Water from wells in this town, is obtained in great abundance, and of excellent quality. Those sunk in the south part of the town, or between the rise of land near the harbor, and twenty rods northerly of the first parish meeting-house, are from forty to fifty-three feet in depth. In other parts of the town, water is obtained by sinking a shaft from ten to thirty feet. A proprietors' well, opposite the Bank, fifty-three feet in depth, was built about sixty years ago, at an expense of more than eleven hundred dollars. Another pro-

1*

prietors' well at the corner of Bartlett and Cabot
streets, was also sunk at great cost.

The principal eminences in the town, are Browne,
Brimble, Cue, Snake, Prospect, Christian, and Bald
hills—on the latter of which, the town, in 1705,
granted Samuel Corning liberty to build a wind mill.
Browne hill received its name from the Hon. William Browne, a wealthy citizen of Salem, who owned
the estate extending to the lane near the corner of
Liberty and Conant streets.   He was the son of Hon.
Samuel and Abigail Browne, and was born May 7th,
1709.   He was educated at Harvard University,
where he graduated in 1727.   In 1737, he married
Mary, daughter of Governor Burnet, who died July
31, 1745.   His second wife was Mary, daughter of
Philip French, Esq., of Brunswick, N. J.   He had
eight children, and during his life-time filled the offices of Justice of the Sessions Court, Representative in
the General Court, and member of the Executive
Council.

About 1750, Mr. Browne erected a splendid mansion on the summit of this hill, to which he gave the
name of "Browne Hall," after a place in Lanca-
shire, England, that belonged to his ancestors.   This
building consisted of two wings, two stories high, connected by a spacious hall, the whole presenting a front
of seventy feet.   The floor of the hall was painted in
imitation of mosaick, and springing from the wall
was a commodious circular gallery.   Adjacent to the
house, was a building occupied solely by the domes-
tics, all of whom were blacks.   The dwelling was
finished in the most thorough and costly manner, and
was furnished in a style corresponding with the
wealth of its owner.   This hall was the scene of

many magnificent entertainments—and on one occasion an ox was roasted whole and served up to a numerous dinner party. The farmhouse stood at the foot of the hill. About 1761, Mr. Browne removed this delightful residence from the hill to a site near Liberty corner. He lived but about two years after, and expired suddenly in his field, of apoplexy, April 27th, 1763, aged 54. A manuscript note in the Archives of the Worcester Antiquarian Society, says: "He was a most polite gentleman, well read in history and geography." He bequeathed a gilt cup to his son William, which once belonged to the lady of Bishop Burnet, and £1000 old tenor to a society in England for propagating the gospel among the American Indians. After Mr. Browne's decease, the estate became the property of Richard Derby, Esq., of Salem. During his occupancy of it, February 22d, 1790, the barn was burned, and thirty-six head of cattle with it. The estate was subsequently purchased by the late William Burley, who disposed of the mansion, which was removed in parts by several purchasers.

BROWNE HALL.

From this hill, opens to the beholder a prospect of surpassing beauty and grandeur. His eye scans an

immense panorama of hill and dale, of forest and
lawn, teeming with animation, and sending up to his
ear the hum of busy life—the lowing of herds and
the cheerful notes of the feathered tribes, blending
rural sounds with the bustle of town and city. Before him, Beverly spreads out as a map, dotted with
churches and school-houses—those objects here in
New England, so happily and gloriously united, and
that bring to his mind's vision the spirit of puritan
forecast, which provided simultaneously for the culture of the intellect and the improvement of the heart.
A little to the north lies Wenham, with its charming
lake ; and still further on, the solitary spire of Hamilton church is seen, pointing heavenward, and relieved by the rich back-ground of Ipswich hills. Turning
himself slowly round, his eyes rest successively on
the valley of Topsfield, remarkable for the superior
intensity of its atmospheric light, while the far-away
mountains veil their heads in clouds—on Danvers
Plains, the Salem Village of "the olden time," whose
proverbial enterprize has obliterated almost every
memorial of the painful and fatal scenes of witch-
craft-folly—on Salem, the city of peace, where the
godly Higginson planted and nurtured the vine
whose prolific energy fruited the New England
churches — on Marblehead, with its iron-bound
shore, emblematical of the hardy spirit of its enterprizing and patriotic inhabitants, and to promote the
moral good of whom, the pious Avery encountered a
watery grave; and, finally, to perfect the view, on
Massachusetts Bay, which, flashing with silvery
light, tossing in giant sportiveness her glittering
foam-cap aloft, mingling her charms with indented
shores, rugged promontories, and countless patches of

russet and green, and bearing on her proudly heaving bosom, the sails of many and distant climes, stretches out and out, as if to mock the feebleness of sight, until she receives and reciprocates the embrace of the mighty Atlantic.

A prospect, of nearly equal beauty, is afforded from Cherry Hill, formerly the estate of the late Joseph White, of Salem, but now the property of Capt. John Hammond. Its proximity to Wenham Pond,* one hundred and seven acres of which lie within the limits of Beverly, the distant view of the ocean, the various scenery of the surrounding country, combine, with the salubrity of its situation, to render it one of the most desirable residences in this vicinity. The mansion, as seen through a long avenue of fruit trees, shaded at its upper termination by two finely branching elms, presents a handsome appearance; and from its top Capt. White, with the aid of a glass, frequently descried his vessels making the port of Salem before their approach was known in the city. A delightful and extensive view of the harbor and adjacent region is had from the summer-house in the

---

* The surface of this beautiful sheet of water measures 320 acres, and is 34 feet higher than the flow of the tide at the head of Bass river. It is well stored with fish, and is much resorted to by the lovers of piscatory amusements. Alewives formerly came up to this pond to spawn, but the dam on Ipswich river, and other obstructions, have nearly stopped their access to it. The water is very pure, and the proximity of the rail-road affords facilities for profitable engagement in the ice business during the winter months. On the northern side of this pond is a conical hill, called Peters' Pulpit. It is said Hugh Peters, one of the early ministers of the First Church in Salem, once addressed a large audience from its top. His text was, John iii. 23, " At Enon, near Salem, because there was much water there." Enon was the original name of Wenham, and the territory of Salem, at that time, joined it.

garden of Mr. George Brown, from the cupola of
Bell's building, and from various other points. The
picturesque view afforded from Ellingwood's Point,
is unsurpassed by any water prospect in this vicinity; and the admirer of nature, who stands on Paul's
Head, at the opening and close of day, will see the
sun rise from his watery bed with a glory, and de-
scend behind the western hills with a gorgeousness,
of which Italy itself might be proud.

Nature has beautifully delineated Beverly, and
marked it for a town. The southern quarter, opposite Salem, combines, for commercial purposes, the
advantages of a commodious and safe harbor, salu-
brious air, and dry, elevated land, well suited for
building. From Essex Bridge, the elevation along
the rail-road track, towards Newburyport, gradually
increases till it reaches more than fifty feet, the summit
level at the corner near Col. Jesse Shelden's, when it as
gradually slopes toward Wenham. The streets are of
commodious width, and generally ornamented with
shade trees; and several, running easterly from the
main street to the marginal one threading the harbor,
present a very handsome appearance. The principal
highways, all of which are bordered with many excellent farms, are, the road leading from Salem to
Newburyport, which makes the main street of the
town,—the road to Cape Ann, which, as it winds its
way along the seashore the whole distance, affords
an exceedingly pleasant and romantic drive,—the
road through Rial Side to Danvers Neck,—Conant
street, which intersects Liberty street (running from
the Neck to the Topsfield road), and leads to Danvers Plains,—and the road from the second parish
meeting-house to Topsfield.

The road from Essex bridge to Wenham is exceedingly crooked, having many acute angles and large curvatures, besides innumerable smaller sinuosities. In this respect, however, it is not singular. Before a way had been discovered of passing from Woodberry's Point, to a settlement made very early at the head of Bass river, except by following the seashore and the margin of the river, it is said a heifer was driven from the Point to the latter place around the shore, and left to remain there. The animal, not liking her new abode, set out to return home through the woods, which she reached before her driver. Instead of pronouncing her bewitched, as probably would have been done some fifty or sixty years later, her tracks were traced, and a path thereby discovered, which subsequently became a road of communication between the two places. The road thus laid out by this four-footed commissioner of highways, has not, since that time, been improved much in its direction. Two hundred years still leave us in possession of many highways, whose numerous windings bear ample testimony to the same scientific origin, and it is quite possible that the road first mentioned was surveyed and laid out by an engineer of a kindred corps.

The natural advantages of Beverly, to which reference has been made, have not been neglected. From the Salem side, the town, with its wharves, storehouses and shipping, presents the compact aspect of a commercial place. As the stranger crosses the bridge, and enters the heart of the main village, he is favorably impressed with the air of comfort and business which the numerous handsomely finished dwellings and shops exhibit; nor is he less gratified as he proceeds, when the well-tilled fields, substantial farm-houses, and picturesque scenery of the second parish open to his view. It is no vain boasting to say, that this town combines as many natural and acquired advantages as any other, of similar territory and population, in Essex county. Nor, it is believed, will the lover of nature elsewhere find more ample means for indulging the senses, or wider scope for the exercise of imagination.

SETTLEMENT.

BEVERLY originally formed a part of the Naumkeag territory, belonging to John, Sagamore of Agawam, which also included Salem, Marblehead, Manchester, Wenham, Danvers, part of Topsfield and of Middleton.* This chief gladly welcomed the colonists, to whom he looked for protection against his powerful enemies, the Tarrantines, and made them a free grant of this entire territory. In 1700, the grandchildren of the Sagamore set up a claim to Beverly, which was cancelled by the payment of £6 6s. 8d., and a formal deed taken.

It was supposed by the late Rev. Dr. Bentley, whose familiarity with the early history of this country entitles his opinions to great weight, that the first settlement within the original limits of Salem was made on Bass river or "Cape Ann Side," as it is styled in the ancient records. He pointed out a spot near Tuck's Point, as the locality of the first fort

---

* Naumkeag, it is well known, was the name of Salem. Mather writes it *Nahumkeick*, on which he has the following comment: "I have somewhere met with an odd observation that the name of it was rather Hebrew than Indian: for *Nahum* signifies comfort, and *Keick* signifies an haven; and our English not only found it an *haven of comfort*, but happened also to put an Hebrew name upon it; for they called it Salem, for the peace which they had and hoped in it: and so it is called unto this day."—*Magnalia, vol.* 1, *p.* 63.

2

erected for the protection of settlers. But since his decease, the error of this opinion has been satisfactorily ascertained. The fort referred to was established on Naugus' Head, nearly opposite fort Pickering, at the entrance of Salem harbor.

The first permanent settlement in this town was effected by Roger Conant, John and William Woodberry, and John Balch, about 1630. It commenced at Curtis Woodberry's Point, whence it extended to Mackerel Cove and other parts. There are reasons for the belief, that at an early period, perhaps not long before the settlement of Salem in 1626, Beverly was an Indian residence. In removing the earth on the westerly margin of Bartlett swamp in 1834, flat stones placed in a circular form, on which fire had been made, and also charcoal and clam-shells, were found near a spring of fresh water. Similar remains have been discovered on the shore west of the mouth of Bass river.

According to a current tradition, one of the first houses erected in this town, was on Woodberry's Point, near the residence of John Prince. It was a large double house, constructed for defence against an enemy, and called the garrison house. It was framed of oak after the fashion of the times, and was taken down about forty years ago. A settlement by an Ellingwood (probably Ralph) was early made on Fox's or Ellingwood's Point. The flats from the old ferry-way to this Point, were granted by Salem to one of the Ellingwood's, in compensation for supporting a pauper by the name of Lambert. The deed of this grant is extant.

There is a tradition, that the first child born in this town, was of the name of Dixey. William Dixey settled on Bass-river-side soon after Conant; and if the tradition is founded in fact, it is probable this child was his. Dixey was admitted freeman 1634, and died in 1690, aged 82.

On 27th October, 1647, the inhabitants of Mackerel Cove were, on petition, released from being called to watch in Salem, except in seasons of danger; and in 1665, the Bass river settlement was permitted by the General Court, to exercise some of the powers of a town, though still subordinate to Salem. These were, to choose selectmen, and raise the charges to be defrayed by and within themselves—to provide for the poor that desired to inhabit with them—to choose their constables and surveyors of highways, and whatever other officers it might be necessary to employ,—with a distinct understanding, however, that in town and country charges, in common interest and concern, and in the choice of Deputies to the General Court, they were to act in concert with Salem.

Three years subsequent to this arrangement, Oct. 14, 1668, Bass-river-side was incorporated as a distinct township by the name of Beverly, and Salem was required to furnish suitable lands and bounds. These bounds excluded Rial-side, and all the territory within the present limits of the town, west of Bass river and Horse brook, which were not set off from Salem until 1753.

The first town meeting subsequent to incorporation, was held Nov. 23, 1668, at which Capt. Thomas Lothrop, Wm. Dixey, Wm. Dodge, sen., John West and Paul Thorndike, were chosen selectmen. These officers were sometimes called *townsmen*, a name significant of their public character, and were selected from among the most worthy of the citizens. For

a long time "they united in their office the powers
and duties of Overseers of the poor, Assessors of
taxes, Surveyors of highways, and at one time,
judicial powers to try civil causes of small amount.
And although their powers are now more restricted,
they are still looked up to as the fathers of the town,
whose prudential affairs they are to order and man-
age according to a sound discretion."

Great dissatisfaction appears early to have existed
with the name of the town; so much so, that in 1671,
Roger Conant, with thirty-four others, petitioned the
General Court for its alteration. As the petition
assigns all the known reasons for a change, it is
given entire, with the orthography unaltered.

Petition of Roger Conant, May 28, 1671.

To the honored General Court, consisting of Magistrates and Deputees, (the 28th of the 3d month,
1671.)

The humble petition of Roger Conant, of Bass
river alias Beverly, who hath bin a planter in New
England fortie yeers and upwards, being one of the
first, if not the very first, that resolved and made
good my settlement under in matter of plantation
with my family in this collony of the Massachusets
Bay, and have bin instrumental, both for the founding and carriing on of the same; and when in the
infancy thereof it was in great hazard of being de-
serted, I was a means, through grace assisting me,
to stop the flight of those few that then were heere
with me, and that by my utter deniall to goe away
with them, who would have gon either for England,
or mostly for Virginia, but thereupon stayed to the
hassard of our lives

Now my umble suite and request is unto this honorable Court, onlie that the name of our towne or plantation may be altered or changed from Beverly and be called Budleigh. I have two reasons that have moved me unto this request. The first is the great dislike and discontent of many of our people for this name of Beverly, because (we being but a small place) it hath caused on us a constant nickname of *Beggarly*, being in the mouths of many, and no order was given, or consent by the people to their agent for any name, until we were shure of being a town granted in the first place.

Secondly. I being the first that had house in Salem, (and neither had any hand in naming either that or any other town,) and myself with those that were then with me, being all from the western part of England, desire this western name of Budleigh, a market towne in Devonshire, and neere unto the sea as wee are heere in this place, and where myself was borne. Now in regard of our firstnesse and antiquity in this soe famous a collony, we should umblie request this small preveledg with your favors and consent, to give this name above said, unto our town. I never yet made sute or request unto the Generall Court for the least matter, tho' I thinke I might as well have done, as many others have, who have obtained much without hazard of life, or preferring the public good before their own interest, which, I praise God, I have done.

If this my sute, may find acceptation with your worships, I shall rest umbly thankfull, and my praises shall not cease unto the throne of grace, for God's guidance and his blessing to be on all your waightie proceedings, and that iustice and righteousness may be everie where taught and practised throughout this wilderness, to all posterity, which God grant. Amen.

Your worships' umble petitioner and servant,

ROGER CONANT.

At this time Conant was upwards of eighty years old, and it may be presumed the name of his native Budleigh possessed for him the charm of early association. But neither his venerable age, the services he had performed, nor yet " the umble desire and request" of a very considerable part of the male inhabitants of the place, availed to obtain the object of his petition. And June 1, 1671, the Court gave for reply, that " the magistrates having perused and considered this request, see no cause to alter the name of the place as desired, their brethren the deputies hereto consenting." Beverly in England, is a town of considerable note in the East-riding of Yorkshire, and was once the residence of John de Beverly, Archbishop of York, who died May 7th, 721. It is probable that from this town Beverly in Massachusetts derived its name, and though the present generation may sympathise with the aged Conant and his associates in the disappointment of their request, they will not regret that the original corporate name was retained in preference to the less euphonious one of *Budleigh*.

Roger Conant, as stated in his petition, was born in Budleigh, England, in April, 1591. He was the son of Richard and Agnes Conant, and grandson of John Conant, who descended from worthy parents of Gettisham, near Honiton, and whose ancestors were of French extraction. He was brother to Dr. John Conant, of Exeter. College, one of the Assembly Divines. In 1623, he emigrated to Plymouth, where he remained until 1625, when, in company with Rev. Mr. Lyford, he removed to Nantasket. He remained there but a short time, and proceeded to Cape Ann, where he was invested with the superintendence of the Dorchester company engaged in the fishery and agricultural pursuits, being in fact the first Governor in the Colony of Massachusetts Bay, though not the Chief Magistrate of a Province. The trial of a year at Cape Ann, was sufficient to satisfy Conant and his company, that the prospect of gain was hopeless, and in 1626 he removed to Salem as a more favorable locality, and settled on the neck of land between Collins' Cove and the North River. His principal companions were John Woodberry, John Balch and Peter Palfrey. Here he was severely tried by the disaffection of most of his company, who, through privation, the fear of Indian hostilities, and an invitation to accompany their late pastor, Mr. Lyford, to Virginia, were strongly inclined to abandon the settlement. In this critical juncture, he remained firm and true to the interests of the company. He declared his intention to continue though all should depart; and by his decided and hopeful tone, revived the drooping courage of his associates, and induced them to relinquish their design.* He discharged the principal offices in Salem for several years, and represented that place in the General Court. He was an original member of the first church in Salem, and was made freeman in 1630. In 1635, he received, in connexion with several others, a grant of land at the head of Bass river; and on his petition

* Mather's Magnalia, i. p. 62.

as "an ancient planter" in 1671, the General Court
granted him 200 acres more.* He took a patriarchal
interest in the affairs of this town until his decease,
Nov. 19th, 1679, in the 89th year of his age. Mather
styles him "a most religious, prudent and worthy
gentleman;" graces that eminently qualified him for
the duties he was called to discharge, and which, in
one instance at least, enabled him to adjust a difficulty between contending parties at Cape Ann that
threatened bloodshed.†

Roger Conant had four sons, Lot, Roger, Exercise
and Joshua. The latter died in 1659.

Lot, probably the oldest son, was born in 1624,
and was among the original members of the first
church in this town in 1667. He had ten children,
viz: Samuel, John, Lot, Elizabeth, Mary, Martha,
William and Sarah, (twins,) Roger and Rebecca.
In 1662, he lived in Marblehead.

Roger, his second son, was the first male born in
Salem—on account of which, in 1640, he received a
grant of twenty acres of land. He came to Beverly
with his father, and previously to 1674, resided in

---

* The grant from Salem runs as follows : "4th of the 11th
month, (Jan.) 1635. That Capt. (William) Traske, Jno. Woodberry,
Mr Conant, Peter Palfrey and John Balch, are to have 5 farmes, viz :
each 200 acres a peise, to forme in all a thousand acres of land
together, lying and being at the head of Bass river, 124 poles
in breadth, and soe runin northerly to the river by the great pond
side, and soe in breadth, making up the full quantity of a thousand acres, these being laid out and surveyed by vs.

JOHN WOODBERRY,
JOHN BALCH."

Palfrey never settled on his grant. He removed to Reading,
where he died July 15th, 1663.

† Hubbard's Hist. N. E. pp. 106—111.

Marblehead. He had a son Roger, who had a son Ebenezer, born Dec. 30th, 1698.

Exercise was, probably, born in Beverly. He was baptized at Salem, Dec. 24, 1637; was made freeman 1663, and was set off with other petitioners for a church in this town in 1667. He appears to have been an active and useful citizen, and represented the town in General Court, in 1682, 1684. The births of three of his children are recorded, viz: Elizabeth, Josiah and Caleb.

John Woodberry, another of the original settlers of this town, came from Somersetshire, England, under the direction of the Dorchester company, which established itself at Cape Ann about 1624. He came to Salem with Conant, Balch and others, in 1626, and the next year went to England as an agent for procuring supplies. He returned in 1628, and was made a freeman in 1630. In 1635, he was chosen deputy to the General Court—and again in 1638, besides which, he was appointed to several offices of trust in town. He was an original member of the first church in Salem. In 1636, he received a grant of two hundred acres of land on Bass river. He was an energetic, faithful and worthy man, and took an active part in the settlement and transactions of the colony. He died in 1641, having lived to see his perils, sufferings and toils contribute to prepare a refuge for his countrymen.

Humphrey, son of John Woodberry, was born in 1609, came to N. England with his father in 1628, was admitted to the church in Salem 1648, was member of the first church in Beverly at its formation, was chosen deacon in 1668, and was living in 1681. Peter, son of Humphrey, was born in 1640. He was made a freeman in 1668, and elected representative in 1689. He also filled the office of deacon, and died July 5th, 1704, aged 64. Peter, jr. his son, was born in 1664, and died Jan. 8th, 1706, aged 42 years. He also filled the office of deacon. He owned the estate, now the property of Mr. Benjamin Woodberry, in the second parish, and resided in the same house. His widow, Mary, survived him fifty-seven years, and died Nov. 20th, 1763, in the 90th year of her age. Peter, jr., had also a son Peter, who was born June 20th, 1705, and died May 14th, 1775. John, a son of the last named Peter, was born Nov. 8th, 1743, and died Sept. 3d, 1813, in the 70th year of his age. He had six children, viz : John, Peter, Hannah, Mary, James and Benjamin. The homestead has remained in the family since the first settlement.

Josiah Woodberry, son of the first named Peter, was born June 15th, 1682, and lived in the second parish. He had a son Peter, who removed to Mt. Vernon, N. H. (then Amherst,) in 1773, and died at Antrim, N. H., aged 85. His son, Hon. Peter Woodberry, was born in Beverly in 1767, and removed to New Hampshire, with his father. He engaged in mercantile and agricultural pursuits. He was about fifteen years member of the House of Representatives, two years a State Senator, and for more than thirty years held the commission of Justice of the Peace. He died at Francistown, N. H., in 1834. He had five sons, Hon. Levi Woodbury, late Secretary of the U. S. Treasury, P. P. Woodbury, George Washington, (settled in Latantia, Miss.) Jesse and James. His wife was the daughter of James Woodbury, who was born in Beverly, removed to Mt.

Vernon, N. H., 1782, and died at Francistown, 1823, aged 86. James was an under officer in Col. Robert Rogers' regiment of Rangers, and was near Wolfe when he fell at the storming of Quebec. The sword he wore in that service is now in the possession of a descendant.

William Woodberry, brother to the first named John, is mentioned in the Salem records in 1639, and his wife Elizabeth in 1640. He had a son Nicholas who died May 16, 1686, aged about 69. He married Anna Paulsgrave, who died June 10, 1701, aged about 75. His daughter Abigail married an Ober, and died Jan. 28, 1727, aged 86. Nicholas had a son Nicholas, born in 1657, died Oct. 13, 1691, aged 34. From John and William Woodberry, all bearing that name in New England probably descended.

John Balch came from Bridgewater, Somersetshire, England. He was an original member of the first church in Salem; was made freeman in 1630, and held various offices of trust. He settled on his grant of land at the head of Bass river, near the present residence of Mr. John Bell, where he died in 1648. He was an intelligent, exemplary and useful citizen. He was twice married, and had three sons, viz: Benjamin, born 1629; John, married to Mary, daughter of Roger Conant, and drowned in crossing the ferry to Beverly, Jan. 16, 1662; Freeborn, who went to England and never returned.

Benjamin had Samuel, b. 1651, d. 1723; John, b. 1654, d. 1738; Joseph, killed at Bloody Brook; and Freeborn, b. 1660, d. 1729. Freeborn lived near Wenham pond. His first wife was a Knowlton, by whom he had Freeborn, (who removed to Bradford,) Benjamin and Mirriam. His second wife was Eliza-

beth Fairfield, by whom he had Elizabeth, Abigail,
Tabatha, William and Mary.   William, son of Freeborn and grandson of Benjamin, was minister of
Bradford—b. 1704, graduated 1724—d. 1792.   He
had seven children, one of whom, William, was
father of Benjamin Balch, of Salem.

Samuel Balch, son of Benjamin, sen., married
Sarah Newmarch 1675—was chosen deacon of the
first church, Oct. 26, 1704; married for second wife,
Martha Butman, 1721; d. Oct. 14, 1723, aged 72.
He had eleven children, viz: Joseph, John, Peter,
Martha, Samuel, Benjamin and John, (twins,) Phebe,
Cornelius, Abigail and Thomas.

John Balch, son of deacon Samuel Balch, b.
1654; married Hannah Denning, Dec. 23, 1674; d.
1738.   He had Israel, Sarah, Caleb, Joshua, David
and Roger.   He owned a large real estate in the
second parish.

To the names of Conant, Woodberry and Balch,
it will be proper to add those of Brackenbury and
Lothrop, as among the most valuable of the early
settlers of Beverly.

Richard Brackenbury came over in Governor Endicott's company in 1628.   The first public business
with which his name is coupled, is in a joint commission from Salem with William Woodberry, Ensign
Dixey, Mr. Conant and Lieut. Lothrop, to "lay out
a way between the ferry at Salem and the head of
Jeffrie's Creek," to "be such a way as a man may
travel on horseback or drive cattle," with the alter-
native, that "if such a way may not be formed,
then to take speedy course to set up a bridge at
Mackerel Cove."   He was a member of the first
church in Salem in 1628, and was made a freeman

in 1630. In 1636, he received a grant of 75 acres of land. He was a member of the first church in Beverly, and took a lively interest in its affairs. His death occurred in 1685, at the age of 85. He left descendants, but the name has become extinct in this town.

Capt. Thomas Lothrop emigrated from England, and during his whole life was distinguished for intelligence, activity and efficiency in public affairs. He settled on " Bass-river-side," where he received a grant of land in 1636. He became a freeman in 1634, and a member of the Salem church in 1636. He represented Salem in General Court for the years 1647, 1653 and 1664, besides holding other important offices. He assisted in founding the first church in 1667, and after the incorporation of this town, he was chosen a selectman, and re-elected to that office from year to year, until his death. He was also chosen representative for several years, and was extensively employed in almost all the public affairs of the town, both civil and ecclesiastical.

In 1644, Lothrop was a lieutenant under Captain Hawthorn, and in 1654, had a captain's command under Major Sedgwick at the capture of St. Johns and Port Royal. He was very desirous of obtaining a bell for the meeting-house in Beverly, and applied to Major Sedgwick for one at St. Johns, but that being already promised, his wish was gratified at Port Royal, by being put in possession of the bell belonging to the "new Friary" of that place, which he transferred to this town. In this expedition Thomas Whittredge and Edward Rayment, of Beverly, held lieutenants' commissions, and William Woodberry, Humphrey Woodberry and Peter Wooden,

3

were pilots. The "plunder" amounted to £740.*

In the early part of King Philip's war, Captain Lothrop was selected to command a company of infantry in the Massachusetts forces, and ordered to the western frontier of the province. This company, styled "the flower of Essex," consisted of young men selected from the best families of the several towns in the county. At this time, the country now embraced in the county of Worcester and the Connecticut river counties, was infested by hostile Indians, and this company performed much hard service at and in the vicinity of Brookfield, making extensive marches through the northern woods in search of the enemy. Hadley being made the head-quarters of the troops stationed in that quarter to protect the settlers, it became necessary to increase the supply of provisions. A considerable quantity of wheat having been preserved in stacks at Deerfield, it was deemed expedient to have it threshed and brought down to Hadley. Capt. Lothrop and his company volunteered as convoy. They passed with safety through the level and closely wooded country, well calculated for a surprize, and at Muddy Brook in South Deerfield, considered themselves, in a great measure, free from danger. The forest here was hung with clusters of grapes; and as the wagons dragged through the heavy soil, it is not unlikely that the teamsters, and possibly a part of the company, may have dispersed to gather them. At this moment of fatal security, seven or eight hundred Indians poured a deadly fire from their ambuscade; and before the sanguinary conflict ceased, Capt. Lothrop and nearly the whole of his command were destroyed. The number who perished, includ-

* Provincial Records.

ing the teamsters, is variously estimated from sixty to ninety, among whom were Josiah Dodge, Peter Woodberry and John Balch of Beverly. The postscript of a letter dated Sept. 22, 1675, and addressed by the Council to Richard Smith in the Narragansett country, gives the following account of this melancholy affair : " This morning we received sad intelligence from Hadley, that upon Saturday last, Capt. Lothrop, with about 60 men, being appointed to conduct from Deerfield to Hadley with carriages and cattle, they were surprized by abundance of Indians that lay in ambushment, and received a dreadful blow, insomuch that about 40 of Capt. Lothrop's men and himself were slain. Capt. Moseley being not far off, engaged with the Indians and fought several hours, and lost 11 men ; others also were slain that were belonging to the carriages, so that the next day they buried 64 men in all. The Indians were judged to be more than 500 men.*

Not long after the " black and fatal day," wherein, says Dr. Increase Mather, " were eight persons made widows, and six and twenty children made fatherless, and about sixty persons buried in one fatal grave," a rude monument was erected near the spot to perpetuate the memory of the slain ; but becoming dilapidated by time, another was erected in 1835, the cornerstone of which was laid Sept. 30th of that year, with appropriate solemnities, and an address by Hon. Edward Everett.

Capt. Lothrop, at the time of his death, was about 65 years of age. He was married to Bethiah, daughter of Joshua Rea, but had no family, and the name in this town is now extinct. His estate, which, as

* Provincial Military Records.

before stated, was received by a grant from the government, was situated in Mackerel Cove, and his house stood near the dwelling of Ebenezer Woodberry. He gave some property to the town; and in 1837, one of the public streets received his name. His widow was married to Joseph Grafton; and his sister Ellen, who came over with him from England, and inherited his property, became the second wife of Ezekiel Cheever, the celebrated schoolmaster at Boston.

"King Philip's war," spread consternation throughout the province. During that brief but sanguinary contest, twelve towns in Massachusetts, Plymouth and Rhode Island, were destroyed, six hundred buildings, mostly dwelling-houses, were burned, and six hundred of the inhabitants fell in battle or were murdered. * Beverly participated in the general alarm; and, as precautionary measures, forts were erected near the meeting-house, at Bass river, at Mackerel Cove, and "near the house of John Dodge, sen." At an early period, and probably previous to this time, a party of hostile savages, it is said, surprized and carried off a family from this town by the name of Foster. They were taken finally to Canada, and seven years elapsed before they recovered their freedom and returned.

In the expedition against the Indians at fort Narragansett in 1675, the following persons from Beverly were engaged, commanded by Capt. Joseph Gardner, of Salem, whose fall, Dec. 19th, was universally lamented. William Balch, William Bonner, Lot Conant, Christopher Read, (wounded,) William Ferryman, Christopher Browne, Moses Morgan, John

* Everett.

Traske, William Allen, John Clark, Richard Huss-band, Thomas Rayment, Ralph Ellingwood, Henry Bayley, Thomas Blashfield, John Ellingwood, Joseph Morgan, William Dodge, Jonathan Biles, William Rayment, Elias Picket, Samuel Harris, John Dodge.*

June 24, 1662, Lawrence Leach died, aged 82. He was proposed for a freeman at Salem in 1630, and was a member of Salem church before 1636, when the town granted him 100 acres of land. He had four sons, Clement, Richard, John and Robert. Clement was married and lived in England. Richard died in 1647, and left a son John, who inherited the estate of his grandfather at Rial-side, known as the "Leach farm." Robert left a son Robert, who was living in 1695. Lawrence Leach held various offices in Salem. The usefulness of his life gained respect for his memory. His widow Elizabeth, died about 1674.

Sept. 20, 1677, a committee of the General Court, consisting of Samuel Appleton, John Whipple and John Fuller, came to Beverly, and after examining the grounds of claim laid by the town, to about 500 acres of land, made a favorable report, which was accepted by the court. This was subsequently reconsidered, and new commissioners were appointed, Oct. 2, 1678, to settle the bounds between Salem Village, Beverly and Wenham.

In the year 1681, great excitement was produced by a claim advanced by the heirs of John Mason to all the territory between the Merrimack and Naum-keag rivers. Of this excitement Beverly partook. The General Court was memorialized, and Rev. Mr. Hale, Capt. Dixy and John Dodge, sen., were chosen

* Provincial Records.

3*

to attend a convention at Ipswich, " to present such
pleas and evidences for the title of the town to its
territory as had been agreed upon," and to unite with
that body in drawing up " something to be presented
to his Majesty, by such messengers as the General
Court shall send."

Among the most material witnesses, were Richard
Brackenbury, William Dixy and Humphrey Woodberry. They testified that the Massachusetts company purchased of the Dorchester company, all their
houses, boats, servants and right at Cape Ann, before
Gov. Endicott's arrival, who subsequently "took
possession of Cape-Ann-side, and soon after laid out
lots for tillage there." It was further given in evidence, that the Indians had been protected by the
colonists who settled at Salem; that they had " free
leave to build and plant" where they had taken up
lands; that the same year or next after they came
to Salem, they cut hay for cattle, which they brought
over on Beverly side, and that they had been in
" possession of Beverly side ever since."*

This claim was agitated until 1691, when the heirs
of Mason, weary, probably, with hereditary litigation,
sold their interest to Samuel Allen, a London merchant, who failing to succeed in a suit instituted
against one of the largest landholders, petitioned the
king to be put in possession of the waste land, which
included all uninclosed and unoccupied lands within,
as well as without, the bounds of settled towns. This
petition was granted; but being again unsuccessful
in subsequent suits, a compromise with the Assembly
of New Hampshire was negotiated, which was broken
off by his sudden death in 1705. In 1706 and 1707,

---

* Annals of Salem, pp. 268, 269.

his son, Thomas Allen of London, prosecuted his claim, but with no better success than his father. After his death in 1715, John Tufton Mason, a grandson of John Mason, suffered a recovery of entail in the Courts of New Hampshire, on the ground that the sale to Allen in 1691, having been made in England, was invalid. Under this recovery, he sold all his interest, in 1746, to several of the principal gentlemen of the province, who, anxious to terminate this perplexing business, relinquished their claim to the towns which had been settled and granted within the limits of their purchase, and adopted a very liberal and popular policy in their grants of other towns. And thus, after a period of nearly one hundred years, the controversy was closed, and the inhabitants of Beverly, as well as all settlers between the Merrimack and Naumkeag rivers, were relieved from further apprehensions concerning the validity of their possessions.*

Nov. 8th, 1686, John Lovett deceased, aged about 76. He was born in 1610, and was one of the eight admitted inhabitants of Salem, July 25th, 1639. At the "seven men's meeting," Nov. 3, 1665, he received a grant of two acres of marsh ground lying near the old planter's meadow in the vicinity of Wenham common. He came early to Beverly, and was at different periods surveyor of highways, constable and selectman. By his will, dated Nov. 8, 1686, it appears he held a large real estate which was devised principally to his children, John, Joseph, Abigail, Mary, Bethiah, and his grandson George Standley. He bequeathed a set of cooper's tools to his son John, and also twenty acres of land on the east side of

* Belknap.

"dirty hole," lying between the lands of his son
Joseph, and his son-in-law George Standley. This
land, now so valuable by its buildings and improvements, is on the east side of Cabot street, somewhere
between the south meeting-house and the bank. Mr.
Lovett's wife, Mary, for whom he suitably provided,
and made executrix of his will, was admitted to the
Salem church, Sept. 1, 1650, and was one of the
petitioners for the formation of the church in Beverly.
She died June 1695, aged about 80.

John Lovett, jr., to whom the old burying ground
lot belonged in 1672, died Sept. 10, 1727, aged about
91. He bequeathed a considerable estate to his
children, Simon, John, Samuel, Benjamin, Susanna
and Bethiah—to his grandchildren, Peter and Bethiah
Shaw, Susanna Sikes, and to the widow of his grandson, Thomas Lovett. He was admitted to the church
Dec. 12, 1714, when about seventy-eight years of age,
to which he left a small legacy. From the first
named John Lovett, all of that name in this town
probably descended.

In 1690, an expedition against Canada was carried
on under the direction of Sir William Phips. For
this enterprize, a company was raised in Beverly by
Capt. William Rayment, who joined the land forces,
amounting to about 2000 men. The fleet employed
to transport the army arrived before Quebec, Oct.
5th, and disembarked 1200 or 1300 effective men.
All attempts to obtain possession of the city failed,
and on the 11th, the army was compelled to return
on board the vessels, which immediately sailed for
New England. Great expectations had been formed
of this expedition. The provincial government had
warmly encouraged it, and, to render it more popular,
held out the idea that the expenses would be entirely

defrayed from the spoils of the enemy. So signal a failure not only produced universal disappointment, but involved the province in a severe pecuniary embarrassment. According to a statement made by Gov. Shirley in 1746, this expedition "cost the single province of Massachusetts about £50,000, with the loss of an abundance of their young men by a malignant fever that raged in the camp, and several distempers that happened in their way home, and gave this province so deep a wound that it did not recover itself in many years after."*

Capt. Rayment and his company endured privation in common with the army, and were subsequently rewarded by the grant of a township of land. He was a useful and respected citizen, represented the town in General Court, and held various other offices of trust and honor. In 1691, he was indemnified by the town for loss sustained as its commissioner in the time of Sir Edmund Andros. He owned an estate in the second parish, and lived near the dwelling-house of Mr. Isaac Babson. His children were Mary, born April 29th, 1688—died Jan. 20th, 1689; William, born Feb. 11th, 1689-90; Daniel, born Nov. 25th, 1691; Paul, born Jan. 22, 1694-5.

In one of the early French wars, a merchantman sailing from this port, was taken by the enemy and carried into one of the West India Islands. The captain, anxious alike for himself and the owners, pled earnestly for a release, and finally succeeded in obtaining it on condition of paying a stipulated ransom. To do this, it became necessary to return to Beverly for the money, which his captors would not permit except he left a hostage. Accordingly, one of

* Provincial Records.

the crew, named Hill, was consigned to their custody. He was placed in prison, with the threat that unless the captain returned on a specified day, all food should be withheld until his arrival. With these terms distinctly declared, he sailed for Beverly. On his arrival, some little delay in procuring the necessary funds occurred, which being overcome, he once more spread his canvass for his port of destination. But this delay had nearly proved fatal to poor Hill. The day appointed for his captain's return closed, and no vessel appeared. The dreaded threat was immediately executed. Both food and water were withheld, and for eight or nine days the unfortunate hostage suffered all the pangs of unappeased hunger and the horror of apprehended starvation. Happily, however, almost at the moment when human aid would cease to avail, the vessel arrived, the ransom was paid, and Hill was set at liberty. He gradually recovered from the feeble state produced by privation, and lived several years to relate, though always with tears, the sufferings endured in a French prison.

In 1670, notices of town meetings were first posted on the meeting-house, previously to which they were called by personal warning. In 1683, Beverly became a lawful port of entry, annexed to the port of Salem, and in 1684 was required to assist in building a house of correction in that town. In 1687, the inhabitants becoming neglectful of town meetings, a vote was passed imposing a fine of ten shillings on all future absentees.

Although the town records begin in 1665, no town clerk was chosen until April 11, 1690, when Andrew Elliot was elected, and his compensation fixed at 30s. in money or 40s. in *pay*, i. e. produce. Up to this period, the records had been kept by the selectmen,

whose doings are blended with those of the town.
Elliot was a native of Somerset county, in the west
of England. He came early to Beverly, and became
a member of the church in 1687. He appears to
have enjoyed the entire confidence of his townsmen,
and was frequently chosen selectman, representative,
&c., and was sixty-three years old when he entered
upon the duties of town clerk. He suffered under
the arbitrary administration of Sir Edmund Andros,
on account of which, the town made him a grant.
In 1686, he was one of the five witnesses taken from
Beverly, to attend at the execution of the Indian
deed of the town of Salem. He wrote a fair hand,
and was very circumstantial in his record of events.
The following entry of the decease of his son, is a
specimen of his method : " Andrew Elliot, the dear
and only son of Andrew Elliot, whose mother's name
was Grace, and was born in East Coker, in the county
of Somerset, in old England, being on board a vessel
appertaining unto Phillip English, of Salem, one
Bavidge being master, said vessel being then at Cape
Sables, by an awful stroke was violently thrown
into the sea and there perished in the water, to the
great grief of his said father, the penman hereof,
being aged about 37 years; on the 12th day of September, about 10 o'clock in the morning, according to
the best information, in the year of our Lord, 1688."

The second volume of town records he commences
as follows : " 3d of Nov. 1685, then this book was
improved for the town of Beverly, as a town book
to record the town concerns by the selectmen of said
town successively. For former concerns in this matter, any concerned may have recourse unto a former
parchment-covered old book extant, and likewise for
some antient records of marriages, births, and buri-

als, which said year was the first year of the reign
of our sovereign lord, King James secundus.

"Truth justifies herself when falsehood comes to naught.
How few improve the first, but with the last full fraught;
Oh thou tyrant custom, what havoc dost thou make,
Thy cruel bonds, fetters and clogs, most men do captivate."

He died March 1, 1703–4, aged 76 years.

Andrew Elliot, a merchant in Boston, who suffered
by the great fire in 1711, was his great grandson, and
Rev. Andrew Elliot, a distinguished clergyman of the
same city, was his great, great grandson. The
daughter of Andrew Elliot, the merchant, was
married to Nathaniel Thayer, and was grandmother
to the late Rev. Dr. Thayer, of Lancaster.

Mr. Elliot was succeeded in office by Robert
Woodberry, who discharged its duties with great
fidelity. He married a daughter of "farmer West,"
was the grandfather of the late James Woodberry at
the farms, and lived in the same house. During his
life-time, he held most of the important offices in the
gift of the town. He was a good penman, and was
almost universally employed in drafting deeds and
other instruments in writing required by the inhabitants of the town.

Another town officer worthy of notice in this connexion, is Robert Briscoe, who, from 1690 until he
removed from the place in 1726, held the various
offices of selectman, assessor, treasurer and representative, besides other important trusts in town
and parish. He was a native of the west of England, but at what time he emigrated to this country is not known. His name is first mentioned in
the town records in 1686, and in 1708, he became
a member of the church. His wife was of a noble

family; but marrying contrary to the views of her friends, they were induced to come to America. He possessed considerable property, and traditions are fresh of the superior style in which his dwelling was furnished. His house stood nearly opposite the first parish meeting-house, and was taken down about forty-four years ago. It was elegant in its day, and is now well remembered for its peculiar form, and its appendages and decorations. In 1712, he presented the town with a bell for the use of the meeting-house, and in 1718, he gave a silver cup to the church. He appears to have been a generous and public-spirited man, and his purse was always at the command of the town in anticipation of any want. His first wife, Abigail, who was a member of the church, died June 1st. 1724, aged 52. His second wife was Mrs. Elizabeth Dudley, of Exeter, N. H., in which town he resided at the time of his decease. Among the legacies he left, was £10 to Rev. Thomas Blowers, £20 to the poor of Beverly, £10 to the poor of Exeter, £10 to the Rev. John Odlin, of Exeter, a silver tankard to the church in the same town, and to his negro boy Cato, £20, a cow, and at 24 years of age, his freedom. In 1832, one of the public streets was named in honor of him, and likewise in 1842, the grammar district school-house received the name of " Briscoe Hall. "

In 1694–5, one half of the town tax was paid in grain, at the following prices : Indian corn, 3s ; rye, 4s ; barley and barley malt, 4s ; and oats, 2s. per bushel. About this period, the difference in the par value of silver and *pay*, or produce, was 33⅓ per cent.

In 1707, Robin Mingo, a negro slave, the property of Thomas Woodberry, was married to Deborah Tailor, an Indian woman. Before the ceremony was

4

performed, she agreed to live with her husband's master and mistress during his life, to be then "dismissed with only two suits of clothes suitable for such a person." July 15, 1722, Mingo received the rite of baptism, and was admitted a member of the church. He was, at the time of his death in 1773, the property of Nicholas Thorndike. From him, *"Mingo's Beach"* is supposed to have derived its name. The number of slaves in this town in 1754, was twenty-eight.

The year 1727, was memorable for an earthquake, which occurred about 20 minutes before 11 o'clock, P. M., Oct. 29th. It was felt through the colonies, and made strong religious impressions on the minds of many in this town and other places. Nov. 18, 1755, a few minutes past 4 o'clock, A. M., another earthquake was experienced, more violent in its motions, and of longer duration than any previously felt in this quarter of the globe. Its greatest violence in this town, was felt in the neighborhood of Colon street, where several chimnies were thrown down. Stone walls were also prostrated, and "the pewter shaken from the shelves" in other parts of the town. Both in Beverly and Salem a change in the quality of the water in the wells was noticed. Water which had previously been soft and suitable for washing, became hard and unfit for that purpose.

Of the citizens of this town who occupied a conspicuous position, and took a leading part in public affairs, between 1730 and 1767, Robert Hale, Jr. was distinguished for activity and influence. He was born February 12th, 1702–3, and baptized on the 21st of the same month. When between 15 and 16 years of age, he was employed to keep the grammar school, and again, at a more mature age, in 1730. In 1721 he was graduated at Harvard College, to the philosophical department of which he presented a solar microscope and magic lantern, in 1764. Immediately upon leaving college, he commenced the study of medicine, under the direction of Dr. Manning, of Ipswich, and about 1723 engaged in a practice that soon extended to all the neighboring towns.* In 1723 he was married to Elizabeth Gilman, daughter of Col. John Gilman, of Exeter, N. H., who became the mother of three daughters; Elizabeth, Rebeccah, born May 27, 1730, died April 27, 1732; and Rebeckah, born Feb. 5, 1732-3, died Aug. 23, 1736. Mrs. Hale died Aug. 19th, 1736, in the 35th year of her age. His second marriage was with Elizabeth, youngest daughter of Hon. John Clarke, of Boston, Dec. 21, 1737.

The energy of character, sound judgment and business capacity of Dr. Hale, were early appreciated by his townsmen, by whom he was chosen to fill the various offices of surveyor, selectman, assessor, town clerk and treasurer; besides the duties of which, he discharged those of justice of the peace, and collector of excise for Essex county. As chairman of the school committee, he took an active and efficient part in the measures adopted to improve the school system of the town. For thirteen years he represented the town in the General Court, during

---

* Col. Hale commenced an account-book in 1723, still extant, with the following sentence: "Crescit nummi amor quantum pecunia crescit." In this book is an inventory of his property, amounting July 10, 1729, to £1155,13,3, free from incumbrance. Of this sum, he received from his father's estate, £790,10,5, and of his mother's thirds, £300. In a note to this inventory, he says: "As my father died five years before I came of age, it cost me £300 at least, out of my estate, for my education, so that by marrying and industry, with God's blessing, I have gained £365 in about six years."

which time he was chairman of several important
committees, and a member of many more, and particularly of the committee to inquire respecting the
impressment of certain seamen in Nantasket Roads,
by officers of the British navy, an event made memorable in our history by being the occasion of serious
riots in Boston.

In 1726, Dr. Hale made a public profession of religion, by uniting with the first church, then under the
ministry of Rev. Thomas Blowers.   In 1735 he was
engaged in controversies and discussions growing out
of ecclesiastical difficulties in the first church in Salem, and in settling the form of church discipline in
the first church in this town; and from 1728 to 1743
inclusive, the parish records present ample evidence
of his abundant labors and powerful influence in the
management of ecclesiastical and parochial concerns.

In 1740, the pecuniary embarrassments of the province led to various projects for relief.   Among these
was an institution known as the Land Bank, with a
capital of £150,000, predicated on real estate.   Of
this company Col. Hale was a manager, by whom
the plan of operations was drafted.   This scheme,
from the hope it inspired, was favorably received by
a large body of the people, but met with determined
hostility from Governor Belcher and his council;
and when Col. Hale presented a copy of the plan to
be recorded in the secretary's office, it was returned
as an indignity.   The enmity of the governor prompted him to visit his displeasure upon all persons connected with the institution.   He issued a proclamation declaring his determination to dismiss every officer, civil or military, who persisted "in being any
way concerned, or giving any encouragement whatsoever, to the passing" of the Land Bank notes;

and Col. Hale, unwilling to sacrifice his independence, as well as to prove faithless to an enterprize in which he had conscientiously embarked, tendered his resignation to the governor.

The course pursued by the governor, in dismissing civil and military officers on the grounds referred to, was regarded as an unwarrantable usurpation of power; and the exasperation it produced seriously threatened open rebellion. Energetic measures were adopted to prevent an outbreak. Public sentiment, however, could not be controlled, and so powerfully was it felt in the royal councils, that in 1741 his excellency was recalled, and succeeded in office by William Shirley.* Gov. Belcher was doubtless honest in his intentions of reform, but injudicious in the use of means. He was subsequently placed in the government of New Jersey, in consideration, it is supposed, of the " terrible shock" to his feelings produced by his removal.†

---

* Since writing the foregoing, I have been favored with the perusal of a letter in the possession of Mr. Robert Peele, of Salem, written by Thomas Hutchinson to a friend in this country, dated London, May 14th, 1741, from which the following extract is made : " I suppose you will have the first news of Mr. Shirley's being appointed our governor by a vessel which sailed a few days ago from Swanzy. Several incidents have occurred to promote it. The collector's place was promised Mr. Shirley's family, and it is said is now insisted on for Mr. Franklyn, and this was a way to satisfy both. Your two countrymen, Waldo and Kelly, claim the merit, and say it is owing to their gratifying the Duke of Grafton, by making interest for Lord Euston at Coventry, where they have spent a month, first and last, soliciting his election. But I had it from Lord President's own mouth, that Governor Belcher's security for some time had been his steady conduct in the affair of the money, and that his brother Partridge, patronizing the Land Bank when before the House of Commons, had done his business."

† Hist. Mass. Currency.

4*

In 1745, Dr. Hale received the commission of colonel, and commanded a regiment in the expedition against Louisburg. This expedition was projected by Governor Shirley. The land force employed consisted of 3,200 men from Massachusetts, 300 from New Hampshire, 300 from Rhode Island, and 500 from Connecticut, all under the command of Gen. William Pepperell. The naval force, for co-operation, was from England, and commanded by Commodore Warren. For this enterprize a company was enlisted in Beverly, under the command of Capt. Benjamin Ives, son-in-law to Col. Hale. "The hardships of the siege were without parallel in all preceding American operations. The army was employed for fourteen nights successively, in drawing cannon, mortars, &c., for two miles, through a morass, to their camp. The Americans were yoked together, and performed labor beyond the power of oxen, which labor could be done only in the night, or in a foggy day; the place being within clear view and random shot of the enemy's walls."* Of these fatigues, Col. Hale's regiment freely partook. His position was one of imminent danger, and, though a part of the time suffering from disease, he proved himself an efficient officer.†

The fall of this "Dunkirk of America," upon fortifying which twenty-five years of labor and thirty millions of livres had been expended, astonished all Europe, and filled the colonies with joy. But though the merits of Gen. Pepperell were acknowledged by the government, who conferred upon him the title of baronet, and placed him in the command of a regi-

* Adams' Hist. N. E. pp. 123, 124.
† See plan of encampment in Bancroft's Hist. U. S.

ment in the British establishment, there were not wanting those in influential stations, who, moved with an unworthy jealousy for British glory, sought in public and private to undervalue the services of the provincial troops. Even Sir Peter Warren, blinded by self-esteem, or swayed for a moment by an influence inconsistent with the generous frankness that characterizes a noble mind, sanctioned by his silence, at least, the libellous tales of American inefficiency. The claims of Gen. Pepperell's army to the meed of approbation, had, however, an honorable advocate in the person of a high-minded Briton, who was in the expedition, and who was an eyewitness to their toil and bravery. He affirms that their zeal, unwearied labor, and prompt execution of orders, entitle them to the appellation of heroes, and suggests that modesty should have dictated to Sir Peter Warren to disclaim all honor in the enterprize, other than that arising from the blockade of Louisburg with his squadron.*

Col. Hale was sensibly alive to American honor; and this ungenerous attempt to wrest from the provincial forces the tribute of approbation justly their due, deeply wounded his sensibility. In a letter to his friend, Col. Pickman, adverting to an account of the siege given in a London magazine, he says: "it is well known to every one engaged in the expedition, that the British fleet never fired a gun, nor lost a man, except by sickness, though they have the credit of taking the place;" and he imputes the exclusive praise of British prowess to a prevalent impression in England, that it was "impossible that a

---

* Letter from "a British merchant," Mass. Hist. Coll., first series, vol. i., p. 110.

New England man could be good for any thing " of
a military character, an imputation which he repels
with becoming contempt, and instances Braddock's
defeat and Sir H. Walker's loss of vessels in the
Canada expedition, as disasters that would never
have occurred, had not the British commanders been
too proud to receive advice from provincial officers
and New England pilots. The great error of the
British government, in all their provincial enterprizes
which failed of success, he shows, consisted in the
appointment of foreign officers to the command of
troops raised here; when between the former and
latter there was no reciprocity of respect or confidence. While at Louisburg, Col. Hale enclosed a
piece of ground for cultivation, which is still familiarly known to our fishermen, who visit it, as Col.
Hale's garden.

The influence acquired by Col. Hale, as a member
of the General Court, and his prominence in public
affairs generally, probably led to the appointment he
received from the Legislature, in 1747, of commissioner to New York, to adopt measures in relation to
the general defence.

In 1755, when the government of Massachusetts
Bay had determined on an expedition against the
French, and the reduction of Crown Point, Col. Hale
was selected by Governor Shirley as a suitable agent
to lay the subject before the government of New
Hampshire, and solicit their aid. His commission
bears date Feb. 22d, 1755, and the same day he received from the governor a series of instructions, by
which he was to conduct the negotiation. They run
as follows :

" You are hereby directed forthwith to proceed to Portsmouth, with my despatches to his excellency, Benning Wentworth, Esq., Gov. of that Province. Upon your arrival there, and appearance either before the Governor and Council or the Genl. Assembly of that Province, or before the Governor alone (as you may have opportunity), you are strongly to solicit the joining of that government with this and the other two governments of N. Eng. &c. in a vigorous and speedy prosecution of the expedition proposed in my speech to the Assembly of this Province, and to contribute towards the execution of it, that government's quota of men and provisions, set forth in the said Assembly's Resolves, a copy of which, as also of my said speech, will be delivered to you : and you are in a particular manner, among such reasons and arguments as shall occur to you, for inducing them to join in the said expedition, to urge those which are contained in my aforesaid speech, and in my letters to the respective Governors, copies of which last shall likewise be delivered to you.

" In case you shall not be able to induce the said government to join in the prosecution of the said expedition, upon the terms proposed in the before mentioned resolves of the Great and Genl. Assembly of this Province, you are to desire of them to let you know whether they will join in it upon any, and what, other terms, together with the reasons of their non-compliance with those proposed by this government.

" Lastly. You are, from time to time, to transmit to me accounts of your proceedings herein, and the progress you make in the discharge of this commission, either by the post or express, as the occasion may require ; and upon finishing your negociations with that government you are to return to Boston, and lay an account of your whole proceedings therein, with the final answer of the said government, before me.

" You are to make use or not of the inclosed vote of the Assembly, dated the 27th of Feb., according to your own discretion. You are to endeavor to induce the government of New Hampshire to raise a greater number of men than what is mentioned as their quota, in the resolves of the Assembly, dated Feb'y, provisionally, viz : in case the government of New York shall not raise the eight hundred men allotted to them to raise.

" W. SHIRLEY."

The appointment of Col. Hale on this service was most judicious, and met the entire approbation of Governor Wentworth. In reply to a letter from Gov. Shirley, urging the necessity of the expedition as an effectual means of checking the encroachments of the French, and proposing to give the command to Col. William Johnson, on account of his superior military knowledge, and his extensive influence over the Indians of the six nations, to which he heartily assents; Gov. Wentworth adds :

"With respect to Col. Hale, he will always be well received by me, with the power you are pleased to invest him with; but lest some of our wrong-headed people should make opposition to what he is charged with from your Excellency, and thereby injure the common cause, I should think it best not to make his business public until he has consulted me, for a little matter will sometimes overset the best concerted measures. He may therefore come in a private manner, and if he can convert the Exeter members, who, I am certain, will oppose this expedition, he will gain a great point, if not a miraculous one."

Thus commissioned and instructed, Col. Hale proceeded to Portsmouth, in fulfilment of his agency. The aspect of the business in its earlier stages, may be learned from the following letter to Governor Shirley, dated

"PORTSMOUTH, March 15, 1755.
" SIR :
I have your Excellency's of yesterday by express, bro't me to Mr. Wentworth's, just after dinner with him and the secretary, &c., so that I immediately laid before them the enclosed papers, which may be of use.

"My last to your Excellency was yesterday morning by the post, when I informed that I was just going to attend the committee of both Houses. They consist of four of each House. I had little occasion to say much about the necessity of the expedition, being forestalled by the papers sent to Gov. Wentworth, with which the secretary (one of the committee) had made them acquainted; only I had taken some pains with some in a private way before. The difficulty was about the quota and want of money, as in my last. When I had endeavored to answer all the objections offered in the committee on these two heads, and some others less interesting, I withdrew, first telling them I would be glad to know their report before it was given in.

"Accordingly, in the afternoon they sent for me, and informed me they had agreed to 100 men. Your Excellency can better imagine, than I express, my situation. I soon found it to be the sense of the whole committee. I renewed all my former arguments, but in as different lights as I could, and added others, which (being a little reason) then occurred to me. They heard me with candor and attention, and after about an hour and a half, I took my leave; first desiring they would take till the morning to consider the consequences of such a report. This morning early, Col. Gilman, of Exeter, (one of the committee) came to my lodgings, as I had desired him over night. We began upon it again and went through every thing, but it did not then appear to make any real impression on him. Being uneasy, I followed him to the lower House, called him out, and urged some things which had escaped me in the former conversation. He seemed better satisfied, and left me about half after ten to go to the committee. About one, Col. Atkinson sent for me to go with him to dinner with the governor. On the road down he told me they had just finished; that the committee had agreed to 500; but to find subsistence only till they arrived at the place of rendezvous, intending they shall go the nearest way through the woods. I asked him how in that case they would do for shelter by the way. He said they should send none but such as should be content to sit down on the ground and cover themselves with their heads. Every one of the committee, he said, had agreed to the report, and he was encouraged it would pass the House—of the board, was no danger. The committee are of the most leading men.

"On Monday, the report will be made, after which I shall move for an addition, conditionally, that N. York find no men, but provisions, &c., having already hinted at it, but not caring to urge it till the grand point was secured. I confess I am not yet out of pain about the quota; there being many of the other members who don't seem inclined to enter into the reasons why they should raise half so many men as we, when their province has but a sixth part so many as ours.* I shall give my whole attention to the affair, until it has the government fiat, and hope to send your Excellency the best news by the next post. I should by no means have troubled your Excellency with so long and particular a detail, if I had not thought that my instructions required it. If, in that particular, I have misunderstood them, I ask your Excellency's excuse, being, sir,

"Your most obedient,

"Humble servant,

"ROBERT HALE."

"P. S. Those Piscataqua men will want at least 20 whip saws, to cut logs into boards for sheltering the army.

"P. S. 2d. Every branch here affected to wonder how our Court could assume to prescribe to each government its quota, but took no exceptions to our leading the way."

The following letter to Hon. John Osborne, chairman of the committee of war, in Boston, furnishes some further particulars of this negotiation :

"BEVERLY, April 13, 1755, evening.

"SIR:

"When I waited on Gov. Wentworth, at Portsmouth, on Friday evening, he told me he had that day signed the act relating to the expedition, which is conformable to the vote I brought from that court when last there; but, as New York are now to provide men instead of warlike stores and provisions, as our court, by the vote of Feb. 27, expected, and as we raise three hundred men more than we at first proposed, I hoped that N. Hampshire would make some addition. Accordingly, I next morning went to the Court House and desired that the house, as soon as met, would adjourn, and permit me a conference with them. They accordingly did, and I was with them an hour and half, and urged every thing in my power to persuade them to find subsistence for their men, at least part of the time, and their quota of warlike

---

* In 1754 there were but 7000 ratable polls in New Hampshire.

stores, but without effect. They let me know that they apprehended five hundred men, subsisted to the place of rendezvous, and raised and paid by them during the expedition, was their full quota of charge, compared with Massachusetts, and much more compared with Connecticut, Rhode Island, and New York; and though I'm very sure they are mistaken with respect to us, yet they continued so firm that they did not deliberate half an hour before they determined not to make any addition to what they have already done.

"Indeed, this has cost them five weeks' constant application, which, being a session of unusual length for them, and they having been, for some days, in hopes to rise that day, 'tis not to be wondered at that they did not incline to begin (as it were) anew.

"Their court is adjourned to the 23d instant, when I hope, if Gov. Shirley, by letter to Mr. Wentworth, shall think fit to renew his instances relative to subsistence, warlike stores, and the encouragement to the Mohawks, they will be induced to do something, though I fear it will not be much. As to sending any person there again, it don't appear to me to be necessary, though if any gentleman has a mind to show his superior talents at negotiation, he will have my hearty wishes for success: I have no great opinion of my own. I shall, however, by next post, write to two or three of the principal gentlemen of that house, and endeavor to prove to them the necessity of their doing something more, that their minds may be a little prepared to receive some impressions next session. In the mean time, Gov. Wentworth assures me he shall raise all the men he is able to, even beyond the five hundred, which may be a great service to us, if our levies should not be complete.

"I am very sorry my journey has been so fruitless, but I think no endeavors of mine have been wanting to show that I am the Province's and,

"Sir, your most faithful,
"Obedient servant,
"ROB'T HALE.

"P. S. I have a very great desire to know how many men of the four regiments were raised in this province, and how many in New Hampshire. I suppose it not difficult to find out by inquiry of the officers; and though it might give your honor some trouble, yet, as it may be of considerable use, I beg the favor I may have the account as soon as may be."

The commission of Col. Hale was conducted with great skill, and with entire satisfaction to Gov. Shirley, whose letters pending the result, partake more of confidential friendship, than of official formality. In a letter dated March 16th, he writes: "It is a peculiar satisfaction to me, that a gentleman in whose capacity to conduct so intricate an affair, as well as important an one as this is, I have the utmost confidence, hath the management of it." After some little delay and several interviews with committees, to whom Col. Hale presented the subject in the light best adapted to obtain their concurrence, he succeeded in securing five hundred men as the quota of New Hampshire, which, though one hundred less than the number designated by Massachusetts, was a far more favorable result than the opposition manifested, warranted him to hope for.

On his return home, Col. Hale entered with interest into the arrangements of the expedition ; and, to aid those under whose direction they were made, he furnished a schedule, predicated upon his military experience, of the principal articles necessary for the service. His talents and service entitled him to a command in this expedition; and from a fragment of a letter to Gov. Shirley, now extant, there is ground for the inference that he had reason to expect it. But from causes unknown, probably from an apprehension on the part of the appointing power that his health was inadequate to the fatigues of field-service, instead of such appointment, he received an offer of a medical post, which he respectfully but pointedly declined.

In 1761, Col. Hale received from Governor Francis Bernard, a commission of sheriff for Essex county, the duties and responsibilities of which office, he discharged with characteristic fidelity.

The Land Bank before referred to, unlike almost every other enterprize with which Col. Hale was connected, failed of answering the expectations of its founders; not so much perhaps from the imperfections of the scheme, as from an opposing influence originating in a quarter difficult to reach and equally so to resist. But though the course pursued by him in this matter, was one that he could review with satisfaction, prompted as it had been throughout by the purest motives, still, the failure was a source of deep mortification; and the suspicions of fraudulent management afloat at the time, entirely unfounded as they were in regard to the managers generally, and peculiarly unjust as directed against Col. Hale, wrought upon a sensitive nature, and seriously affected his health and spirits. His highly honorable and useful life was terminated by lingering sickness in 1767, in the 65th year of his age.

The decease of Col. Hale was a severe loss to this town. For a period of more than forty years he had been connected with its affairs, and was frequently its agent for the accomplishment of local objects. The many reports drawn up by him which are found in the church, parish and town records, display a talent for drafting papers in a concise, energetic and business-like manner; and the appearance of the town and parish records, at the several periods when he was clerk, show his accuracy and ability in the execution of that office. His character was every where sustained for persevering industry and active enterprize. He exerted a controlling

influence over those with whom he was associated,
and his qualifications to govern were freely admitted.
Yet in the exercise of this power, he was actuated
by the dictates of morality and religion. Few are
now living who remember him in life, but tradition
abounds and is redolent with the mention of his virtues.

Col. Hale, during his life-time, owned and occupied the estate that had been the property of both his
father and grandfather, and which is now in the
possession of his descendants. He left no sons. His
eldest daughter, Elizabeth, was married to Mr. Benjamin Ives, who died about 1773. Robert Hale Ives,
a son by this marriage, was born July 18th, 1744,
and soon after his grandfather's decease, was connected with the public affairs of the town. His son,
Thomas Poynton Ives, was born in Beverly, April
9th, 1769, and for forty-three years was an eminent
merchant in Providence, R. I., where he died April
30th, 1835, aged sixty-six years. He was of the
house of Brown & Ives, than which none in this
country has maintained a higher character for integrity and well-directed enterprize, and in which his
sons, Moses and Robert Hale Ives, are now part-
ners. He was distinguished for untiring industry,
high mercantile probity, unostentatious benevolence,
generous hospitality, and ardent love of country.
He was twenty-four years president of the Providence Bank, and fifteen years president of the Sav-
ings Institution in that city. He was a friend and
liberal benefactor of Brown University, and for forty-
three years a member of its board of trustees. To
the community with which he was so long identified, he bequeathed an example of unblemished hon-

or, and of faithful service for the good of others; and to his children, not only ample fortune, but what is far more valuable, the record of a father's worth— the simple dignity of his name and character.

5*

REVOLUTIONARY PERIOD.

In the events which preceded the revolution, and which resulted in the establishment of an independent republic, this town took a lively interest; and its contributions, in talents and treasure, were large and efficient. The repeal of the odious, as unwise, stamp act, in 1765, was celebrated with illuminations, bonfires, and other demonstrations of triumph. The various infractions of colonial rights, on the part of Great Britain, were condemned in the most decided language; and from time to time measures were adopted for resisting oppression, and for obtaining a redress of grievances. The town unanimously concurred in the non-importation plan; and with a zeal scarcely inferior to that which animated the Boston "tea party," sought to abolish the use of the article, for the sale of which the East India Company held the monopoly. This movement found more grace in the eyes of those by whom it was commenced, and who yielded to the promptings of the sternest enthusiasm, than in the sight of the gentler sex; for though, to use the expression of a living witness,* "the women were all liberty men, and threatened to scald the tories," still the delicious infusion of the China plant was a luxury all were not quite prepared to

---

* Ebenezer Rea.

repudiate ; and many amusing traditions are extant, of expedients practised for its secret enjoyment, secure from the indignation of the sterner sex, whose patriotic ardor enabled them to maintain the most rigid self-denial. These arts, however, were sometimes thwarted, and the "drawings" of the "tea-caddy," to the chagrin of an expectant coterie, were despoiled of their aroma by an unseen, but liberal deposit of "Virginia twist."*

In the preliminary measures to which reference has been made, the town proceeded with moderation. No threats of revolt were uttered, but a determination was firmly expressed to preserve the inviolability of their rights. In a letter of instruction, addressed to their representative, Henry Herrick, Oct. 21, 1765, they say, "We cannot, without criminal injustice to those glorious princes, King William and Queen Mary, or to the memory of our venerable fathers, nor without the highest injustice to ourselves and to posterity, consent to yield obedience to any law whatsoever, which, by its natural constitution or just construction, deprives us of the liberty of trial by juries; or of our choosing meet persons to represent us in the assessing or taxing our estates for his Majesty's service. And we do accordingly advise and instruct you, our representative, to refuse your consent, in any such case, and do all that in you lies, to prevent all unconstitutional drafts upon the public treasury." In the same letter, they express their unqualified disapprobation of the riotous attack upon the house

* A hearty patriot coming home unexpectedly one day, found a company of his wife's neighbors assembled to tea. He said nothing, but revenged himself by putting a large "quid" of tobacco in the tea-pot. Sometimes, to escape detection, the ladies drank their tea in the cellar.

of Lieut. Gov. Hutchinson, and others, and declare, "that such is our abhorrence of such riotous and mobbish behavior, that we are fully determined, as a town, to stand by each other in suppressing such disorders at all hazards," though, at the same time, as at a subsequent meeting, they were opposed to the loss being remunerated from the public treasury.

It would be interesting, did the limits of this volume permit, to transcribe the transactions of the various town meetings, from 1765 to the close of the revolutionary struggle in 1783, as illustrative of the patriotism and devotion which animated every breast.

On the 17th Sept., 1768, they chose Henry Herrick a delegate to join with delegates from Boston and other towns in convention, to consult and advise on the state of the province, in which, however, he was to abstain from any act of disrespect to parliament, and of disloyalty to the King. In their further instructions to him, as representative, May 22, 1769, they say, "We apprehend that no power on earth can justly deprive us of our essential rights, and that no man can be safe, either as to his life, liberty or property, if a contrary doctrine should prevail ; therefore we recommend to you a firm, but prudent opposition to all unconstitutional measures."

Among other important measures adopted by the town, was the appointment of a committee of correspondence and safety, which consisted, at different periods from 1773 until the close of the war, of John Leach, Benjamin Jones, Henry Herrick, Samuel Goodridge, Josiah Batchelder, Jr., Josiah Batchelder, Joshua Cleaves, Larkin Thorndike, Joseph Wood, Nicholas Thorndike, William Bartlett, Andrew Cabot, Joseph Orne, Benj. Lovett, Jr., Nathan Leach, Caleb Dodge, Joseph Rea, Livermore Whittredge,

Benjamin Smith, William Longdell, Edmund Giles,
Jonathan Conant, John Conant, Isaac Thorndike,
Isaac Chapman, Thomas Stephens, John Lovett, 3d,
William Dodge, William Taylor, and Asa Leach.
Of the letters addressed by this committee to the
central committee in Boston, the three following
have been preserved:

" *To the Committee of Correspondence for the town of Boston:*
" GENTLEMEN:

" Inclosed you have the transactions of this town, in consequence of the resolves of the metropolis of this province, and the
letter of correspondence herewith transmitted, whereby you will
perceive the sentiments of this town with regard to the common
cause in which we are all concerned. In the name of the town
we return thanks for the early care, taken by the town of Boston,
to communicate the most early intelligence of any alarming circumstances that they have, with regard to any infringements on
our rights as Christians, subjects, or colonists.

" And, gentlemen, inasmuch as we are all concerned in one
common cause, we shall esteem it as a favor of a free correspondence, that we may have the most early intelligence of any interesting events of a public nature, as you live in the metropolis, that
we may concur with you in any salutary constitutional measures
for the good of all; and are, gentlemen, with the greatest regards,
" Your most humble servants,

" JOHN LEACH,   SAMUEL GOODRIDGE,
BENJ. JONES,   JOSIAH BATCHELDER, Jr.
HENRY HERRICK,
" BEVERLY, JAN. 11, 1773."

The transactions referred to in the foregoing letter
were the doings of town meetings held Dec. 21,
1772, and by adjournment, Jan. 5th, 1773, at which
it was affirmed that " the rights of the colonists
in particular as men, as Christians, and as subjects, are studiously, rightly and justly stated by
the committee of correspondence for the town of

Boston," and Col. Henry Herrick, the representative
from Beverly, is instructed to "endeavor, as much
as possible, in a legal and constitutional way," to
effect a redress of the "intolerable grievances" to
which the colonies had been subjected, and to secure
the preservation of all the "rights, liberties and
privileges, both civil and sacred," guaranteed by the
charter. Instructions, similar in their tenor, were
given to Josiah Batchelder, Jr., who was chosen representative to the General Court, Sept. 26, 1774.

To the Same.

"BEVERLY, Nov. 10, 1773.

"GENTLEMEN:

"Yours of the 21st Sept. we have received and observe the
contents, and are sensible of the justness of the sentiments
thereof, in which we harmonize, and are fully of opinion that no
other measures can be come into so salutary as a strict union of
all the colonies for a redress of the many grievances the colonies
labor under from the acts of parliament imposing duties on certain
articles for the express end of raising a revenue on the people of
the colonies without their consent, out of which revenue the governor and other great officers are paid, whereby they are independent of this province for their support,—as also many other
grievances, which are so well known we shall not at this time
enumerate. We are heartily sorry to hear the petition of our assembly hath not been regarded by our most gracious sovereign
(as we have been informed), which we fear will be disagreeable to
many of his majesty's faithful subjects in America. As we live
at a distance from the metropolis, and can't possibly have the first
intelligence, we shall esteem it a favor from you, of any intelligence, and shall heartily concur with you in any salutary measures for the recovery of our just rights: and are grieved that his
majesty is deaf to the complaints of his subjects in America, who,
we think, are as faithful subjects as any in his dominions. We
are sensible that the good people of this town are fully in the sentiments you have exhibited to us in your several letters, for which
we are obliged to you, and hope you will still continue to write to

us of every thing of a public nature you may think worthy of a communication.

"We are, gentlemen, your humble serv'ts

"And entire friends,

"SAM'L GOODRIDGE, *Clerk.*"

"Signed by order of the Com. of}
Cor. for the town of Beverly. }

To the Same.

"BEVERLY, Jan. 4, 1774.

"GENTLEMEN:

"Yours of Nov. 23d, 1773, and the inclosure, we have received, but not till the 11th ultimo, for which we return our warmest thanks. As early as possible we communicated yours to our town, but the inclemency of the weather hindered a general attendance of its inhabitants. The meeting was adjourned to this day. Inclosed you have the resolution they then came into, by which you will perceive the sentiments of this town. We heartily concur with you in every salutary measure for preventing the enslaving or ruining ourselves and posterity. But we hope, gentlemen, we shall have a union amongst ourselves and all our brethren of the several colonies on this continent, which we think will be the best means to obtain a redress of the many grievances we at present labor under.

"We are, gentlemen,

"Your sincere friends and humble serv'ts,

"By order of the Committee of Correspondence,

"SAMUEL GOODRIDGE, *Clerk.*"

The following resolution referred to, was adopted at a town meeting, Jan. 4, 1774, in the following words:

"That the method of introducing tea into this province in the method proposed by the British ministry, for the benefit of the East India Company, is justly and fairly stated by the inhabitants of the town of Boston; and that it is the sentiment of this meeting, that they will always, in every salutary method, cheerfully join with our brethren of the town of Boston, and every other town in this province, in withstanding every unlawful measure tending to enslave us, or to take our money from us in any unconstitutional manner."

A true copy : attest,

JOSEPH WOOD, *T. Clerk.*

On the 6th and 7th September, 1774, a county convention was held at Ipswich, to consider the situation of public affairs, in which this town was represented by Benj. Lovett, Samuel Goodridge, and Joseph Wood. Of this convention Jeremiah Lee, of Marblehead, was chairman, and John Pickering, jr. of Salem, clerk. In the report made by a committee, which was unanimously accepted, they express their loyalty to the king, and their readiness to support with their lives and fortunes, his person, crown, dignity and constitutional authority. "But," they add, " by the horrors of slavery, by the happiness attending virtuous freedom, we are constrained to declare, that we hold our liberties too dear to be sported with, and are therefore, most seriously determined to defend them. This, in the present dispute, we conceive may be effected by peaceable measures. But though, above all things, slavery excepted, we deprecate the evils of a civil war; though we are deeply anxious to restore and preserve harmony with our brethren in Great Britain; yet, if the despotism and violence of our enemies should finally reduce us to the sad necessity, we, undaunted, are ready to appeal to the last resort of states; and will, in support of our rights, encounter even death, sensible that he can never die too soon, who lays down his life in support of the laws and liberties of his country."

To an attentive observer, it was evident that a crisis in American affairs was near—that a drama, the closing act of which was known only to the Ruler of the universe, was soon to open. The 19th of April came, mild and with summer's loveliness. The sun rose with unclouded splendor, and the husbandman went forth to his peaceful pursuits, and each man to his calling. Soon the scene changed. Groups were gathered at the corners of the streets in earnest conversation, men were seen hurrying to and fro, drums beat to arms, and stern determination was depicted on every countenance. What had given rise to this commotion? The appearance of a messenger, proclaiming as he went, that a detachment from the British army in Boston, had the night before left the city in silence, to seize and destroy military stores deposited at Concord. The effect was electric. The fire of patriotism burst forth with volcanic power. Capt. Joseph Rea, who commanded a company of militia, mounted his horse and posted with all possible dispatch to the Farms with the intelligence, proclaiming it aloud by the way. Capt. Caleb Dodge and others, following his example, rode off in other directions. The call to resist this act of aggression, met a hearty and united response. The farmer left his plough in the field, the mechanic his work-shop, and the merchant his store; and before 3 o'clock p. m. a large proportion of the male population of the town, capable of bearing arms, had gone forth, or were assembled in preparation to march to the rescue.

The consternation felt by the more timid portion

6

of the female population, in prospect of being left
defenceless, was great. A large number having by
mutual instinct collected together, their condition
was freely discussed. "Our husbands and sons are
gone," they despondingly said, "and none are left
to protect us. If the regulars come during their absence, what will become of us, what shall we do?"
"Do?" exclaimed a stout-hearted mother present,* a
fair representative of many hearts bold and determined as her own ; "Do? who cares for the regulars?
Let them come ; and if they do not behave themselves, we'll take our brooms and drive them out of
town."

The British troops paid dear for their success at
Concord, and their subsequent wanton devastations
when returning to Boston. The blood shed at Lexington was the signal for retaliation. The provincials, finding life and every thing valuable at stake,
assumed their native valor and returned the fire at
Concord bridge with deadly effect. As the troops
retreated, the discharge of musquetry was kept up
without intermission from walls, fences, houses,
trees and barns, until they were met by a reinforcement under the command of Lord Percy, who with
two field-pieces kept the provincials at bay for a
time. The people, however, flocking in from all
quarters in great numbers, the attack was renewed,
and a galling covered fire was continued until the
enemy reached Charlestown, having one hundred
and fifty men killed and wounded, and some taken
prisoners.† Of the men from Beverly, Reuben Ken-

* Mrs. Hannah, wife of Josiah Batchelder, jr.
† Journals Prov. Congress, Mass. pp. 662, 681, 682.

nison was killed, and Nathaniel Cleaves, Samuel Woodberry and William Dodge were wounded.*

The effects of this outrage upon the inhabitants of Beverly, were such as might be expected on a people who understood, and were determined to maintain, their rights. In May, the selectmen paid £26.10.6 for blankets to be supplied to the army, raised for eight months by the province. Other sums were subsequently appropriated for the same purpose, and purchases were made of the householders who cheerfully parted with a part of their family stock for the public use. In the work of supplies, female patriotism was warmly engaged during the whole revolutionary contest. Cloth was woven, stockings were knit, and garments made for the soldiers to a large amount, and every call for aid was cheerfully and promptly met.

On the 16th Jan., 1775, Josiah Batchelder, Jr., was chosen to represent the town in a provincial congress to be held at Cambridge, "to consult and deliberate upon such further measures as, under God, shall be effectual to save this people from impending ruin, and to secure those inestimable liberties derived from our ancestors."

This year the town voted to raise fifty-six minute men, including officers, who were to parade two half days in each week, during the pleasure of the town, to learn the military art. The vote for paying the minute men creating dissatisfaction, as no other towns had adopted the practice, it was repealed Feb. 29th, just one month after its passage. A mili-

---

* The widow of Kennison, after marrying a second time, died Oct. 22, 1842, aged 89. She retained in her possession till her death, the shirt worn by her first husband when killed.

tary watch, of sixteen persons, in four divisions, was established, and a watch-house for each division ordered to be built. The committee of correspondence were also directed to appoint a captain and other necessary officers, with a sufficient number of men, to exercise the cannon in the fort or breastwork on Woodberry's head, for which service they were to be paid a reasonable sum. They were likewise directed to enlist " a number of men, to make up forty in the whole, to repair to the fort, as their alarm-post, in case of an alarm."

One morning in the autumn of 1775, a privateer schooner sailed from Beverly on a cruise. She had not been long out, when she was discovered by the British ship of war Nautilus, of twenty guns, who immediately bore down upon her. The superior force of the enemy induced the captain to put back. The chase was continued until he gained the harbor and grounded on the flats. It being ebb-tide, the Nautilus came to anchor outside the bar, and opened a fire on the town. The meeting-house being the most conspicuous object, several shots were aimed at it, one of which penetrated the chaise-house of Thomas Stephens, destroying his chaise, and another struck the chimney of a house on the opposite side of the street, scattering its fragments in every direction. This unceremonious assault proved too much for the equanimity of its patriotic occupant. He seized his musket, and rushing to the beach, returned the compliment with hearty good will. Immediately upon the commencement of firing, many females residing in exposed situations, hastily retired to places of greater security. There were some, however, who, " made of sterner stuff," paid little attention to this demonstration of hostility, and continued their domestic occupations as though nothing uncommon was going on. Of this class, was a good lady, the wife of a devoted friend to American freedom, who was at the moment engaged in preparing a batch of bread for the oven. The house she occupied was directly in the range of the meeting-house, and liable to be struck by every discharge. Her brother, anxious for her safety, came in, and informing her of the danger, desired her to take her child, and proceed by a circuitous route to a place beyond the reach of the enemy's guns, while he would rally a company to resist any attempt to land. To this she demurred; she felt no alarm. Besides, her oven was heating, the bread was nearly ready, and as to leaving before it was set in, she could not think of it ! She was finally prevailed on to forego this resolution and retire. As she was passing around the south-eastern corner of the common, curiosity prevailed over apprehension; and, climbing upon the wall, she stood in full view of the enemy's vessel, surveying the scene, until a cannon-ball striking the earth near her, gave decided intimation that it was time to depart.

The alarm spread rapidly, and soon men were seen with their fire-arms hurrying from every quarter to the defence of the landing. Among the earliest on the ground, was Col. Henry Herrick, an active member of the committee of correspondence, and whose patriotic spirit greatly contributed to the energetic action of the town in furnishing men and supplies for the army. The confusion of the moment did not make him forgetful of the dignity of his official character; and with characteristic regard for effect, and disregard of danger, he appeared on the beach in full military costume, a conspicuous mark

6*

for the enemy's aim. The commander of the Nautilus soon found himself in an awkward position. Owing to an unlucky choice of anchorage, the receding tide left his vessel aground, which careened so that he was unable to bring a single gun to bear. In the mean time, the citizens of Salem opened a fire upon her from the Hospital point, with several four and six pounders, while a number of good marksmen, concealed among the rocks on the Beverly side, rendered it hazardous for an officer or man to appear on deck. In this condition, without power to offer a single token of his good or ill will, he lay until dark, when, the tide floating his vessel, he weighed anchor and stood out to sea, carrying with him no very pleasant recollections of his introduction to the citizens of this town.

The importance of fortifying the town was now apparent. Breastworks were thrown up on Woodberry's point and Paul's head, and furnished with cannon, and measures were adopted to procure a supply of ammunition. The committee of safety applied, through William Bartlett, Esq., the navy agent, to General Washington for assistance, who directed the following reply:

"CAMBRIDGE, 13th Dec. 1775.
" SIR:

" Your letter of the 11th, with a petition from the committee of correspondence for the town of Beverly to his Excellency, is come to hand. The General desires me to inform the committee that he would have great pleasure to comply with their request in the fullest extent, could he do it consistent with that attention which he must pay to the safety of the whole; that you may spare them such pieces of cannon as are not at present absolutely necessary for the armed vessels; that you may also spare them such a quantity of the shot that is on board the brig, as they may think necessary for their immediate use, taking from the committee an obligation to return the same, or the value of them, because these articles must be made good to the captors and the continent.

"As to the article of powder, that is of a very delicate nature ; but to show his willingness to serve the good people of Beverly, it is his Excellency's desire that you keep in your possession what powder you have found on board the prizes, making an immediate return of the quantity unto him. If it should so happen that the town and harbor is attacked by the enemy, the General consents that you lend the same unto the committee, at the same time taking their obligation, for reasons as before assigned for the shot. This is the most effectual way his Excellency can think of to answer the prayer of their petition, and this you will please to communicate unto them.

"I am sir, your most ob't serv't,

"STEPHEN MOYLAN, P. T. S.

"WILLIAM BARTLETT, ESQ."

In Jan. 1776, the town voted to hire twenty-four men to guard on the seacoast by night-watches, at West's beach and near Benj. Smith's house. Of these watches Benj. Smith and Azariah Woodberry were appointed captains, and £100 were provided to defray the expenses of guarding the town. At this time, Col. Glover, with the 14th regiment of the continental army, was stationed here, who maintained a watch at the fort.

The progress of events had now prepared the public mind for the declaration " that these United Colonies are, and of right ought to be, FREE AND INDEPENDENT STATES;" and in anticipation of such a measure, the town, at a meeting June 13, 1776, twenty-one days before it transpired, voted, that should the Continental Congress, for the safety of the colonies, declare them independent of Great Britain, they solemnly pledged " their lives and fortunes to support them in it." The General Court having recommended to the towns to consider the proposed articles of confederation and union among the states, the town, at a meeting Feb. 4, 1778, empowered and instructed its representative to act and do anything relative thereto, that in his judgment would be most for the public good. May 22d, the constitution of government devised by a convention of the State, having been laid before the town for its consideration, it was rejected by a vote of 22 to 3; and George Cabot, Rev. Joseph Willard and William Bartlett, were appointed a committee to draft instructions to the representative, expressing the reasons of dissent. It is an elaborate and interesting document, evincing a thorough acquaintance with the subject; and while it disclaims all disposition " to prevent good order, and encourage anarchy and opposition to equal government," it claims the right of opposing, " with a decent, but manly and zealous freedom," any form which they conscientiously think " does not tend to the public welfare."

In 1778, a requisition was made on the town to reinforce the army in Rhode Island; and the three captains of the militia companies, assisted by their subalterns, were authorized to obtain the quota on the best terms possible, " giving the preference to town inhabitants."

Paper money had at this period so much depreciated as to demand an effort for its improvement; and July 12, 1779, Geo. Cabot and Joseph Wood were appointed delegates to a convention to be held at Concord, for the purpose of " adopting such measures as shall be necessary to carry into effect, by common consent, the important object of appreciating the paper currency." At a subsequent meeting, the proceedings of this convention were highly approved. A county convention having been held at Ipswich, Aug. 19, to regulate the prices of labor, produce, and other articles, the proceedings were approved and adopted by the town, and a committee appointed to prepare a list, and cause it to be printed, for the use of the inhabitants. This list comprises nearly one hundred articles, from which the following are selected : West India rum, £6.6.0 per gal. ; N. England, £4.16.0; molasses, £4.7.0; coffee, 18s. per lb. ; chocolate, 24s. ; corn, £4.16.0 per bush.; rye, £6 ; beans, £7.10.0; house carpenter's labor, £3.6s.8d. per day ; mason's, 80 to 92s ; shoeing a horse all round, plain, £5.8.0 ; neat's leather or calfskin shoes, £7.7.0 ; making suit of clothes, superfine broadcloth, £18 ; spinning 20 knots linen yarn, 10s. 8d ; mug of flip or toddy, made of good W. I. rum, 15s ; a good dinner at the tavern, £1.1.0 ; sexton, for digging the grave of a grown person, £4.10.0. These prices were those paid in currency, and not in silver, one dollar of which, in 1781, was equal to $40 of the new emission paper, and $3200 of the old.

In 1779, a fine of £5400 was assessed on the town by the General Court, for failing to supply the number of militia required by a previous resolve; and March 13, 1780, a petition for its remission was prepared. The petition stated, that the town had ever been a steady friend and firm advocate of the revolution, and that the present delinquency was a consequent of "early and punctual compliance with precedent requisitions," which had exhausted them of men and much money. Appeal is made to the public records, in evidence " that their quota of the

continental army in 1777, and the many levies of
militia, had been furnished with a steadiness equalled in but few other places;" to which it is added,
" that as a town they had furnished more men, and
been at greater expense in carrying on the war, than
almost any other town, in proportion to their abili-
ties"—a fact that the proceedings of numerous town
meetings, from 1765 to 1783, conclusively demon-
strate.

In August, this year, George Cabot and Joseph
Wood were elected delegates to a convention to meet
at Cambridge, on the 1st Sept. following, for the
purpose of framing a new State constitution.   At
the town meeting in May, 1780, it was submitted for
consideration ; and, after being read and discussed,
it was referred to Josiah Batchelder, George Cabot,
and Rev. Joseph Willard, " to revise, examine, and
make such remarks on the same as they might think
best."   At an adjourned meeting the subject was
further discussed, and the report of the committee,
together with sundry proposed amendments and instructions, was adopted by a unanimous vote.

From the commencement of the war until its termination, this town was largely engaged in privateering. Between March and November, 1781, fifty-
two vessels, carrying 746 guns, with crews of 3940
men, were fitted out and chiefly owned in Salem and
Beverly.*   Among the successful commanders were
Captains Eleazer Giles, Elias Smith, Hugh Hill, and
Benjamin Lovett.   In 1776, Capt. Giles sailed from
this port in a brig of ten guns, and soon after fell in
with a fleet of merchantmen, laden with stores,

* Felt's Annals.

bound from Jamaica to London, four of 'which he succeeded in capturing, viz: the ship Lucia, 400 tons, brigs Alfred, Success, and another, name unknown, of 300 tons each. On another cruise he was less successful. Falling in with a British vessel, of equal or superior force, and relying on the boasted bravery of a newly shipped crew, he gave battle. Immediately upon the attack, a portion of his men proved by their conduct that his confidence in their bravery had been misplaced; and after a short, but sharp engagement, in which he was wounded, he was compelled to surrender, and was carried into Halifax.

Capt. Smith, a courageous and dignified officer, commanded the ship Mohawk, of 20 guns, and cruised off the West Indies. In 1781 he fell in with, and after a short engagement captured, a Guineaman of 16 guns, which he sent into Beverly. When the captain came on board to surrender his sword, he was presented to Capt. Smith, who stood abaft the wheel, clad in a sailor's coarse pea-jacket, with a red bandanna tied round his head, as a substitute for a tarpaulin. " Do you command this vessel, sir?" inquired the captain of the slaver. " Yes, sir," replied Smith, folding his arms, and with characteristic politeness making a very low bow, " in the room of a better."

Capt. Hill, who came early to this country from Ireland, commenced privateering in the Pilgrim, of twenty guns, the building of which he superintended at Newburyport. He was a brave and generous officer, and distinguished for humanity to his prisoners. On one cruise, while sailing with the English ensign at mast-head as a decoy, he was boarded by the captain of a British vessel of war, who not suspecting the character of his entertainer, remarked that he was "in search of that notorious Hugh Hill." Unprepared at the moment for an engagement with so formidable a foe, Capt. Hill replied that he was on the look-out for the same individual, and hoped soon to meet him. After spending some time on board without penetrating the disguise, the officer departed. In the course of a few days, Captain Hill again encountered his visiter. The American flag was immediately run up, and an engagement ensued, which resulted in the capture of his British antagonist, who, with his vessel, was sent into Beverly. Capt. Hill's principal theatre of action was the coast of Ireland, where he captured many vessels, and greatly annoyed British commerce. After leaving the Pilgrim, he commanded the Cicero, and took several prizes. Probably more captured vessels were brought into this port than into any other in New England, the cargoes of which furnished important and seasonable supplies for the continental army.

Among the enterprizing and successful commanders not engaged in privateering, was Capt. John Tittle. During the revolutionary war, he sailed in a letter of marque, in company with two other vessels, for a port in France. They were fallen in with by three British cruisers; and as, from the superiority of force, resistance appeared vain, Tittle's companions bore off before the wind, with the hope of escape. One succeeded, and the other was captured. In the meantime, Capt. T. was attacked by two of the enemy, and, nothing daunted, returned their fire for the space of two hours, by which time all his canvass above the lower yards was shot away. The crew, overcome with fear by the seeming desperation of their situation, began to abandon the guns—whereupon the captain drew his sword, and ordering them back to duty, threatened to run the first man through who again left his quarters. At this moment the third enemy bore up, and hailing Capt. T. commanded him to strike his colors. To this he replied, " It will be time enough to strike when compelled;" and then addressing the crew, " we'll try them a little longer." The battle was continued another hour with great spirit; when a shot taking effect between wind and water, silenced one of the enemy, and night coming on, they all drew off and left Capt. T. to pursue his voyage without further molestation.

Foremost among the officers and soldiers in the revolution, from this town, and eminent also as an enterprizing and valued citizen, was Col. Ebenezer Francis. He was born at Medford, Mass., Dec. 22. 1743, and in 1764 removed to Beverly.

His opportunities for acquiring an education in youth, had been quite defective. But, by diligent self-culture, he had early fitted himself to engage extensively and successfully in business transactions, and to take a respectable stand by the side of the best educated and informed, in the prominent stations he afterwards occupied before the town and his country. Notwithstanding the disadvantages, in this respect, under which he had labored, and which he had been obliged by himself mainly to overcome—probably induced, in no small measure, by this very circumstance—he took a warm and efficient interest in the schools. And it is worthy of mention, as evincing at once his interest in them and his resolute spirit, that in one instance, when the scholars of one of the districts, (now called the Cove district,) had risen against their master, and compelled him to abandon

7

his post, he immediately undertook the government
and instruction of the school, and very soon not only
quelled the rebellion, but restored a wholesome state
of discipline and improvement.

In 1766 he was married to Miss Judith Wood, by
whom he had four daughters and a son. He was
actively and extensively engaged in business till the
war broke out. He had, however, taken a deep interest in the political agitations which preceded it.
Convinced that resort must finally be had to arms in
deciding the controversy between this and the mother
country, he paid much attention to military science
and exercises himself, and encouraged it as far as he
could in his fellow-patriots. His three brothers partook of the same martial spirit, and all of them became officers in the revolutionary service. By his
stature, which was tall and imposing, as well as by
talents and character, he was fitted to command.
Accordingly, he at once occupied a prominent stand
among those who, on the first shedding of blood,
were ready to take up arms. In less than three
months from the commencement of hostilities, he received a captain's commission from the Continental
Congress, which was dated July 1, 1775. Early in
the following year, he had risen to the rank of Colonel, and commanded a regiment stationed on Dorchester heights, near Boston, from Aug. to Dec.
1776. Under his prompt and thorough discipline,
his men were shortly trained; so that in his regimental orders of Aug. 29, 1776, he " flatters himself
that they will soon attain that degree of soldiership
that will be but a little inferior to the most veteran
troops." By a commission dated Nov. 19, 1776, he
was authorized by Congress to raise a regiment in

the State of Massachusetts ;—which was raised, under the name of the 11th Massachusetts regiment,
and retained that designation through the war. At
the head of this regiment, Col. Francis marched in
Jan. 1777, to Ticonderoga. With that regard for
religion, which was a characteristic of his life, he—
previously to setting out on the march—had his regiment assembled to attend religious services in the
meeting-house of the first parish. Those who remember that occasion, express in glowing terms their
recollections of its interest and solemnity. Associated with him on that perilous expedition into the
wilderness, were many brave and noble spirits, and
some of them highly educated. His revered and
beloved pastor, Rev. Mr. Hitchcock, of the second
parish, in Beverly, and afterwards minister of a
church in Providence, R. Island, accompanied the
regiment as chaplain, having succeeded in that station the celebrated Dr. Cutler, of Hamilton. Henry
Herrick, a graduate of Harvard College, and, after
the war, a distinguished teacher in Beverly, was
adjutant of the regiment. Moses Greenleaf, collector
of Newburyport, under the federal government, and
father of Prof. Greenleaf, now of the law college, at
Cambridge, was a captain in it. A private journal
of Capt. Greenleaf, which is now in the library of
the Massachusetts Historical Society, narrates the
principal events which occurred while the regiment
was stationed at Ticonderoga, and afterward, on its
retreat, with the rest of the garrison, before the over-
powering forces of Burgoyne. From that is gathered
the following graphic, though melancholy sketch of
the closing scenes in the life of Col. Francis. "14th
June, heard enemy's morning gun—Indians and

others near—skirmishes. 2d July, enemy advance, with two frigates of twenty-eight guns and fifty gun-boats—land troops about two miles from us. Saturday, 5th July, at 12 o'clock, spied British troops on the mountain overlooking Ticonderoga—at 9, received the disagreeable news of leaving the ground. At 2, next morning, left Ticonderoga—at 4, Mount Independence; after a most fatiguing march, arrived same day at Hubbardton, (near Whitehall, N. Y.), twenty-two miles from Mount Independence—supped with Col. Francis—encamped in the woods, the main body going on about four miles. Monday, 7th July, 1777, breakfasted with Col. F. At 7, he came to me, and desired me to parade the regiment, which I did : at $7\frac{1}{4}$ he came in haste to me, told me an express had arrived from Gen. St. Clair, informing that we must march with the greatest expedition, or the enemy would be upon us,—also, that they had taken Skeensborough, with all our baggage ;—ordered me to march the regiment—immediately marched a part of it. At twenty minutes past 7, the enemy appeared within gunshot of us ; we faced to the right, when the firing began, which lasted till $8\frac{3}{4}$ a. m., without cessation. Numbers fell on both sides ; among ours, the brave and ever to be lamented Col. Francis, who fought bravely to the last. He first received a ball through his right arm, but still continued at the head of our troops, till he received the fatal wound through his body, entering his right breast ; he dropped on his face. Our people, being overpowered by numbers, were obliged to retreat over the mountains, enduring on their march great privations and sufferings." Thus fell, in the prime of manhood, one of the most promising officers of the revolution,—

one whose bravery and valor, friends and foes alike were forward to acknowledge—whose worth, the aged, that knew him, still delight to recount, and whose untimely loss they yet with flowing tears lament.

The following excellent letter from his pastor and the chaplain of his troops, conveyed the sad tidings of his fall to her, who was most nearly and deeply interested in the event.

"Moses Creek, July 21, 1777.

"Dear Mrs. Francis:

"My heart is filled with compassion and sympathy for you, while I relate the melancholy tale of the fall of my dear friend, the Colonel. You will consider this event as under the government of that God, who has an undoubted right to do as seemeth Him good, and therefore, endeavor to command your passions into a silent submission to His will. If there is any consolation in the gospel, I think you may accept it. I doubt not, your loss is his greater gain : I can witness to his uniformly good conduct in the army, in discountenancing vice, and encouraging virtue ; in setting before his men an example of sobriety, and an attendance upon duties of piety. No officer so noticed for his military accomplishments and regular life as he. He lived universally beloved, the loss of him as generally lamented. While these things make you look upon your loss the greater they might administer to you unspeakable consolation. He was not unmindful of the dangers of the field, being appointed to bring up the rear-guard. He supposed it probable they might be attacked, and therefore, desired me to take care of his knapsack with what was in it, if I could not save anything else, which I did, though I lost my clothes by doing it. He was in good spirits when I parted with him the evening before the retreat. He mentioned his being equally exposed to fall with others, but seemed willing to commit himself to Providence, and leave the event. His conduct in the field, is spoken of in the highest terms of applause. He has embalmed his name in immortal fame. I must conclude by wishing

7*

you all Divine supports. Trust in God. He will provide for you and the fatherless children.

"From your sincere and affectionate friend,

"E. HITCHCOCK."

Subjoined are extracts from " Travels in America, by a British officer," who was in the battle of Hubbardton, and afterwards quartered as prisoner in the vicinity of Boston.

" The rear guard of the enemy was composed of chosen men, commanded by a Col. F., who was reckoned one of their best officers.

" At the commencement of the action the enemy were every where thrown into the greatest confusion; but being rallied by that brave officer, Col. Francis, whose death, though an enemy, will ever be regretted by those who can feel for the loss of a gallant and brave man, the fight was renewed with the greatest degree of fierceness and obstinacy.

" A few days since, walking out with some officers, we stopped at a house to purchase vegetables. Whilst the other officers were bargaining with the woman of the house, I observed an elderly woman sitting by the fire, who was continually eyeing us, and every now and then shedding a tear. Just as we were quitting the house she got up, and bursting into tears, said, ' gentlemen, will you let a poor distracted woman speak a word to you before you go?' We, as you must naturally imagine, were all astonished; and upon inquiring what she wanted, with the most poignant grief and sobbing as if her heart was on the point of breaking, asked if any of us knew her son, who was killed at the battle of Hubbardton, a Col. Francis. Several of us informed her that we had seen him after he was dead. She then inquired about his pocket-book, and if any of his papers were safe, as some related to his estates, and if any of the soldiers had got his watch; if she could but obtain that in remembrance of her dear, dear son, she should be happy. Capt. Ferguson, of our regiment, who was of the party, told her, as to the Colonel's papers and pocket-book, he was fearful they were either lost or destroyed;

but pulling a watch from his fob, said, 'there, good woman, if that can make you happy, take it, and God bless you.' We were all much surprized, as unacquainted that he had made a purchase of it from a drum-boy. On seeing it, it is impossible to describe the joy and grief that was depicted in her countenance; I never in all my life beheld such a strength of passion; she kissed it, looked unutterable gratitude at Capt. Ferguson, then kissed it again; her feelings were inexpressible; she knew not how to express or show them; she would repay his kindness by kindness, but could only sob her thanks; our feelings were lifted up to an inexpressible height; we promised to search after the papers, and I believe at that moment, could have hazarded life itself to procure them."

This watch is now in the possession of Col. Francis' son, Ebenezer Francis, Esq. of Boston.

John Francis, a brother of Col. Francis, was born in Medford, Sept. 28th, 1753, and previously to the revolutionary war, removed to this town. At the commencement of the struggle for freedom, he entered the service of his country. He was an adjutant in the regiment commanded by his brother, and fought by his side in the battle of Hubbardton. He subsequently held the same office in the regiment under the command of Col. Benj. Tupper, and continued in the war during the first six years, an active and rising officer. He was in several battles, was wounded at the capture of Burgoyne, and retired, with honor, from the army. In 1786, he raised a company in Beverly and Danvers, and marched in Col. Wade's regiment, to suppress Shays' rebellion. He was captain of the militia company in the second parish, and afterwards commanded the Beverly regiment. He was also for many years a selectman, and served in other important municipal offices. He was amiable in his domestic relations, and much esteemed for his hospitality and cheerfulness. He died July 30th, 1822, in the 69th year of his age.

Capt. Joseph Rea, of whom mention has been made in the preceding pages, was the son of Gideon Rea, who owned and lived on the estate now the property of Mr. Edward T. Proctor, in the second parish. He was born in 1736, baptized by Mr. Chipman, Aug. 1, the same year, and died in 1798, in his 63d year. He was an efficient member of the committee of correspondence, and commanded a company enlisted in Beverly and Lynn, sent to the aid of Washington, in New Jersey. His sons were Isaac, Gideon, Joseph and Ebenezer.

Ebenezer Rea is still living, at the advanced age of eighty-two. He was fifteen when the battle of Lexington took place, and retains a vivid recollection of events that transpired in this town during the revolutionary war. In 1778, he enlisted under Capt. Jeremiah Putnam, of Danvers, from whose company he was drafted, with others, to fill up a regiment stationed at East Greenwich, R. I. After his term of service expired, he shipped on board the Resource, Capt. Richard Ober, of Beverly, and sailed for the West Indies. On the voyage he was taken by a British sloop-of-war, and carried into Jamaica. Here, instead of being confined as prisoners, he and a part of the crew were transferred, as sailors, to the frigate Pelican, Capt. Collingwood, afterwards second in command with Nelson at the battle of Trafalgar, and for more than a year was not permitted to go on shore.*

_____

* Capt. Collingwood is described, by Mr. Rea, as of a tall, commanding figure, dark complexion, with black eyes, from whose piercing glance nothing on shipboard escaped. He was a rigid dis-

While cruising on that station, in August, 1781, the Pelican encountered a severe hurricane, and was wrecked on the rocks of Morant Keys. Four of the crew were lost. The remainder succeeded in reaching a small, uninhabited island, on rafts, where they remained ten days, with but little food, and were taken off by the Diamond frigate, which came to their relief from Jamaica. On returning to that island, Mr. Rea and several of his shipmates were put on board the Hinchinbroke, and one day, while lying at Port Royal, they obtained permission to go on shore. Tempted by so favorable an opportunity, they determined to desert from a service into which they had been forced, and, if possible, return to their native land. The resolution was more easily formed than executed. Unforeseen obstacles beset their design : and, after wandering up and down the island for twenty-five days, inventing various stories to escape suspicion, and heartily wishing more than once that they had never undertaken a plan so seemingly impracticable, they were forced to return to the very place from which they started. Fortunately, they unobserved got on board a cartel ship, bound to Havana, with Spanish prisoners, the commander of which was in want of seamen. They frankly informed him who they were and what they had done, and he, with a kindness for which they hardly dared to hope, shipped them at once for the voyage. On arriving at Havana, they were paid off and discharged, and Mr. Rea then took passage for Boston

---

ciplinarian, but kind to the crew, not permitting the petty officers to impose upon them. He never used profane language, and often on the Sabbath officiated as chaplain.

on board a brig commanded by Capt. Henry Higginson. When on soundings, off New York, the brig was taken by a British cruiser and carried into that port. He was immediately put on board the Jersey prison-ship, where he was confined from January to May, 1782, when he was exchanged and returned to his friends.

Sept. 14, 1774, Major John Leach deceased, in the 74th year of his age. He was among the active whigs of the early part of the revolution, and was a member of the committee of correspondence in this town at the time of his death.

In the preceding February of this year, a donation was made by the town for the relief of the poor in Boston, consisting of two barrels of sugar, one barrel of rum, five and a half quintals of fish, one hundred and five pounds of coffee, two cheeses, eight pairs of women's and five pairs of men's leather shoes, one hide of upper-leather, three curried calf-skins, sixteen pounds of chocolate, ten pounds of pork, twenty-five pounds of flax, one barrel of flour, one and a half bushel of corn, and £31 9s. 10d. in money. Some of the poor of Boston were also quartered upon the town.

In 1775, a scarcity of bread appears to have been apprehended, as the supplies by water were mostly cut off; and, at a town meeting held on the 19th June. two days subsequent to the battle of Bunker Hill. the selectmen were ordered to purchase 1500 bushels of grain and ten casks of rice, to be disposed of by them in the best manner, for the use and benefit of the town. A similar precaution in relation to ammunition was adopted, and a fine of ten shillings was imposed on any one who should " unnecessarily waste or fire off any charge of powder."

At a meeting held in April, 1776, the town declined sending delegates to a convention held at Ipswich, "relative to an equal representation by every man's having a like voice in the election of the legislative body of this colony;" but, at a subsequent meeting, a committee was appointed to sign, in behalf of the town, the memorial agreed upon by that convention.

The year 1777 was distinguished by a riotous proceeding, in which the gentler sex were the principal actors. The merchants of this town, in consequence of the little confidence they had in a constantly depreciating paper currency, refused to sell the West India commodities in their possession, at the stated prices. This determination gave great offence, and under the excitement of the occasion, a number of women resolved to redress the grievance, forcibly or otherwise. One cold November morning, a company of about sixty, wearing lambskin cloaks with riding hoods, marshalled by three or four leaders, one of them bearing a musket, marched in regular order down Main and Bartlett streets to the wharves, attended by two ox-carts. They proceeded to the distil-house, where a quantity of sugar, belonging to the estate of Stephen Cabot, deceased, was stored. In the meantime, the foreman of the distillery, to whose custody the goods had been committed, locked the gates at the entrance of the passage leading to the store, and stood sentry within, to prevent the ingress of the assailants. Finding themselves opposed, they called to their aid a reinforcement of men, who, with axes, soon demolished the gates. The gallant foreman still maintained his post, and made a bold demonstration of resistance. His fair assailants, nothing daunted, pressed vigorously to the onset, and seizing him by the hair, which was not of nature's growth, were proceeding to execute summary vengeance, when he eluded their grasp by leaving his artificial covering in their hands—and fleeing all but scalpless to the counting-room, locked himself in for safe-keeping. The work of victory then commenced. With the co-operation of their volunteer reinforcement, these gentle expounders of "women's rights" forced the doors of the store, and rolled out two hogsheads of sugar, which were placed on the carts in attendance. The affair had now assumed a serious aspect, and several other merchants having a quantity of sugar on hand, and unwilling to risk the consequences of resistance and possible defeat, entered into a negotiation, which resulted in an agreement, on their part, to sell each a barrel of sugar to the female dictators, at the stipulated price, and receive paper money in payment. With this treaty the war closed, and the valiant band dispersed. The sugar was carted to the house of the principal leader, who kept a shop, and was there dealt out in convenient parcels, according to treaty engagement. Acting as agent in the business, she received and paid over the money to the owners of the sugar, with whom an amicable settlement was subsequently made for the quantity forcibly taken.

It is but just, in closing this brief account of a proceeding in which the ludicrous and the serious are blended, to remark, that few seaport towns having so much foreign trade as this had in times past, and so much privateering and other maritime business, have been so distinguished for their uniform, orderly submission to the laws of the land. The single departure from this course here related, probably had the effect of inducing greater caution among the well-disposed, and occasioned their prompt interference to check the first motions towards any disorderly pro-ceedings.

The year 1788 is an epoch in the history of Beverly, marked by the establishment of the first cotton mill in America; that of Slater's, at Pawtucket, having been commenced in 1790. A building of brick was erected in the second parish, near "Baker's corner," at the junction of the Birch-plain and Ipswich roads, and a company of proprietors incorporated Feb. 3, 1789, without any exemption or privilege, except that of acting as a body corporate. Great expectations were entertained from the introduction of manufactures into the country on an extensive plan, at this early period. A periodical of the day, describing this factory, says, "that an experiment was made with a complete set of machines for carding and spinning cotton, which answered the warmest expectations of the proprietors. The spinning-jenny spins sixty threads at a time, and with the carding machine, forty pounds of cotton can be well carded per day. The warping machine and the other tools and machinery are complete, performing their various operations to great advantage, and promise much benefit to the public, and emolument to the patriotic adventurers." This establishment was visited by Gen. Washington, on his tour through the country in 1789. Not realizing the anticipations of the proprietors, they abandoned it as a body corporate, and the business was carried on by individu-

als, who subsequently erected a mill at the head of
Bass river, for the purpose of spinning cotton by
water-power. This enterprize proving unprofitable,
the machinery and buildings of the cotton mill were
finally removed, and the brick factory was destroyed
by fire in 1828. In 1841 a steam factory was incorporated, and a large amount of stock subscribed, but
operations were temporarily suspended for more favorable times.

The first election for governor, and other state officers, subsequent to the ratification of the constitution of the United States, was held in Beverly this
year, April 8th, at which John Hancock received
155 votes for governor, and Elbridge Gerry 17. For
lieut. governor, Benj. Lincoln received 158 votes,
and James Warren 17.

The winter of 1780 is known as the hard winter.
The snow fell seven successive days in December, to
the depth of four feet on a level. The cold was intense, and for thirty days the sun made not the
slightest impression on the snow, even in southern
aspects. Many persons perished ; and in this town,
from scarcity of fuel, a considerable number of fruit
trees were cut down.

May 19, 1780, is distinguished as the *dark day*.
The sun rose clear, but soon assumed a brassy hue.
About 10 o'clock, A. M., it became unusually dark.
The darkness continued to increase till about 1
o'clock, when it began to decrease. During this time
candles were necessary. The birds disappeared and
were silent, the fowls went to their roost, the cocks
crew as at day-break, and every thing bore the
appearance and gloom of night. The alarm produced by this unusual aspect of the heavens was great,

and tradition has preserved many anecdotes of terror.
An old gentleman of rather singular turn, supposing
the judgment-day at hand, dressed himself with unusual care, and taking his silver-headed cane walked
out into the field to await the event. As the darkness came on, Mr Willard, who possessed some rare
instruments, took a station on the common to make
observations, and was soon surrounded by a large
number of his parishioners, who gazed on his operations with awe and wonder. Mr. W. paid no attention
to the conjectures and expressions of alarm uttered in
his hearing, and calmly pursued his investigations.
In the midst of these, a person of excitable temperament came running from the seashore, exclaiming in
accents of terror, " the tide has done flowing!" " So
it has!" replied Mr. Willard, who, with admirable
presence of mind took out his watch—" so it has, for
it is just high water."

The night succeeding the day was of such pitchy
darkness, that in some instances horses could not be
compelled to leave the stable when wanted for service. About midnight the clouds were dispersed,
and the moon and stars appeared with unimpaired
brilliancy. This phenomenon is supposed to have
been occasioned by the smoke arising from extensive
fires in Maine, New Hampshire and Vermont, and
which, owing to the clearness of the air and light-
ness of the winds, had accumulated over this region
in immense quantities. This year was also remarkable for the brilliant appearance of the aurora borealis,
which, from the description, must have been more
magnificent than the display witnessed on the evening
of Dec. 11, 1830.

On the 4th of September, the first town meeting

was held for the election of governor, lieut. governor and councillors, pursuant to the provisions of
the new constitution, when the following votes were
given.   For governor, James Bowdoin, 29; John
Hancock, 16.   For lieut. governor, John Hancock,
29; Benjamin Greenleaf, 14; James Bowdoin, 2.
The first representatives under the constitution, were
Larkin Thorndike and Jonathan Conant.

This year, Col. Henry Herrick deceased.   He was
an active agent in all the first revolutionary movements, and for many years represented the town in
General Court.   He frequently presided at the numerous town meetings held to consider the public concerns, at a time when it required a good degree of
moral courage for any one to appear conspicuously
in acts and measures of doubtful result, and in event
of failure, placing him in the position of a rebel
against the King and the government of Great Britain.   His house stood on the site of the present
residence of Ebenezer Meacom.   His family consisted of eight children, viz: Joseph, Pyam, Henry,
Joanna, Elizabeth, Nancy, Mary and Ruth.

The peace of 1783 was hailed in this town with
demonstrations of the liveliest joy.   This year the
town refused its assent to the proposition for holding
and keeping at Ipswich, all the courts of law and
offices of register of deeds, register of probate, and
clerk of the courts of common pleas and general
sessions of the peace, and instructed its representative, Mr. Dane, to govern himself accordingly.   In

1784, £1200 were voted to be raised for the service of the town and the payment of debts. In 1785, Mr. Dane was elected a delegate to Congress, and was succeeded as representative by Larkin Thorndike. In 1786, the pecuniary difficulties and embarrassments of the town, in common with every part of New England, were very considerable, arising in part from debts contracted during the war, the general stagnation of commerce, and the burdens of taxation consequent upon the revolution. This year the "Shays' rebellion" occurred—to suppress which, a regiment of militia was marched from Essex county under the command of Col. Wade, of Ipswich, an officer in whom Washington, during the revolution, reposed the utmost confidence. In 1787, the votes for governor were 125, of which John Hancock received 77, and James Bowdoin 48. The same year George Cabot, Joseph Wood and Israel Thorndike, were chosen delegates to represent the town in the State convention to be held in Boston, Jan. 1788, for the purpose of taking into consideration the constitution or frame of government for the United States, proposed by the federal convention.

Between 1786 and 1789, town offices went begging. So many persons chosen declining to serve, resort was had to a fine as a compulsory measure to complete the proper organization. The greatest difficulty was experienced in obtaining persons to serve in the office of constable, as they were obliged to collect the taxes in their respective wards, a duty which appears to have been peculiarly onerous at that time. To secure the services of these officers, a fine of £5 was imposed on those who refused to accept the office when chosen, or procure a substi-

8*

tute : and even this measure was not always successful, as it appears that, in 1786, seven town
meetings were held between March and October,
before persons would serve rather than pay £5 fine.

In 1790, Larkin Thorndike and Joseph Wood were
chosen representatives, and instructed to attend the
General Court together only on occasions of extraordinary business, and at other times separately. In
1791, the town treasurer was directed to fund the
paper money on hand, or sell it, as he might think
best. In 1792, it was voted that all contracts should
be made and paid in hard money instead of town
orders.

Feb. 22, 1793, Washington's birth-day was celebrated with a display of colors and a ball and supper
in the evening. Among the toasts were the following :

"Agriculture—May we always revere the most
ancient and most useful of arts.

" Manufactures—May a conviction of their utility
in an improved state, make us cherish them in their
infancy.

" Commerce—May it universally be conducted on
the liberal principles of reciprocal advantage."

The proclamation of neutrality, issued by the
President of the United States in 1793, and induced
by the war then existing in Europe, was regarded by
every friend of peace as " a wise and prudent measure, well-timed, founded on fact, and calculated to
secure the honor and promote the true interests and
happiness of the country." The design of that proclamation was warmly seconded in this town. At a
meeting of the merchants and others, held the 25th
of July, of which Moses Brown was chairman, reso-

lutions were unanimously adopted, recognizing its necessity and propriety, as not only announcing to the powers of Europe the equitable disposition of the United States, and tending to produce a reciprocity of friendly sentiments, but also as admonishing all American citizens of the penalties to which a violation of the laws of nations subjected them. In order to preserve "the strictest neutrality between the powers at war," the meeting further resolved, that "should any inhabitant of these States, regardless of all moral and political obligations, fit out or be interested in any privateer or vessel armed to cruise against any nation at peace with the United States, we will endeavor to detect him, that he may suffer the punishment inflicted by the law for such piratical conduct."

The subject of revising the State constitution was laid before the town in 1795, and decided in the affirmative by a vote of twenty-six to ten. In 1796, a petition drawn up by Rev. Mr. M'Kean, William Burley, Israel Thorndike, Moses Brown and John Stephens, was adopted by the town with entire unanimity, and presented to Congress, praying for the immediate fulfilment of the treaty made between the United States and Great Britain.

Soon after the close of the revolutionary struggle, public attention was directed to the vast wilderness of the west as "much to be desired for a possession." Statesmen saw in that immense territory the future seat of civilization and political power. Political economists perceived, in a mild climate, a fertile soil, numerous navigable streams and geographical relations, superior advantages for agricultural, manufacturing and commercial pursuits, as well as for the

support of a dense population ; and capitalists dream-
ed of fortunes to be made by investments there.
The "Ohio fever," as it was aptly denominated,
prevailed throughout New England, and numerous
families left "their pleasant homes, to follow the
guiding hand of Providence to the western realms of
promise." Forty-four years ago, " a long ark-like
looking wagon was seen traversing the roads and
winding through the villages of Essex and Middlesex,
covered with black canvass, inscribed on the outside
in large letters, 'to Marietta on the Ohio.' That
expedition, under Dr. Cutler, of this neighborhood,
was the first germ of the settlement of Ohio, which
now contains a million and a half of inhabitants.
Forty-four years have scarce passed by, since this
great State, with all its settlements, improvements,
canals and growing population, was covered up (if I
may so say,) under the canvass of Dr. Cutler's
wagon. Not half a century, and a State is in existence, (twice as large as our old Massachusetts) to
whom not old England, but New England is the land
of ancestral recollections."* In the afore-named company of emigrants, was the family of Peter Shaw
and several other persons of this town.

1798. The town this year for the first time chose
a health officer, and in 1801 a hospital was erected
on Paul's head at an expense of about $450. This
point was originally the property of Paul Thorndike,
one of the first selectmen of the town after its incorporation, and from him derived its name. A watch-
house was built here as early as 1711.

January 18, 1799. The schooner Alert, of Beverly,

* Everett.

Capt. Jacob Oliver, was taken by three French privateers as she was entering the harbor of Santander, and sent into Bayonne. She was not captured without a noble struggle. With only two guns, she beat off a lugger that led on the attack, and continued the combat with a second, until that was reinforced by a ten-gun schooner, when she was compelled to strike. This outrage upon American neutrality excited strong murmurs among the inhabitants of Santander, and the commander of the fort notified the captains of the French privateers in the harbor, that if they attempted to put to sea after an American vessel came in sight, he would sink them.

From 1773 to 1800, numerous town meetings were held for the adoption of measures to prevent the introduction and spread of the small-pox. A committee of inspection was chosen; a house provided to which suspected persons and their goods were to be conveyed for examination and cleansing; smokehouses were erected, and fences were thrown across the roads, to prevent the passing of persons without inspection. Inoculation with small-pox virus, though several times commenced, never met with cordial approbation—owing, perhaps, to the same prejudice that resisted its introduction into Boston, in 1720. In 1788, it appearing that the practice of inoculation continued, a committee was appointed to inform the masters of all houses infected with the disease, that they were forbidden, under the highest displeasure of the town, and the penalties of the law, to permit any person to come into their house, for the purpose of inoculation, or of passing through the distemper. To carry the intention of the town more completely into effect, all suspected persons were required to undergo fumigation, and inoculation by physicians and all other persons was prohibited after the first day of July. In 1800, the town was thrown into alarm by the introduction of virus from London, supposed to be vaccine, but which unfortunately proved to be the matter of small-pox, or a disease nearly approximating to it, probably the varioloid. A town meeting was the consequence, exhibiting strong symptoms of tumult, but which happily terminated without violence. At this meeting, inoculation either for small or kine-pox, was again prohibited except at hospitals, and various other precautionary measures were adopted. Since 1800, the general introduction of kine-pox by vaccination, has prevented the spread of small-pox here as elsewhere.

In 1803, the town concurred in the petition of John Heard and others, for a turnpike from Beverly to Newburyport. This road was intended to be commenced at Nathaniel Batchelder's blacksmith's shop; and running in a direct line across Dodge's Row near the school-house, to intersect the main road in Hamilton, near Dr. Faulkner's corner. This project was prosecuted no further than to procure an act of incorporation. The same year, $1500 were voted for the repair of the highways.

March 27, 1807, Capt. George Raymond died, aged 99 years and about 3 months. He was the son of Nathaniel and Rebecca Raymond, and was born Dec. 21, 1707. He was in the Cape Breton expedition, and is mentioned in the town records of 1770, as moderator of a meeting at which measures were adopted to suppress the use of tea. He resided, at the time of his decease, in the second parish.

July 4th. The thirty-first anniversary of American Independence, was celebrated with particular demonstrations of joy. The Light Infantry, and other military companies paraded, and salutes were fired from a cannon used to announce the memorable declaration of 1776, at sunrise, noon and sunset. At half past 9 o'clock, the Light Infantry company paraded in front of Hon. Israel Thorndike's mansion, and received the present of a standard; after which, with a numerous company of ladies, the clergy, gentlemen of this and the neighboring towns, and the officers of the third regiment, they partook of refreshments liberally provided by that gentleman. At eleven o'clock a procession was formed and moved to the South meeting-house, escorted by the Light Infantry, a part of Capt. Brown's company, and the Salem Juvenile Artillery, the whole under the command of Capt. Rantoul. Prayers were offered by Rev. Messrs. Emerson and Randall, and an appropriate discourse delivered by Rev. Mr. Abbot, from Exodus 12 : 14. After the religious services, the procession was again formed and escorted to a tent on Watch House Hill, under which about two hundred persons of different politics partook of an elegant dinner, at which Col. Lovett presided. Among the toasts given were the following :

"The Militia : Every citizen a soldier, and every soldier a patriot.

"Our Fisheries : While we draw wealth from those exhaustless mines, with gratitude may we remember the patriots who procured us the blessing.

"Agriculture, Commerce, and the Arts : Together they flourish ; separated they die.

" Schools, Academies, and Colleges : May they be nurseries of science and virtue.

" The Ladies of Beverly, who this day presented the standard to the Light Infantry: May their generous patriotism be long held in grateful remembrance."

Dec. 22d, the long embargo was enacted which was subsequently repealed by the non-intercourse act of March 1, 1809. The political excitement of this period, is shown by the number of votes given at successive elections. The whole number cast in April, 1807, was 588; in April, 1808, 654; in Nov. 1808, 671; in April, 1809, 650. At these times the fishermen and seamen were generally at home, and particular pains were taken to induce every voter to use his franchise.

Jan. 21, 1808, Joseph Wood departed this life, aged 68 years. During a period of more than forty years, he was constantly connected with town affairs. He represented the town in General Court for a great number of years, and from 1771, to the day of his death, nearly thirty-eight years, filled the office of town clerk. He had also been a selectman, and for some years before his decease was an acting justice of peace and notary public. During the whole of the revolutionary war, he was one of the committee of correspondence, inspection and safety, thus occupying a place of great labor and responsibility, which was bestowed only on such as were well known to be zealously devoted to the cause of their country. In 1788, he was a member of the convention for ratifying the constitution of the United States, and the fidelity with which he discharged every public duty, uniformly secured to him the unbounded confidence of his fellow-townsmen.

This year, the town petitioned the Congress of the United States, to suspend the operation of the embargo laws. The petition is recorded at length, and will, in future time, be an interesting document to those who are desirous to become acquainted with all the transactions of that period. The following year, at one of the most numerous meetings ever held in this town, spirited resolutions were unanimously passed, disapproving of the embargo laws, and a petition embracing the substance of these resolutions, was voted to be presented to the General Court, praying for relief.

December 10, 1809, Josiah Batchelder, jr., Esq., deceased, aged 73. He was the son of Josiah Batchelder, who served in the expedition against Port Royal in 1707, under the command of Capt. Benj. James, of Marblehead, and died at the advanced age of 88. Mr. Batchelder early commenced a nautical life, and by energy of character, soon rose to the command of a vessel. In 1761, on his passage from Georgia to St. Christopher, with a cargo of lumber, he was taken by a French privateer, and, after being detained twenty-four hours, succeeded in obtaining the release of his vessel for two thousand three hundred pieces of eight. For the payment of this sum he was retained a hostage on board the privateer; while his vessel, under the charge of his first officer, was despatched to St. Eustatia or St. Christopher for the money. In the meantime he was carried into Martinico and thrust into a filthy prison, from which he obtained release, and proceeded to St. Christopher,

9

where he entered a protest against the whole proceedings.

Mr. Batchelder was early a warm, devoted and
energetic friend to the cause of freedom, to promote
which he made large pecuniary sacrifices. His fellow-citizens honored him with their confidence by
electing him six times to represent their interests in
the General Court. He was also elected a member
of the Provincial Congress in 1775, and again in '76,
'77 and '79, and in both assemblies was placed on
the most important committees. His extensive business and public station made for him a large acquaintance at home and abroad, and his numerous
guests were entertained with a generous hospitality.
For many years Mr. B. discharged, with great acceptance, the duties of a justice of the peace; and
when, by act of Congress, Salem and Beverly were
formed into one district, he received the appointment of surveyor and inspector, which office he held
until his decease. He was thirty-five years a member of the first church, and departed this life, leaning,
with unshaken confidence, on the Christian's hope.

In 1810, the town, by vote, protested against the
removal of the term of the Supreme Judicial Court
from Ipswich to Newburyport. In 1812, soon after
the declaration of war against Great Britain, spirited
resolutions were passed in town meeting, disapproving the proceedings of the government of the United
States, and approving the course of the General
Court and of the Governor in relation to the war.
Delegates were also chosen to attend a county convention at Ipswich. In 1814, a memorial was adopted by the town and ordered to be presented to the

General Court, in reference to the sufferings of the inhabitants from embargo and war. In 1814, an attack being apprehended from the enemy, several families removed to the interior.

On the 9th of June, a barge, from a British ship of war, pursued a schooner belonging to Manchester, towards this harbor. Unable to escape, she was run ashore on Mingo's beach and abandoned. The British set her on fire, but the flames were afterwards extinguished by the neighboring inhabitants without much damage. The alarm occasioned by this affair was followed by a public meeting, at which measures were adopted for the effectual protection of the town. Subsequently, a company of infantry from Haverhill and Methuen, and of artillery from Danvers, were stationed here for the defence of the coast; but the following winter, cause for further warlike preparations was removed by the treaty of peace, executed at Ghent, Dec. 24, 1814, and ratified by the American senate Feb. 16th, 1815.

March 6th, 1819, Mr. Robert Endicott, an exemplary and respected citizen, deceased, aged 62 years. Mr. Endicott was a descendant from Governor Endicott, of the fifth generation. He removed from Danvers to Beverly in the latter part of 1781, being the first of the name that settled here. He married Mary, daughter of Rev. Nathan Holt, of Danvers. Of seven children, two only survive, who, with their families, reside in this town.

In 1820, the question of amending the constitution was submitted to the people, who gave a majority in the affirmative. Four delegates were elected by this town to attend the convention called for that purpose, and which consisted of about five hundred members.

December 22, 1822, William Burley died, in the 72d year of his age. He was a native of Ipswich, and was born January 2d, 1751. He took an active and zealous part in the war of the revolution, and was some years an officer in the American army.

On the 3d of February, 1780, when under the command of Col. Thompson, on the lines near White Plains, Mr. Burley, who was then a lieutenant, was taken prisoner in a severe skirmish with a detachment of British troops. Col. Thompson, who commanded, was also taken, with several other officers and about ninety men. This misfortune was owing to the negligence and imprudence of the Colonel, who omitted the precautions he had been directed to take to guard against any sudden attack.*

Mr. Burley was compelled to remain a prisoner a year and nine months, on his parole, on Long Island, when he obtained his liberty by an exchange. This long captivity, at such a crisis, was a very severe trial to one of his active character and ardent patriotism. The last year of his imprisonment he was allowed the pay and rations of a captain in the continental service.

He left a legacy to this town of five hundred dollars, to be expended for the instruction of poor children in reading and the principles of the Christian religion. This legacy was managed by a committee appointed for the purpose, who bestowed the benefit on such children in different parts of the town as, in their judgment, most required it. A legacy of a similar character was also left to his native town.

August 31st, 1824, General La Fayette, then mak-

---

* Heath's Memoirs, p. 230.

ing a tour of the country he had so signally served by the side of Washington, passed through this town. He was received, as he was every where, with every demonstration of respect. His arrival was announced by a salute of thirteen guns, from Ellingwood's point. An arch was erected on Essex bridge, at the line of the town, beautifully decorated with flowers, evergreens and flags, bearing the inscription, "Welcome, La Fayette, the man whom we delight to honor." On arriving opposite the bank, where was displayed across the street a line of national banners, he was cheered by a concourse of citizens. His carriage and escort halted for a short time, amidst a furious rain, when he was addressed by Hon. Robert Rantoul in behalf of the citizens, as follows:

"GENERAL: The inhabitants of Beverly bid you welcome. We welcome you to our country,—that country which owes so much to your aid in the acquisition of her independence. We receive you not merely as the friend of our beloved country, but as the friend of MAN. Your labors, your sacrifices, your sufferings in the cause of liberty, demand our gratitude. Tyrants receive the commanded adulation of their slaves, but to the benefactors of our race belong the spontaneous effusions of our hearts. Accept our sincere congratulations that you live to witness the order, the prosperity, the happiness that results from our free institutions; and may the evening of your days be solaced with the reflection that those principles of government, to the support of which your life has been devoted, and which alone can secure the enjoyment of rational liberty, are fast spreading their influence through the whole family of man. Wishing you long life and uninterrupted happiness, we bid you farewell."

9*

After an affectionate reply to this address, the General resumed his journey.

In 1827, Capt. John Low died, in the 82d year of his age. He was born in Hamilton, in 1745. He became a resident of Beverly before the revolutionary war, at the commencement of which he forsook his business of cabinet-making, and raised a company for the continental army. After leaving the army he kept a public-house near the ferry-way, and subsequently removed to Lyman, Me., where, until the day of his decease, he enjoyed the confidence of his fellow-townsmen.

In consequence of the alarming prevalence of the Asiatic cholera in various parts of the country, in 1832, a town meeting was held August 4th, at which a committee of nine persons, including the selectmen, was appointed as a health committee, who were authorized to take such measures to prevent its introduction and spread as should be thought necessary. This committee, in discharge of their duty, caused directions to be printed and circulated, in which they recommended attention to personal cleanliness, moderation in the use of food, total abstinence from the use of distilled spiritous liquors, and the exercise of a moral courage that results from a rational confidence in God.

July 4th, 1835. The anniversary of American independence was celebrated in this town on the 3d July, the 4th being the Sabbath, without distinction of party. The oration was by Edward Everett, the present minister from this country to Great Britain, who chose for his subject the early part of the life of George Washington, terminating with the French war, about 1756. This effort of the distinguished orator was one of his happiest. For an hour and a half, he spoke without recurrence to notes, and riveted the attention of a crowded and overflowing audience in the Dane street meeting-house. At the close of the exercises, a numerous company, with invited guests, including twelve revolutionary veterans, repaired to a pavilion erected on the common, where they partook of an excellent dinner. The pavilion was tastefully decorated with flowers and evergreens by the ladies, who were complimented at the table in the following toast:

"The Ladies of Beverly, who have labored for our present accommodation; and with their permission we would mention the *Lady Superior*, whose great industry and good taste have done so much for the beauty and ornament of the scenery about us. May she never consign herself to a cloister less joyous and happy than that which witnesses the festivities of this day."

Hon. Robert Rantoul presided at the table, assisted by several vice-presidents; and although total abstinence from intoxicating liquors did not then generally prevail, yet the example of the president, and some other *teetotalers*, was not lost upon the company; and on the whole, the entertainment may be pronounced one of the most orderly, tasteful and intellectual, of its kind, ever enjoyed by the citizens of Beverly. Among the toasts offered on the occasion was the following, in compliment to the orator:

"The orator of the day: The union of genius, talents and industry, regulated by virtuous principle, will always command respect and esteem from a free and enlightened community. The power of eloquence, when employed to promote harmony, union and peace among friends and neighbors, excites the most grateful feelings, and merits the warmest praise."

This sentiment was responded to by Mr. Everett, in a neat and appropriate speech, which was received with great applause. Addresses were also made by

Hon. Leverett Saltonstall of Salem, and Mr. Blunt of New York. Letters, accompanied with toasts, were read from a number of distinguished gentlemen, who were unable to accept the invitations extended to them.

The committee of arrangements consisted of fourteen citizens, of whom Josiah Lovett, 2d, was chairman. The escort duty was performed by the Beverly Light Infantry. The bells were rung, and salutes fired in the morning and at evening; and after sunset a display of fireworks was made on Watchhouse hill. The celebration was conceived and carried out in an excellent spirit, and the occasion passed off with fewer causes for regret than usually attend festivities of this description.

August 20th, a town meeting was held, at which a series of resolutions were adopted, and a committee appointed to endeavor to obtain a change of the location of the Eastern Rail-road, from the east to the west side of Essex bridge. The objections to the former location, as urged in the resolutions, were, substantially, that the construction of a bridge there would materially injure the anchorage accommodations of the harbor, incommode citizens engaged in the cod fishery, expose the town to fire from engines, endanger the lives of numerous children who must cross the road in going to and from school, and permanently injure the business, prosperity and growth of the place; all of which evils the location of the road west of the bridge would obviate. At an adjourned meeting, Sept. 17th, the report of the committee was accepted, their number enlarged, and instructions given them to continue their efforts to obtain a compliance with the resolutions passed at the first meeting. This object was attained in 1837.

PUBLIC BUILDINGS, AND ESSEX BRIDGE.

BESIDES the houses for public worship, the principal public edifices in Beverly are the town-hall, bank, and almshouse. A large three-story brick building was erected in 1839 on Cabot street, at the head of Bartlett street, by Mr. John Bell, and fitted up for stores, offices, reading-room, etc. It also contains a hall for lectures and other public assemblies, and is known as " Bell's hall." A cupola surmounts the building, affording a convenient " look-out," from which vessels may be seen far away at sea.

The old town-hall occupies an elevated site, a short distance easterly from the main street. It was erected in 1798, by Mr Obediah Groce, of Salem, at a cost of about $2000. It is two stories high, and has a cupola, furnished with a bell. It was originally built to accommodate the grammar-school ; but when completed, a vote was passed to occupy the second story for town purposes, previous to which time town meetings had been held in the first parish meeting-house. It has been variously altered, from time to time, and in 1842 was sold to the grammar district, who gave it the name of BRISCOE HALL.

The new town-hall stands on the east side of Cabot street, a little south of the first parish meeting-house. It is of brick, three stories high, of remarkably correct symmetry, and is highly ornamental to the town. It was originally built for a private residence, by Andrew Cabot, about fifty-five years ago, in the most substantial manner, the walls being very thick. It subsequently became the property of the late Israel Thorndike, who ornamented its ample grounds with numerous fruit and

forest trees, shrubs and plants.   In 1841, it was purchased of the heirs of Mr. T., and altered as it now
appears.   On the first floor are rooms for the school
committee, selectmen, assessors and town clerk.   The
second and third stories are thrown into one, making
a large and commodious hall, with galleries on three
sides, furnished with fixed seats, while for the main
floor moveable settees are provided.   The hall is light-
ed with astral lamps, and the rostrum is furnished
with a sofa and chairs.   The whole interior arrangement is neat and convenient, and reflects great credit
on the gentlemen under whose superintendence the
work was executed, as well as on the mechanics by
whom the labor was performed.   The committee to
whom was committed the care of this enterprize,
consisted of George Brown, chairman, John Safford,
Augustus N. Clark, James Haskell, and Francis
Woodberry.

The hall was opened for public purposes October
26, 1841, with appropriate religious exercises, and
an address from Hon. Robert Rantoul.   The building, with the public square adjoining it, is protected
on its west and south sides by a neat fence of chain,
inserted in granite posts; and is shaded by a number
of beautiful horse-chestnut and elm trees.   Altogether, it is one of the finest and most convenient
buildings for town purposes in the county.

The banking house is also on Cabot street, at the
corner of Central street.   It is of brick, three stories
high, and was built by John Cabot, a brother of Andrew, near the time of the erection of the new town-
hall.

Attention was directed to the wants of the poor,
very soon after the town was incorporated; and one
of the conditions of a contract, made for the support

of a pauper in 1723, was, that he should be kept as a *christian* ought to be kept. As early as 1719–20, a vote was passed by the town to build an alms-house. It was afterwards re-considered, and that purpose was not finally accomplished until 1803, when the house now owned by the town was erect-ed. It is pleasantly situated on a court, running northerly from Cabot street. The house is two sto-ries high, and contains twelve rooms, besides two in the basement; one of which is used as a kitchen, and the other as a work-room. The basement story also contains the necessary cells for the confinement of disorderly persons. The house was very tho-roughly repaired in 1838, at an expense of $2,500, and under its present efficient management, affords a humane asylum for the friendless poor. Land owned, and rented by the town for that purpose, is cultivated by the inmates of this house, who raise potatoes and other vegetables sufficient for their own consumption, and cut hay enough to keep two cows. Among the greatest conveniences obtained for this town by corporate enterprize, is Essex Bridge. On the 26th Dec. 1636, a ferry was established between Salem Neck, or North Point, and Cape-Ann-side, as Beverly was then styled. It was kept by John Stone, who was to receive as passage-money, "2*d.* for each stranger, and 1*d.* for an inhabitant of Sa-lem." The next year (1637) the inhabitants of Bass-River-side, petitioned the court to exempt them from the ferriage fee, on the ground that they did not re-ceive any part of the toll profits; but the prayer was not granted. In 1639, the ferry was granted to Wil-liam Dixy for three years. He was "to keep a horse-boat; to have for a stranger's passage, 2*d*; for townsmen, 1*d*; for mares, horses, and other great beasts, 6*d*.; for goats, calves, and swine, 2*d*.

Jan. 5, 1698–9, the ferry-landing on the Beverly side was laid out by order of the Court of General Sessions of the Peace, on a return by a jury. This landing includes nearly all the flats between Safford & Stone's wharves, and, although not the property of the town, has been until recently a public landing. In 1749, the ferry was let for £3 sterling a year; and the rates of toll were fixed at 6*d*. old tenor, or 1 copper for a passenger, 2 coppers for a horse, 7 for a chair, 9 for a two-wheeled chaise, and 11 for a four-wheeled carriage. In 1783, it was let for £30 a year. A boat was to be kept in the night on each side of the river, and no more than double ferriage was to be required at unseasonable hours.

It appears from the records, that this town claimed a right in the ferry, in opposition to the claims of Salem to an exclusive property. In 1742, it was voted, that the inhabitants feel aggrieved by Salem's taking away their former privilege in passing and repassing the ferry between Salem and Beverly, and a committee was chosen to treat with the selectmen of Salem about the matter, and to report ten days before the subsequent meeting in March. At the March meeting, following, in 1742–3, the report of this committee was considered and accepted, but further proceedings stayed until the action of Salem thereon was ascertained. At a meeting in September of the same year, a committee of five was appointed to use all lawful means for recovering the town's right in the ferry, and Mr. Bollan was retained as counsel. At a meeting, Dec. 26, 1743, John Thorndike, jr. was appointed agent for the town in relation to this dispute, but in what manner it was adjusted, if ever, is unknown.

As population and travel increased, the inconvenience of a ferry must have been proportionably realized, and the erection of Charles river bridge, connecting Boston with Charlestown, suggested the idea of a similar improvement here. The subject was brought before the town at a meeting held June 21st, 1787, on the petition of Thomas Stephens and others, and a unanimous vote was passed to instruct the selectmen to petition the General Court to grant George Cabot and others an act of incorporation, for the purpose of building a bridge. The selectmen, to whom this duty was assigned, were Joseph Rea, John Lovett, 4th, Charles Dodge, Jonathan Conant and Asa Leach. The prayer of the petitioners was granted, though not without opposition, Nov. 17th, 1787. The persons named as corporators, were George Cabot, John Cabot, John Fiske, of Salem, Israel Thorndike, and Joseph White, of Salem, whose shocking murder, in the night of April 6th, 1830, thrilled the community with horror. The first proprietors' meeting was held at the Sun tavern, in Salem, Dec. 13, 1787, of which Nathan Dane was moderator, and William Prescott, clerk.

The first directors were George Cabot, John Fiske, Andrew Cabot, Joseph White, Edward Pulling, Joseph Lee and George Dodge. At the first meeting of the directors, George Cabot was chosen president, George Dodge and John Fiske, vice-presidents, and Thomas Davis, jr. treasurer. Robert Rantoul was chosen president in 1838, and has since sustained the office.

The first pier was laid in May, 1788, and on the
10

24th September of the same year, the bridge was opened for passage. The bridge is 1484 feet long, 32 feet wide, and consists of 93 piers. It has a draw, with convenient piers, hawser, etc. for the accommodation of vessels passing it. Its cost was about $16.000. The stock is divided into two hundred shares, and for several years previous to 1830, sold for about five times the original par value. It is still good property. The proprietors are required to pay to Salem £40 annually, as compensation for the ferry-ways, and £10 to Danvers.

With a view, as it seems, to prevent a diversion of travel from Danvers Neck, which it was apprehended the erection of Essex bridge would effect, a bridge was commenced, and though opposed by the corporation of Essex bridge, completed over Frost Fish river, near where the dam of the Danvers and Beverly iron-works company now is. The feeling in which this work was accomplished, gave it the name of *Spite bridge*, the memory of which time has not entirely obliterated. The right to take toll on Essex bridge was granted for seventy years from its opening, when it reverts to the Commonwealth.*

SCHOOLS AND ACADEMY.

THE history of education in this town, could it be written in detail, would be exceedingly interesting and instructive, illustrating the importance it has ever held in the estimation of its citizens; and show-

* The course of the bridge from Beverly side to Salem, is south 5 deg. west.

BEVERLY, AS SEEN IN THE DISTANCE FROM FROM THE I LEAGUE MILE.

ing the various progress it has made here in common with sister towns. It is probable that provision of some kind was made for the education of children very soon after the settlement in 1630, though nothing relating to the subject is found on record until 1656, when a meeting-house was built, which was also used for a school-house. For aught that is known, this arrangement continued for a period of more than eighteen years, when, Nov. 5th, 1674, a school-house was ordered to be built on the town's land, near the meeting-house, 20 feet long, 16 feet wide, and 9 feet stud. This was also to serve the purpose of a watch-house. At what time this order was executed does not appear. The erection of this building, from causes unknown, was probably delayed several years, as by an arrangement entered into May 19, 1677, with Samuel Hardie, (the first schoolmaster whose name is recorded,) it was stipulated that he should have the meeting-house to teach in during that summer, and some other place during the winter. His agreement with the selectmen, was "to teach ordinary learning according to the utmost of his ability, and to take a faithful account, and receive pay according to ordinary rates." His first contract was for the year, and if the payments of the scholars did not amount to £20, the town was to meet the deficiency; and if the payments exceeded that sum, he was to pay the surplus to the town. He continued to keep the school for several years. He was the son of Robert Hardie, a citizen and haberdasher of London. Jan. 24, 1675, he married Mary, daughter of Samuel Dudley, of Exeter. Nov. 5, 1674, he was chosen clerk of the writs for Beverly; and Sept. 1, 1684, was employed, with Andrew

Elliot, to transcribe the town records into a new book. Besides being a teacher of youth, he is supposed to have exercised the functions of a physician.

At a town meeting Nov. 2, 1686, it was "agreed by said town, with Corporal David Perkins, that the said town should have and did hire of said Perkins, one convenient room or chamber with a fire-room in it, for the space of six months after the date hereof, for the just sum of 10s. in pay, for a place for Mr. John Pearly to teach school in during said term, for the use of said town. And further, it was then agreed that the new selectmen, with the assistance of Capt. William Rayment and Corporal Thomas West, as a committee, were chosen to agree with said schoolmaster, about the terms of teaching for said town, provided that said committee do not exceed £20 in pay, or £10 in money, for said teaching one whole year from the date hereof."

In 1700, in conformity to the law then in force, a grammar-school was established, and Robert Hale, son of the minister, was appointed master, with a salary of £10, and an additional allowance if he kept an English school. The next year the school was kept by Daniel Dodge. In 1704, James Hale, another son of the minister, was the master, who taught writing, reading, casting accounts, Latin and Greek grammar, at a salary of £30. In 1720, the school was kept by Pyam Blowers, son of the minister, who is the last of the early teachers of whom record is made.* In 1782, the grammar-school was

---

* John Rogers, Henry Rust, William Shurtliff and John Cotton, are among the graduates of Harvard College, who were teachers in this school at an early period.

discontinued, for which the town was presented to the Court of Sessions, when it was resumed again and continued without further interruption to 1825, a period of 124 years. The grammar-school was kept in various places till 1798, when it was established during its further continuance in the new house on Watch-house Hill, the second story of which was fitted up for town purposes.

About 1700, attention to the schools declined, but revived again about 1749, when the teacher was required to return a list to the selectmen, of the names of parents and masters, and the number of children and servants belonging to each, that were instructed by him. The selectmen were to tax the parents and masters for the support of the school, except such as they judged proper to exempt, and commit the tax to one of the constables for collection. Any person refusing to pay for his proportion of fuel, was to be punished by his children or servants being denied the privilege of warming themselves at the schoolhouse fire!

At a meeting March 20th, 1749–50, the sum of £32, old tenor, was voted to the inhabitants of the east part of the town, to enable them to keep a school four months in the year. The next year £4.5.8, lawful money, was voted them for the same purpose, and in 1752, it was voted that the grammar-school should be kept in that part of the town in proportion to what they paid towards taxes. From 1754 to 1825, various changes and improvements were made, when the grammar-school was abolished, and a vote was passed to divide the school money raised by the town, among the ten school districts as they now exist, according to the number of ratable

10*

polls. In 1836, the school committee revised the
school regulations, which, at a subsequent town-
meeting were adopted. The books prescribed for
the use of the schools in those regulations, are—Cum-
mings' Spelling Book, New Testament, Young Reader, Introduction to the National Reader, National
Reader, Sullivan's Political Class Book, Wood-
bridge's Geography and Atlas, Colburn's Arithmetic
first part and sequel, Goodrich's History of the
United States, Comstock's Philosophy, Holbrook's
Geometry, Fowle's Linear Drawing, Blair's Rhet-
oric, Colburn's Algebra, Bowditch's Navigator, Worcester's Dictionary, Story's Abridgement, Parker's
Natural Philosophy, Greenleaf's Arithmetic—to
which list others have since been added. It is made
the duty of instructors to exert their best endeavors
to impress on the minds of children and youth, committed to their care and instruction, the principles of
piety, justice, and a sacred regard to truth; love to
their country, humanity and universal benevolence;
sobriety, industry and frugality; chastity, moderation and temperance; and those other virtues which
are the ornament of human society and the basis
upon which a republican constitution is founded:
but no books are to be used in school which are calculated to favor the tenets of any particular sect of
christians.

By the returns of 1841, it appears that the number of persons in this town between the ages of
4 and 16, is 1249, being an increase of 40 since the
census of 1840, and of 122 since 1839. The number
of all ages in all the schools is 1345, of which number 50 are over 16 years, and 46 under 4. The average attendance in the schools in summer, is 504;

in winter, 593; making 152 less than the whole number between 4 and 16. The number of children in primary schools is 817. In 1809, the school money was ordered to be rated at $1.90 for each poll, which is the sum assessed at present. The amount raised by taxes for the support of schools in 1798, was $1140; in 1806, $1600, and for their support last year, $2240.10. The gross amount paid for public and private tuition, including the academy, is upwards of $5000. The schoolhouses, ten in number, were, with a single exception, erected before public attention was awakened, as for the last few years it has been, to the improved construction of such buildings. They are, nevertheless, commodious and in good condition. A convenient schoolhouse was erected in Bass river district in the autumn of 1842.

The report of the school committee, made to the town meeting, March 10, 1806, is recorded at length. This is the commencement of a series of able reports on the state of the schools, which have been continued to this time, with manifest good effect in raising the standard of education. By spreading a general statement of the condition and relative improvement of the schools before all the citizens at the annual town meeting, a more general interest in the subject is excited. Emulation is also produced among the respective districts, which tends to the improvement of their schools. Without this general diffusion of knowledge concerning the schools, any attempts at improvement, made in town meetings, will always be received with an indifference more fatal to success than positive opposition. But the benefit of these reports is not confined exclusively to the towns to which they are made. By a provision of law, a copy of them is required to be sent, with the annual returns, to the secretary of the Commonwealth, for the use of the Board of Education. They are then examined by the secretary of the board, who makes such extracts as he judges may be serviceable, and incorporates them with the abstracts of returns which he makes to the board. These are published in a volume, and a copy sent to each of the towns in the Commonwealth; and thus, an account of any improved method of managing schools, or a useful hint made in a report of one town, may become available to every district in the State.

For the gratifying change effected in the character of the public schools, from 1804 to 1827, the town is chiefly indebted to the school committee, and especially to its chairman, Rev. Dr. Abbot, for that period, whose unwearied devotedness and careful attention to the qualifications of teachers, contributed essentially to elevate the standard of education. Since the impulse thus given, succeeding committees have watched over the schools with unabated interest, and performed an amount of service highly creditable to their public spirit. The requisitions of the law have been conformed to, and a gradual improvement has been made. The condition of the schools at the present time is better than at any former period. In the grammar district arrangements are made by which the poorest children may obtain a good academic education, and if they desire it, be advanced in a collegiate course.

The public schools, it has been justly remarked by one whose age and experience give weight to his words, "ought to be equal to the wants of every class in society; and until they are made so, they do not answer the proper end of their institution. If any class are obliged to separate from others in the EDUCATION of their children, it lays the foundation for distinctions and separations in SOCIETY in riper years, incompatible with those principles of equality which ought to be so carefully cultivated and guarded by all who have at heart the preservation of our political institutions." The public school system was conceived in the spirit of republicanism. It proposes to educate for all the practical purposes of life, the mass, who without its aid must suffer the evils of ignorance, as well as entail those evils on the community. And it further aims to strengthen the arch of republican institutions, and to perpetuate social equality, by bringing together and subjecting to a common training the children and youth of all stations. If the spirit of its conception is kept constantly in view by the guardians of education, this desirable and important result may be obtained, guaranteeing thereby the fulfilment of the fondest hopes of the patriot and philanthropist. How far, or how soon, the public schools will be equal to the wants of every class in society, must mainly depend on the parents and guardians of youth. Laws may do something and school committees may do more; but, unless seconded by those who have the deepest interest at stake, the progress must be necessarily slow. Schools may have a name to live; but while parents and guardians are indifferent to their improvement, it is comparatively little that committees can effect. The destiny of these institutions—colleges of the people, as they have been denominated—is not in the custody of the legislature exclusively, nor yet in the care of a few individuals appointed by the town to examine into their condition from time to time. It is in the hands of parents and guardians, and on them rests the responsibility of their prosperous existence. If parents will do for their children as much as they do for favorite animals—if they will see that their bodies are warmly, comfortably and healthfully housed, and their minds suitably fed—if they will visit the school with something of the interest with which they go to their various employments, and with frequency—if they will exercise their right in demanding high qualifications in teachers, and in nameless other ways second the views and come up to the help of committees and the friends of education, public schools *will* flourish, and the bread thus cast upon the waters will return in an abundant and well-ripened intellectual harvest.

The BEVERLY ACADEMY was projected as a private school in February, 1833, by a number of gentlemen, who associated for that purpose. On the 1st of May following, they purchased an eligible lot of land on the north-easterly side of Washington street, and, dividing the property into thirty-two shares, immediately commenced the erection of a building suited to their object. On the 17th June, the same year, the school was opened under Abiel Abbot, of Wilton, N. H., as principal, and Mary R. Peabody, as assistant. Mr. Abbot was succeeded the next year by Charles A. Peabody, of Tamworth, N. H. He continued only one term, when Edward Bradstreet was employed. On the 30th January, 1835, the proprietors of the school obtained an act of incorporation, and Mr. Bradstreet continued the instruction until 30th June, 1836. His assistant, with some intermission, was Ann W. Abbot. He was succeeded on 25th July following by Thomas Barnard West, who remained principal till his much-lamented death in October last. His assistants have been Mary Williams, Ann W. Abbot and Mary T. Weld. The present principal is Edward Appleton, who graduated at Cambridge in the class of 1835. The average number of pupils has been about 30 of both sexes, more than half of whom were males. The Academy has been from the first under excellent supervision, and has won for itself a deservedly popular reputation.

In 1837, a school was commenced in the second parish, and incorporated as the NEW ENGLAND CHRISTIAN ACADEMY. This school was conducted on the manual labor system, and during its continuance, averaged about 60 pupils. Its preceptor, with the exception of a single term, was Mr. Joseph Henry Siewers. The Academy remained in operation less than two years, when, for reasons of a pecuniary nature, it was closed. The principal university in the United States has found munificent friends among the citizens of this town, who, within about twenty years, have made bequests and donations to it amounting to nearly $50,000.*

COLLEGE GRADUATES.

THE following is a list of persons born in this town, graduated at the several colleges in New England.

* Quincy's Hist. Harvard College.

The list doubtless exhibits less than the whole number, as the means for obtaining an accurate account are necessarily imperfect.

HARVARD. 1686, Robert Hale. 1703, James Hale. 1721, Robert Hale, jr., Pyam Blowers. 1724, William Balch. 1728, Joseph Lovett. 1731, Henry Hale. 1732, Joseph Herrick. 1733, Thomas Balch. 1738, John Chipman. 1767, Henry Herrick. 1777, Jacob Herrick. 1782, Benjamin Bartlett, Larkin Thorndike. 1791, Nathaniel C. Lee. 1799, Joseph Dane. 1806, Daniel Oliver. 1809, Nathaniel K. Oliver. 1810, Thomas Stephens. 1812, Charles Brown. 1813, William Thorndike. 1816, Augustus Thorndike. 1818, Henry K. Oliver (honorary degree). 1820, Ingalls Kittredge, Jr. 1826, Andrew P. Peabody, Robert Rantoul, Jr.

BOWDOIN. George Thorndike (honorary degree at Harvard, 1807). 1811, John M'Kean. 1817, James M'Kean. William Abbott and Isaac Rea (date unknown). 1826, George Trask. Frederick Choate (date unknown).

AMHERST. 1831, Benjamin Ober. 1836, D. Oliphant. 1839, James D. Trask. 1842, Issacher Lefavour.

YALE. Nathaniel Dike, Joseph Shaw.

DARTMOUTH. 1796, Josiah Batchelder (degree of M. B. at Harvard, 1799). 1839, Benjamin Franklin Edwards.

LIBRARIES, READING ROOMS AND LYCEUM.

THE Social Library was commenced by subscription, Jan. 20th, 1802. It was divided into one hundred and thirty-two shares, and an assessment of $5 laid on each share. The $660 thus raised, was invested in a valuable collection of books, selected by Joshua Fisher, Nathan Dane, and Thomas Davis, assisted by Rev. Mr. McKean. This collection has been increased from time to time by donations, and by purchase with sums raised by assessments, until it now contains not far from one thousand volumes. The original share-holders were seventy-two. They now number more than one hundred.

The library is supplied with several of the most valuable foreign and domestic periodical publications, and books are added from time to time by the trustees, who are invested with discretionary powers. The utility and benefit of this institution were sensibly felt soon after its establishment, when books were comparatively scarce and costly, affording, as it did, to many families, the perusal of valuable books not readily elsewhere found; and its usefulness is constantly increasing.

The Mechanics' Association possess a select and increasing library, which affords the means of intellectual improvement to its members. This and the Social Library are kept in the school-committee room, in the town-hall, both of which are open weekly, the former on Thursday and the latter on Saturday, for the delivery and return of books. Connected with some of the churches, particularly the First, are valuable libraries. There is a circulating library kept by Stephens Baker, and several good private collections. But the most striking and important feature in the diffusion, among us, of useful knowledge by books and reading, is the School District Library.

11

It had, for several years, been an object of desire to the friends of education, that something might be effected for the intellectual benefit of a large and constantly increasing juvenile population, who from local and other causes, were not enjoying the advantages to be obtained in populous villages and cities. To this end, a resolve was passed in General Court, 1842, appropriating $15 from the State school fund, to every school district in the Commonwealth that shall raise a like sum for the purchase of a school library. By the establishment of such libraries in each district, the means of intelligence are placed in the hands of every child; and if the books are selected, as they should be, with reference to usefulness, entertainment and moral influence, the result cannot be otherwise than propitious to intellectual and moral development; and it is highly creditable to this town, that the provisions of the resolve are very generally complied with; so that, with the Sunday-school libraries, in each of the religious societies, the youth of Beverly are in the possession of unusual advantages. Simultaneously with the inception of this plan, a publishing firm in Boston commenced the publication of a series of works, under the supervision of the Board of Education, entitled the "Common School Library." It consists of fifty 12mo. volumes, and the same number of 18mo. size, adapted to the capacities of young readers. Taking into view the distinguished character of the board, consisting of gentlemen of both political parties and of different religious denominations, the freedom of the books from sectarian peculiarities, and the superior mechanical execution of the work, these volumes may be pronounced unrivalled by any series ever issued from the American press, and are worthy, as they will command, an extensive patronage.

The other means for general information in this town, are three reading rooms, which are well supplied with newspapers. A lyceum was established here among the earliest in New England, and has been, to this time, successfully sustained.

MERCHANTS.

In the list of distinguished merchants and valued citizens, may be recorded the names of George, Andrew, and John Cabot, Moses Brown, Israel Thorndike, Joseph Lee, John and Thomas Stephens.

GEORGE CABOT was born in Salem, in 1751, and in childhood came to this town. He early engaged in commercial pursuits, and at the age of eighteen became the master of a vessel, in which capacity he visited various parts of Europe. Mr. Cabot belonged to that class of citizens, who have contributed so much to the prosperity of the United States, and who gave occasion to Burke's splendid eulogium on the enterprize and intelligence of New England navigators. His sea-faring life was made subservient to the improvement of a mind naturally contemplative and quick to discern. The countries, customs, and people, with whom his foreign voyages made him acquainted, were regarded with the eye of a statesman and philosopher, and he drew from them enlightened and comprehensive views of human nature and society.

In 1779, at the age of twenty-five, Mr. Cabot was chosen by the town delegate to the provincial congress which met at Concord, with a view to the visionary project of ordaining a maximum of prices. At this time, in the ruinous condition of commerce, it was hoped to cheapen commodities by forcing the holders to sell at reduced and fixed rates. Good sense triumphed over folly, and it was at this congress that Mr. Cabot first displayed that profound acquaintance with the correct principles of political economy, for which, throughout his life, he was most remarkable. Before Adam Smith was known in this country, and twenty years before Say and the continental writers had formed any correct ideas on the subject, he maintained the present prevailing and enlightened doctrines concerning domestic and international commerce.

He was an influential member of the state convention, in 1788, which was called to deliberate on the adoption of the federal constitution; and in securing the dearest interests of the country, was associated with King, Ames, and Parsons. Subsequently to this, he was elected to the United States senate. Of that body he possessed the entire confidence, and was at the same time the confidential friend of Washington and Hamilton, then the eye and ear of the nation. If there be any merit in the financial system reported by Hamilton, and preserved through all the changes of parties, Mr. Cabot is entitled to a large share of it; for upon his commercial knowledge and profound views, not only of finance but of political economy, Gen. Hamilton reposed the most unlimited confidence. The friendship and mutual regard of these two distinguished statesmen continued till the premature and lamented death of Hamilton. Nor was the intimacy between Cabot and Ames less close. They were united in feeling, principle, purity and patriotism.

Mr. Cabot never courted distinctions, and it was with reluctance that he accepted the office of senator.* At the expiration of the fifth year of his service, he resigned his seat, to enjoy once more the congenial calm of private life. In 1793, he removed from Beverly to Boston and though he shunned office and place, his influence continued undiminished. In 1814, he felt himself constrained to yield his preference, and for a short time appeared again in public life, as president of the convention which met at Hartford, just before the close of the late war. Of that convention, so suggestive of subsequent political disquisitions, it is not proposed here to express an opinion. But in sanctioning it with his presence and counsel, Mr. Cabot's age, good sense, and well-known principles, warrant the affirmation, that he followed the suggestions of mature reflection, and acted with the purest motives and views. Indeed, for forty years he was the Nestor, the wise, calm and considerate counsellor, of most of the intelligent statesmen on the federal side, in our State and national governments. Asking nothing for himself, hoping and wishing nothing for his friends, with a mind capable of comprehending the most abstruse questions, and ready to discuss the most simple— without parade, without assumption, applying the powers of a most persuasive eloquence in the most finished language, pouring forth the stores of a mind

* When the Navy Department was created, Mr. Cabot was offered the office of First Secretary by the elder Adams, which he declined.

11*

enriched by various literature and research—he never failed to convince, or inform, or persuade. The great characteristics of his mind, in which all would agree, were simplicity and profoundness. It is impossible to calculate how extensive are the effects of such a mind on the welfare and happiness of a state, and its value can be best realized only by its loss.*

Mr. Cabot died at Boston, April 18th, 1823, in the 72d year of his age, after a painful sickness, which he endured with christian resignation. The author of an obituary notice, and who had for many years known him intimately, says, " No one could converse with Mr. Cabot an hour, without being struck with the correctness of his sentiments, the liberality of his opinions, the fitness of his illustrations, and the propriety and beauty of the language with which his thoughts were clothed. No one could see him, indeed, and mark the proportions of his form, the dignity and grace of his demeanor, and the expression of his manly and intelligent countenance, without being convinced that he was no common man.

" But they who saw him often, and knew him intimately, could best estimate the resources of his mind and the high worth of his character. He had always something new to communicate, for delight and instruction; and they who conversed with him every week and day had never occasion to complain that his stock of thoughts was exhausted, or that there was nothing more to be learned from him. Integrity, firm principle, and a high sense of true honor, were the habits of Mr. Cabot's soul; and with these were blended sympathy, benevolence, and a singular modesty.

* Kirkland's sermon on the death of George Cabot.

"In short, there was in Mr. Cabot's character, a rare union of those qualities which constitute true goodness, and raise man to the high dignity of which his nature is susceptible. To borrow a passage from the eloquent sermon, preached on the Sunday after his interment, by President Kirkland, it may be said with confidence, that 'the enumeration of the principal virtues, considered in relation to ourselves, our fellow-men, and the Deity, is a delineation of his character. He was distinguished by prudence, which seeks lawful advantages by right and appropriate means; by contentment, which acquiesces in a moderate portion of good, is reasonable in wishes, and keeps at a distance from selfish repining, though not without keen sensibility and a constitutional predisposition to anxiety; by fortitude, a spirit collected and resolute in difficulties and dangers, and evincing always an entire superiority to fear; by patience, bearing trials with an equal mind, and especially showing exemplary composure in bodily sufferings; and by modesty, refusing to make pretensions, and display superiority, whilst estimating highly the value of opinion—paying a delicate respect to the impressions of other minds, and pleased with the favorable judgment of his fellow-men. He exhibited the spirit of application and industry, executing seasonably and thoroughly what he undertook; and though less willing than was desired to assume responsible employments, he was far removed from any thing like indolence. He manifested a wise and careful self-government, disdaining the bondage of sense; in pleasures, regarding the boundaries prescribed by nature, by health and by duty. He saw the value of the golden mean in conduct, and cultivated the moderation which prevents virtue from degenerating into vice by irregularity and excess, and which, in relation to distinction and place, rather avoids than courts pre-eminence.'

" Mr. Cabot's religious views, principles and feelings, were in perfect harmony with the whole of his character. A deep sense of his relation to God, was the foundation of his virtue. A firm belief in the divine authority of the christian revelation, was the result of a full and candid examination of its evidences ; and, though he punctually attended on all its ordinances, and was never backward to profess and maintain his convictions of its truth and excellence, his Christianity was yet more in his heart than it was on his lips, and was to be seen in the conduct of every hour, and in all his usual occupations, as conspicuously as on the first day of the week, and in the temple of God. There was neither cant nor levity in his conversation, superstition in his thoughts, uncharitableness in his feelings, nor censoriousness in his judgments. His opinions were not to be shaken by the usual arguments or cavils, for they were formed by impartial and mature investigation ; and he was as well versed in theology as most who teach it. The faith which he had deliberately adopted in the strength of his days, remained to comfort his age, to cheer him in illness, and support him in the hour of death."

ANDREW CABOT was born in Salem, Dec. 16, 1750; and, with his brother, entered largely into commercial pursuits, from which he early retired, after acquiring a handsome fortune. In 1779, he chartered to the provincial government the ship Defiance, of 16 guns, valued at £100,000, paper money, for an expedition to dislodge the enemy from Penobscot, in which she was lost. He purchased a farm in Cambridge, of Lieut. Governor Thomas Oliver, and also an estate of Col. Lechmere, known as "Lechmere Point." He was of lively temperament, was much esteemed for his social qualities, and died after a short illness, May, 1791, in the 41st year of his age.

JOHN CABOT was a representative from this town in the General Court in 1792, and in 1796 was nominated as a candidate for representative to Congress, but declined. He afterwards removed to Salem.

MOSES BROWN was a descendant, in the fifth generation, from Abraham Brown, who, in 1632, settled at Watertown. He was born at Waltham, in April, 1748, was graduated at Harvard College in 1768, and commenced business as a merchant in Beverly in 1772. Espousing the cause of American independence with great zeal, he raised a company of men in 1775, and in January, 1776, joined the line of the American army, as a captain in Glover's regiment ; served in New York and New Jersey, and was at the battle of Trenton. His corps being disbanded, in 1777 he returned to Beverly, resumed business in partnership with his brother-in-law, Israel Thorndike, and continued in active and successful pursuit of it until the year 1800, when he retired with an ample fortune. He always took an important part in public enterprizes. He was one of the largest original proprietors of Essex bridge, connecting Salem and Beverly, and of the Salem and Boston turnpike, and had a leading agency in the construction of these,—which, as great undertakings, and as affording facilities for communication, were for a long time not less thought of than the recently opened railroad between the same places now is. He was a federalist of the Washington school, and in 1808 one of the presidential electors. He united integrity with benevolence, was exemplary in all social and domestic relations, and a generous contributor to public and private charities and associations. He died in June, 1820, and "to afford some farther aid to the theological institution at Cambridge, the government of which is connected with Harvard University, he bequeathed to that important institution two thousand dollars, in the six per cent. stock of the United States, to be applied in any way the government shall determine will best promote the cause of Christianity, and the design and utility of this religious establishment." *

ISRAEL THORNDIKE, one of the most eminent and successful merchants in New England, was born in Beverly, in the year 1755. He had in youth no advantages of education, except those which the public schools of his native town afforded; but he possessed, in the vigor of his own mind, a never-failing spring of self-advancement. The war of the American revolution was an event adapted to call into activity his powers and spirit of enterprize. Embracing with zeal the cause of his country, he became part owner and captain of an armed ship; and the judgment with which he planned his cruises,

* See " Sermons by the late Rev. Abiel Abbot, D. D., of Beverly, Mass.," pp. 154–165; also, "History of Harvard University, by Josiah Quincy," vol. 2, pp. 414–415.

and the intrepidity and diligence with which he conducted them, were rewarded with distinguished success. Having entered into partnership with his
brother-in-law, the late Moses Brown, he engaged,
after the peace of 1783, in an extensive and most
profitable commerce with the East Indies and China.
Sagacity, judgment, industry, strict attention to business, and thorough acquaintance with the details of
every commercial enterprize in which he engaged,
were the chief causes of his success. He was also
an early patron of manufactures; and invested, it
was said, a greater amount of capital in them than
any other individual in New England. By his various pursuits he accumulated an immense property—
amounting, at the time of his decease, to nearly a
million and a half of dollars. In 1810, he removed
his business to Boston, in consideration of the greater
advantages for prosecuting it in that central empo-
rium. He still retained a residence in his native
place, passing a considerable portion of his time
there, and ever manifesting a warm interest in its
welfare. He was eminently social in his feelings;
and none more than he delighted in dispensing a
princely hospitality. In a tribute to his memory,
published soon after his death, it is justly remarked,
that "few individuals, endowed with such mental
powers, appear in a generation." His fellow-citizens showed themselves ready to acknowledge his
superior talents by repeatedly calling him to public
office. At different periods of his life, he was a
member of the convention called for the adoption of
the constitution of the United States, and a representative and senator in the legislature of Massachusetts. He was a generous contributor to patriotic,

charitable and religious objects, and often gave an active agency in their support. In 1806, he subscribed five hundred dollars for the foundation of the Natural History professorship in Harvard University; and also the same amount in 1818, for the library of the theological school. In the same year, being informed that the library of Professor Ebeling, of Hamburgh, was for sale, and that an agent of the King of Prussia was negotiating for it, Mr. Thorndike ordered it to be purchased, at the cost of six thousand five hundred dollars, and presented it to the University; thereby securing to his country one of the most complete and valuable collections of works extant on American history. The first parish of Beverly has a remembrance of his liberal regard, in an addition to its funds of about $2600, received from the sale of an estate presented to it, agreeably to his expressed intentions and wishes, by his sons, to whom it is also indebted for the gift, at the same time, of an elegant chandelier for its vestry.

Mr. Thorndike closed his long career of eminence and usefulness in May, 1832; retaining, to the last, great energy and activity, and expiring calmly, though suddenly, in the bosom of his family, and in the midst of devoted friends.*

Joseph Lee was born in Salem in May, 1744. His ancestors came from England, and were settled in Boston early in the 18th century, where they engaged in mercantile pursuits. At the age of thirteen, he adopted a sea-faring life, and afterwards succeeded to the

---

* See Quincy's History of Harvard University, vol. 2, pp. 411–414, 596.

command of a vessel in the European and West India trade. At a subsequent period he became a merchant and ship-owner, and for many years was partner with George Cabot in the trade to Spain, the West Indies and Baltic. During his residence in Beverly, he was engaged largely in underwriting privately on the shipping of this town, Salem and Marblehead, and was also a director in an insurance office in Salem.

Mr. Lee took no prominent part in the political affairs of the times; and though he held no office in town, he took an active interest in promoting its various municipal concerns. He had a turn for mechanics, especially naval architecture, and was constantly employed in devising improvements in shipbuilding. His models for ships were adopted by many of the mechanics and merchants of Essex and Boston, and led the way in great degree to the great improvement of construction by which superior sailing is combined with an increased carrying capacity. The brig Caravan, built in Salem in 1801, by Briggs, a celebrated builder, and owned by his sons, was constructed on a model furnished by him, and was considered to be, in point of sailing and carrying, in advance of any vessel of her time.

Mr. Lee sought no other emolument for his improvements than the satisfaction arising from a consciousness of having contributed to the advancement of the naval art. He was always ready to furnish information and models to all who consulted him, and to give his personal attendance in a supervision of shipbuilding when within his neighborhood. He took an active part in procuring the erection of Essex bridge, of which he was one of the largest proprietors. For

12

several years he gave his time gratuitously to the care
and superintendence of the bridge, and on his removal
to Boston, received the thanks of the directors and a
piece of plate as a recognition of their estimate of his
services.

Some years previous to his removal to Boston,
which occurred in 1807, that he might be near his
children, who were settled there, Mr. Lee had retired
from the active pursuits of commerce. In the metropolis he was elected a director of an insurance
company, in which office he continued until from
advanced years he voluntarily retired. He died in
1831, at the age of 87. The industry of Mr. Lee
was crowned with success, and his fortune, though
not so considerable as acquired by some who continued in business after he retired, was adequate to the
wants of a numerous family and the promptings of
a benevolent disposition. He contributed freely to
the support of literary and charitable institutions,
and within a year of his death made a donation of
$20,000 to the Massachusetts General Hospital. Mr.
Lee was a man of modest pretensions, and passed
through life without an enemy, and without a stain
upon his character. For the progress of his race he
had a quick and abiding sympathy, and to the cause
of civilization he contributed a full share. To the
close of his life he retained a strong attachment to
the people of Beverly, among whom he spent a considerable portion of his days, and where he is now
remembered as an honorable merchant, and an exemplary, useful citizen.

JOHN STEPHENS was born in this town Oct. 7, 1763.
He was grandson of John Stephens, the friend of

Robert Briscoe, and son of Thomas Stephens, who died in June, 1795, aged 58. Mr. Stephens was distinguished for cheerfulness, energy in business, and patriotism. He took an active part in town affairs, and shared largely in the confidence of his fellow-citizens, by whom he was several times chosen their representative in the General Court. He died of fever after a short illness, universally lamented, Oct. 28, 1801, aged 38.

THOMAS STEPHENS was born May 9, 1769, and early engaged in mercantile pursuits with his brother John. He held the office of town-treasurer, and was often consulted on important town affairs. He was four times elected representative to the General Court, and afterwards held a seat for several years at the senate-board. Firm in the principles upon which he acted, social in his manners and exemplary in his life, he was greatly beloved by all who knew him. He died on the same day, and nearly at the same hour, with his friend Rev. Dr. Abbot, June 7, 1828, aged 59.

THE BAR.

UNDER this head are placed the names of Hon. Nathan Dane* and Hon. William Thorndike.

Mr. DANE was born in Ipswich, Mass., Dec. 29, 1752. He was descended from one of three brothers

* This notice of Mr. Dane, from the pen of Rev. C. T. Thayer, was originally published in the American Jurist and Law Magazine for July, 1835, and has been kindly furnished with some additions, by the author, for republication here.

of that name, who early came over from England and settled in Gloucester, Andover and Ipswich. His father was a farmer of that worthy and substantial class, from which have sprung so many of the distinguished men of our country. His parents are both of them represented to have been respectable and excellent persons, and he always spoke of them with veneration and affection. They had a numerous family—six sons and six daughters,—of whom only two daughters now survive; and one of these, Mrs. Appleton, residing in Beverly, is in her 102d year.

Mr. Dane labored on his father's farm till after he was twenty-one. To this circumstance he often referred as having contributed essentially to that physical vigor and power of long-continued application to study, for which he was afterward so remarkable. It was not till after he was of age, that he enjoyed more than the advantages of a common-school education, which, at that time, were very small; though he was then in the habit of devoting most of the leisure he could command to reading, and his favorite study, mathematics. Soon after he became of age, he resolved to prepare himself for college. This he did in the short space of eight months. He entered Harvard University in 1774, and graduated, with high reputation for industry and scholarship, in 1778. After leaving college he went to Beverly, where he taught a school, at the same time pursuing the study of law under the late Judge Wetmore, of Salem. His surviving pupils speak of him with affectionate respect, as having been a devoted and successful instructor. In 1782, he commenced the practice of law in Beverly, and came almost at once into extensive and profitable

business. He was, however, no fomenter of litigation, but was conscientious in endeavoring to check
it whenever justice or expediency admonished him
so to do, and the effect of his character in this respect has long been visible in the place where, through
his whole professional life, he resided. When clients
came to him under highly excited feelings, he used
frequently to put by attending to their cause till the
next morning—to give them, as he said, opportunity
to sleep upon it.

Though the practice of his profession, till within
about twenty years past, when by growing deafness
he was induced gradually, and at length wholly to
retire from it, continued his chief object, he yet found
time to fill, with honor to himself and advantage to
the community, various important public stations.
In 1782, and the three following years, he was a
representative in the General Court of Massachusetts.
In 1785, '86 and '87, he was a delegate to Congress. In
1790, '94,'96, '97 and '98, he was a member of the Massachusetts Senate. He was appointed on a committee to revise the laws of the State in 1795, and again
to a similar duty in 1811 and '12. In 1794, he was
appointed a judge of the court of common pleas for
Essex county, but very soon after taking the oaths of
office, resigned. He was an elector of President of
the United States in 1812, a member of the Hartford
convention in 1814, and chosen in 1820 member of
the convention for revising the State constitution,
but on account of deafness did not take his seat. In
these and various other civil offices, his services were
eminently efficient and valuable. " While in the
Senate of Massachusetts, he is said to have been distinguished by his ability in debate, knowledge of
12*

public business and capacity for discharging it, and
the uprightness and directness of his views. The
journals of the old Congress, in which he continued
till the adoption of the present constitution of the
United States, show that he was appointed on nearly
every committee of any importance. It was in this
assembly that he reported the celebrated ordinance
for the government of the territory of the United
States north-west of the river Ohio." "We are accustomed," said Mr. Webster, in the U. S. Senate during the debate on Foot's resolution in 1830, "to praise
the lawgivers of antiquity; we help to perpetuate
the fame of Solon and Lycurgus; but I doubt whether
one single law of any lawgiver, ancient or modern,
has produced effects of a more distinct and marked
and lasting character than the ordinance of '87.
That instrument was drawn by Nathan Dane, then
and now a citizen of Massachusetts. It was adopted,
as I think I have understood, without the slightest
alteration; and certainly it has happened to few
men, to be the authors of a political measure of more
large and enduring consequence. It fixed, forever,
the character of the population in the vast regions
northwest of the Ohio, by excluding from them invol-
untary servitude. It impressed on the soil itself, while
it was yet a wilderness, an incapacity to bear up any
other than freemen. It laid the interdict against personal servitude, in original compact, not only deeper
than all local law, but deeper, also, than all local constitutions. Under the circumstances then existing, I
look upon this original and seasonable provision as a
real good attained. We see its consequences at this moment, and we shall never cease to see them, perhaps,
while the Ohio shall flow." To have been the drafter

of the ordinance of 1787 alone, it has therefore, not without justice been said, is glory enough for any man.

Mr. Dane, besides, took an active interest in many objects of general improvement and benevolence. His liberal donation of $15,000, (which he bestowed in his lifetime, and the first rich fruits of which he lived to see and enjoy), to the Law College of Harvard University, is well known. It resulted immediately in the establishment of the Dane Professorship of Law, which has since been " adorned by the learning and talents of Mr. Justice Story, and from which he has sent forth those immortal works that have excited the admiration of the jurists of Europe, and first called their attention to the jurisprudence of our country." Mr. Dane was a member and supporter of the Massachusetts Agricultural Society, the Massachusetts and Essex Historical Societies, and the American Antiquarian Society. To the Indiana and Michigan Historical Societies, of which, in gratitude for his being the author of the ordinance which constitutes the fundamental law of those states, he was elected an honorary member; and to the Dane Law Library of Ohio, for the same reason bearing his name, he was a donor. He was also one of the founders of the Massachusetts Temperance Society, (the first established society of the kind,) was for several years president, and contributed to its funds. Not only did he lend his aid to these general objects, but he interested himself in those which were on a smaller scale, and near home. For instance, during the distresses consequent on the embargo of the last war, he devised a plan for a society to relieve the poor of his own town, by

furnishing them work, which was formed and
proved beneficial in its operation, and to which he
was himself a liberal contributor in money and personal services.

While he was thus engaged in public labors, he
found time for much private study, as the results of
his retired exertions abundantly show. His great
work, " A General Abridgement and Digest of American Law, with occasional notes and comments," in
nine volumes, has long been before the world. It
was published in 1823 and 1829, and is regarded
a monument of immense industry and learning.
While that was in progress, he was also employed
on another work, of nearly equal extent, entitled a
Moral and Political Survey of America, which he
left complete in manuscript. The objects of this
survey, as stated by himself, are " First, to bring
into view the moral and political principles of the
various parts of America, from its discovery by Co-
lumbus in 1492, to the establishment of the federal
constitution in 1790; tracing those of civilized
America to their true sources in the old world;
making federal America the principal object : Secondly, to form a just idea of the moral and political
condition and character of men here, in the same
period : Thirdly, useful reflections on proper occasions, especially in regard to that character and
those principles of law and liberty, on which has
arisen a great and enlightened nation in United
America—principles most essential to the preservation of its present condition : Fourthly, to do a little
towards preserving in our country, a manly, moral
character, ' a moral regulated liberty,' where this
character and this wise union of law and liberty,

are so very important, and where a vicious character and licentious liberty would soon destroy self-
government." The following extract from the preface is subjoined, both as relating to the work itself,
and as possessing the interest of an autobiographical
sketch. "Taking into view the author's other labors, public and private, especially his other vol-
uminous writings in print and manuscript, some may
doubt if he has had sufficient time properly to form
and revise this work, by no means a small one. If
any such doubts do or shall exist, a mere sketch of
his long life, method, and course of study, will, it is
believed, at once remove them, and show how much
common talents, in sixty years and more of studies,
accompanied by unceasing industry and exertions,
may accomplish. So far as there may be any merit
in the author's writings, professional labors, and
public services, state and federal, it is to be attributed entirely to his industry, method, and course
of studies. As much extended as are his writings,
facts that may be briefly stated will show, there has
been no need of haste or want of time. By several
years' labor on a farm, a constitution good in itself
was much strengthened and confirmed. In the same
years, by mathematical studies, his mind acquired
the habits of close thinking and patient investigation.
His firm constitution, and unwearied habits in
thinking, and persevering industry, enabled him in
eight months to prepare for admission into Harvard
College, on examination in the usual manner, in the
year 1774. The same firm constitution, patient
habits, and untiring mind, have enabled him since
to study and write at least twelve hours a day.
Neither the care of children, nor the cares or want

of property, have interfered with his studies. In
May, 1782, he began to collect materials for this,
and his law work. Since leaving college, in 1778,
he has confined his studies and writings principally
to the subjects of law and politics, history and biography, morals and religion. He has always, since
he commenced these studies, used common-place
books, some of which are preserved; and has ever
made his public and professional business, and his
writings, go hand in hand and afford aid one to the
other. Are not sixty years of such studies nearly
equal to the studies of three common lives, in time
and industry? It is here proper to state that, in
1782, when the author, in fact, commenced this and
his law works, there were only fragments in the
country on either subject, and he came to the resolution to make his collection of materials on both
subjects as extensive as possible, so as to produce
something like a whole on each. Could he now be
carried back to the age of twenty-eight, and find the
copious writings now existing on each subject by
others, probably he would not think of engaging in
either case. Though no other person has ever produced a general code, or abridgement of American
law, or a general survey of all parts of America any
way like this, yet the writings of others on these
topics are now copious and very valuable. But being the writings of numerous distinct and scattered
authors, they are in numerous distinct and scattered
parts. Of near thirty histories, by as many authors,
each one is only the history of a single state. It
will be found on inquiry, that near half of the chap-
ters in this work are peculiar to it, but a small part
of which is to be found in any other writings pub-

lished; and where the information given can be found elsewhere, it is generally in a scattered state, and not embodied, as in this work. Indeed, no one has ever attempted to embody in a general work, the morals and politics of all parts of America, for three centuries and more, including statistics largely, and religion as far as it is a part of the constitutions and laws. In fact, no work of this kind has any other author attempted of any part of America."

The "Survey" evinces unquestionably great research, and comprehends a vast amount of information. But it is marked with the same neglect of style, which is so obvious in Mr. Dane's other writings. His object, when composing, always seemed to be to pursue the thought before him, and simply to make his views intelligible to others. He had no graces of style, either native or borrowed; neither did he ever seek for any. To instruct and convince—not to fascinate and delight—was his aim. For truth—to acquire and communicate it—did he chiefly concern himself; for its dress he cared little or nothing.

In all he did, indeed, in his habits and manners generally, he was rigidly simple. He went straight forward to whatever object he had in view, without any parade either in the preparation or execution. When he spoke, whether in town meeting or in more public bodies, his eloquence was that of fact and argument—perfectly plain, the expression of strong conviction, without any of the arts of oratory. He was uniformly prompt, punctual, and systematic. He had a particular time and a particular way for doing everything he undertook; and no person could be more industrious and persevering in the accom-

plishment of what had once been undertaken.   His
life throughout was one of constant and wonderful
diligence.   There was, too, an elevation in his aims,
which betokened no common man : and possessing,
as he did, a spirit and energy in executing, propor-
tional to the capacity for conceiving them, it is not
strange they were so admirably completed. He was,
we must admit, signally favored in their completion
by the health he enjoyed, having never before his
last illness been confined to his house by sickness
more than two days at a time, and that very rarely.
He no doubt, did much to preserve his health, by
regularity and temperance in diet, and by exercising
every day in the open air. He took regular rather
than a great deal of exercise, and that was walking
chiefly.

The qualities of his intellect were altogether of
the solid kind. By his cast of mind, as well as by
habit, he was inclined to the severer and graver
studies. He had little acquaintance with the lighter
branches of literature; never read a novel before
Scott began to publish, and his romances he read
principally for their historical value; though his
reading became more various after he retired from
the practice of law. His judgment was singularly
discriminating and well-balanced. Few ever lived
who were less biased by passion or prejudice.   He
was thus formed, on most contested points, to pursue a medium course, and to be a moderate man in
any party with which he might be connected.   For
the same reason was he likely, more than most others, to be correct and stable in his opinions on all
subjects.

In the management of public affairs, he was cautious, firm, sagacious, and able ; and in conducting his private business, he exerted corresponding skill. It may be mentioned as confirming this last remark, that though he was long in the practice of loaning money to many different individuals, he never, in this way, incurred pecuniary loss.

He was a truly upright man. To a female friend who, at the time he was preparing for his profession, rallied him with saying, "So, you mean to be an honest *lawyer*," he replied, " I mean to be an honest man." And his whole subsequent career attested the sincerity and strength of this early resolution.

He possessed great goodness of heart. He was blessed with singular evenness of temperament, and was remarkably free from the indulgence of resentful or vindictive feelings. Instances might be named, of his returning liberal benefactions for ingratitude and injury. In domestic life, he was ever conciliating and kind to those with whom he was there connected. To the excellent partner of his life, to whom he was united for fifty-five years, and who survived him, he was a devoted husband. Without children of his own, he was as a father to many. Several of his relatives he assisted to a liberal education, and others he aided in establishing respectably in life. If a prudent economy reigned in his family, so also did a ready hospitality. Though his mind was habitually braced to severe thought and study, he was not without social feeling. Among his particular friends, he not seldom showed a high relish for humor and lighter conversation; and he had a choice fund, with which at times he delighted to entertain them, of anecdote and reminiscences respecting the sages and worthies, and the important scenes and transactions with which, in his long and eventful life, he had been connected. As an instance of the interesting recollections which would thus occasionally drop from him, it may be mentioned that, not many months before his decease, he stated, in conversation, that it was not till the celebrated ordinance of '87 was on the eve of its passage, that the thought occurred to him of inserting the clause by which slavery was forever excluded from the states north of the Ohio; thus presenting the striking reflection, that by the mere after-thought, as it were, of a single individual, acting fifty years or little more ago, and then a young man and comparatively unknown, such mighty consequences should result to the millions now living, and the many more millions to live, in that extensive and very fertile region.

Mr. Dane was not a person of naturally quick sensibilities. So unvaryingly did his impulses obey his judgment, that one who did not know him well might sometimes have been induced to doubt their strength, and at least to suppose him more just than generous. But that he had strong attachments, not a few who were the objects of them will attest. That he was benevolent, his various bestowments, public and private, amply prove. For all objects that seemed to him good, he was interested. For his country he certainly had a sincere love. From early life to almost his latest moments, he watched narrowly its interests. By the faithful performance of his duties as a legislator and statesman, he labored for it; he did scarcely less by his writings. When our Union was threatened by the doctrines of nullification, he looked with intense anxiety to the issue, and showed, by a pamphlet amounting to a considerable volume, which he prepared and published in his eightieth year, that he was then as willing to labor for his country's good as he had been in his meridian vigor. And even when confined to his chamber and bed, and up to the day of his death, he kept along with the course of public events, making frequent inquiries respecting them—inquiring particularly, and with evident solicitude, concerning the difficulties with France, which constituted, at that time, the most engrossing national topic.

He was, moreover, a religious man and a Christian. He believed in the divine origin of Christianity with a firm conviction, and after thorough examination of its evidences. Few laymen have spent so much time in the study of theology. During more than fifty years, he had been in the habit of passing his sabbaths—excepting the hours of public worship, which he attended constantly—in theological pursuits, which would make (as he computed it) between seven and eight years given expressly to the subject. He preserved his acquaintance with Greek to the last, and commonly read the New Testament in its original language. Of the Hebrew he also had some knowledge, and sometimes referred to it in examining the Old Testament. He was well versed in biblical criticism, and understood well most of the theological controversies of the day. In his unpublished work, he has treated quite at large the subject of religion, so far as it is connected with and recognized in our constitutions of government. But he was not in theory only a Christian; he was practically devout and religious. There was found among his papers a prayer, which he composed many years since for his own use; and which would be found

by all a valuable help to devotion. He was conscientious in his attendance on the public institutions of
religion, and to its ministers he proved himself, by
his attentions, his counsel, and his substance, peculiarly a friend. The best evidence, however, of his
being at heart a Christian, was his life; that child-
like purity, which was free equally from the contam-
ination of gross or polished vice—that perfect sincerity, which scorned low intrigue and every form of
deceit—that untiring diligence, with which he improved his talents, and consecrated them to worthy,
useful, and high ends. His death was serene, beautiful, and happy. Three months previously, he was
seized with a paralytic affection. The shock came
upon him in the midst of perfect health. But it was
received without alarm, and in entire submission to
the divine will. From that time his strength gradually decayed, and he gently sank away to rest.
He retained to the last a delightfully composed cheerfulness. He felt—and no one could more truly say—
his work was done. Rarely has there been one that
had proposed to himself so much, who lived to see
his objects so fully accomplished. And if then, and
even before, there was, as he reflected on his exertions and the success which had attended them, a
complacency bordering on weakness, it was certainly
a pardonable self-satisfaction. His reason never, for
a moment during his illness, forsook him. He continued, almost to the closing scene, to converse with
his friends on such subjects of a general nature as
had usually interested him, as well as on those relating immediately to his expected departure. Only
a few hours before his death, he gave directions respecting his burial, and with the same collectedness

took leave of the relatives that surrounded his dying bed. He died Feb. 15, 1835.

For consistency and integrity, a well-spent life and a peaceful death, it would be difficult to find his superior. Such a life and such a death are the best illustration of the reality and the value of virtue and religion. The example they contain may justly be held forth for imitation, not merely to those of the same profession, but to all young men, and to all of whatever age, who would secure the most desirable distinctions for themselves, and be the best benefactors of their country and race.

A monument is erected over his grave, which is of pyramidal form, about ten feet in height, and composed of beautiful white marble, resting on a block of dressed granite. The inscription, written by Judge Story, is as follows :

" In memory of the Hon. Nathan Dane, L.L.D. A revolutionary statesman ; an eminent jurist ; the author of an Abridgment and Digest of American Law ; the founder of the Dane Professorship of Law in Harvard University. His private life was distinguished for simplicity, integrity and dignity ; his public life for wisdom, fidelity, and patriotism. He lived and died a Christian. He was born on the 27th of December, 1752. He died on the 15th of February, 1835.

" His fame belongs to his country. Let the gratitude of future ages cherish it."

On one side of the monument is the following inscription, commemorative of his amiable and much-lamented wife.

13*

" In memory of
Polly, wife of Nathan Dane.
Of singular purity, benevolence and piety;
An ornament and rich blessing to her
Family, to the Church and to society;
And having through a long life been
Faithful in all its relations,
She expired in Christian faith and hope,
April 14, 1840, aged 90 years.

HON. WILLIAM THORNDIKE was born in Beverly,
Jan. 1795. He early gave indications of genius and
talents of a high order, of regard to the principles of
morality, and of reverence for religion. His father,
Capt. Nicolas Thorndike, for most of the early part
of his life, was employed abroad; and he, like many
other great and good men, was mostly indebted to
the tender care and instruction of a pious mother,
for the formation of a character of virtue, of early
piety, of kind and affectionate dispositions. This
character, thus formed in childhood, was developed
in his youth, and exemplified in manhood in all the
various relations in which he was called to act.

He was fitted for college under Dr. Benjamin
Abbot, at Phillips Academy, in Exeter, and entered
Harvard College in advanced standing. He was distinguished by close attention to his studies, and by
exemplary conduct, and graduated with distinction
in 1813, at the age of 18. On leaving college, he
studied law with the late Hon. Nathan Dane. In
1816, he was admitted to the bar of Essex county,
and soon commenced the practice of law, at Bath,
Maine. On the 4th July, 1816, he pronounced an
oration in Beverly, at a celebration of American
independence. After he had become established in

the business of his profession, at Bath, he was married to Miss Nancy Stephens, daughter of John Stephens, Esq., of Beverly. The happiness of this connexion, the result of esteem, friendship and love, formed in early youth and commenced with the most flattering prospects, was blasted by death. One short year separated this happy couple, and left the survivor bereft of both wife and her infant offspring. This event, if not the cause, was soon followed by feeble health and depression of spirits, which occasioned the abandonment of his profession, when prosperity and advancement were on the point of crowning his well-established reputation, as an advocate and counsellor. He then returned to the circle of his friends in his native town, and there engaged in commercial pursuits. Here his worth was well known, and his popularity was unrivalled. He was immediately placed in those public offices and employments, which—happily for New England—are generally bestowed on talents and worth, in her towns. Within a short period, he became a director of all the principal monied institutions in the place, and was elected to the offices of selectman, overseer of the poor, and one of the school committee; in which last capacity, he devoted much time and labor to the improvement of the schools. He rightly appreciated the importance of this sphere, in which there is room for the occupation of the best talents, and for that persevering exertion which finds little reward other than the high consciousness of performing duties, the future consequences of which will be experienced in a glorious progress of society in knowledge and virtue.

In 1826 and '27, he was a representative from

Beverly, in the General Court.   His retiring disposition prevented his taking a conspicuous part in the debates of the House, or in its business; but his sound judgment, purity of motive, and general intelligence, were laying the foundation for more extensive usefulness in the other branch of the legislature. In 1828, he was elected a senator for the county of Essex, and was re-elected in '29, '30, '31, and '32. In the last of these years he was elected president of the Senate.   As a member of that body, he was indefatigable in the performance of those labors which fall on its more industrious and active members, with greater weight, from the smallness of their number, compared with that of the House, and from the practice of investigating subjects of legislation by joint committees of both branches.   On certain emergencies, he displayed in debate a spirit, eloquence, and capacity, equal to the greatest occasions.   His ease of manner and quickness of apprehension were peculiarly adapted to the duties of a presiding officer.   While president of the Senate, his wisdom, impartiality, decision and firmness, secured the confidence of all concerned in its transactions. In the spring of 1832, he was elected president of the National Insurance Company, and afterward, of the Hamilton Bank, located in Boston.   These offices came to him unsolicited and were accepted with reluctance—particularly at leaving his friends and various avocations in his native town for a residence in the city; and they were entered on with the understanding, that he might resign them at the expiration of a period, the larger part of which had passed at the time of his decease.

In his relation to the first parish and church in

Beverly, his services will always be remembered with gratitude. For several years he superintended the first parish sunday-school, and with great success. He was at the same time superintendent of that school, and president of the Massachusetts Senate; and the spectacle was at once beautiful and touching, of the same individual admirably discharging and gracing those so different stations.

His chief aim in conducting the sunday-school, was to make it, to teachers and scholars alike, a scene of mutual improvement and satisfaction. Discarding the principle of emulation, which had previously been resorted to here—as it is even now elsewhere—he sought (as he said in a report on this subject,) "to secure the attention of the scholars to the duties required of them, by engaging their affections, and offering as a reward for faithfulness, not the record of their good deeds, or the tempting allurements of gifts, but the smiles of a kind and endeared instructer, and the satisfaction of an approving conscience,—feeling anxious that purer motives should stimulate the mind and swell the heart, than those which proceed from the promise of pecuniary rewards, or the display of acquisitions, the only value of which is in their secret influence, and the tone they give to character and principle."

He was eminently a religious man. His faith was enlightened and liberal, as well as earnest and firm. He stood on the great principle of the entire independence of the mind of all human authority in the grand concerns of religion. His sympathy and fellowship were not with those who merely interpreted scripture as he did, but with those who, believing in divine revelation with sincerity, conformed their

hearts and lives to its precepts, as understood by them.
What he most desired for himself, and delighted most
to see in others, was unswerving deference to moral
and religious principle ; and it was the possession
of this which imparted a crowning lustre to the simple dignity, the genuine independence, the amiable
temper, and earnest spirit, which marked both his
public and private life.   In the midst of all this
worth and usefulness, having acquired a prominence
in the public regards rarely attained by one no farther
advanced in years, and when deservedly esteemed
one of the most valuable and promising characters,
of which not only his native town but the Commonwealth could boast,—consumption, that widely fatal
disease, before which so large a portion of our race
falls—fastened upon him ; and after lingering for
some months, he expired, July 12th, 1835, in the 41st
year of his age.   It is not extravagant eulogy to say
of him, that he was one whom all might wish to
resemble, and lament to lose.   Though the verdure
of seven summers has come and faded on his grave,
there are memories of him, deep and many, in the
heart of this community, which have not and cannot
fade.   His manly form, his features beaming intelligence and sensibility, his benignant smile, his unassuming yet engaging manners. and above all, his
talents and virtues, the good he did and the greater
good he would—had he lived—have done, altogether
constitute an image delightful to cherish, and that
will not soon pass away.

PHYSICIANS.

The practising physicians, resident in this town since 1677, so far as ascertained, are Samuel Hardie, Robert Hale, Robert Hale, Jr., John Herrick, Benjamin Jones, Israel Woodberry, Isaac Spofford, Larkin Thorndike, Joseph Orne, Nathan Lakeman, Barnard Tucker, Elisha Whitney, Joshua Fisher, Abner Howe, Josiah Batchelder, Ingalls Kittredge, Wyatt C. Boyden, Ingalls Kittredge, Jr., Augustus Torrey, Joseph Torrey, and Edward Bradstreet. The six last-named are now in practice here. Of Drs. Hardie and Robert Hale, Jr., mention has been made elsewhere.

Robert Hale, son of Rev. John Hale, was born November 3d, 1668. He received his education at Harvard College, where he graduated in 1686, in the 18th year of his age, and in 1690 became a member of his father's church. His attention was early turned to divinity, the study of which he pursued with a view of entering the ministry. In this design he received encouragement from an uncle residing in England, who left him a legacy in 1691. During his father's absence as chaplain, in the Canada expedition of 1690, he supplied the pulpit; but the state of his health compelling him to relinquish "that best of employments," as he styles the clerical profession, he engaged in the practice of medicine, in which he continued until his decease in 1719, aged 51 years.

In 1693, Mr. Hale appears to have suffered much from physical debility. In a letter to his father, dated " Preston, 22d, 11th," in which there is a mingled strain of despondency and christian resignation, he says : "I find myself heir to my mother's distempers ; would to God I might of her graces." At his mother's decease he came in possession of a property in Sarum, England, which was managed for him several years by Bennett Swayne, Jr., of London. In 1701, he succeeded Dr. Hardie as master of the grammar-school, and subsequently was a selectman, justice of the peace, and a representative to the General Court.* His widow was married in 1720 to Col. John Gilman, of Exeter, N. H. The latter part of her life was spent in this town, in which she died.

Mr. Hale had two sons and a daughter; Robert, Henry, and Rebecca.

Dr. HERRICK was a practitioner here in 1721.

Dr. JONES was a native of this town. He had an extensive practice, and was highly respected. He was a member of the second church, is frequently mentioned in the parish records, and appears to have taken an active interest in its affairs. He died about 1778. His first wife was Ginger Leach, and his second Sarah Endicott, of Danvers, who died in 1797, aged 78.

Dr. WOODBERRY, son of Samuel Woodberry, was born in Beverly, March, 1734, and pursued his medical studies with Dr. Putnam, of Danvers. He mar-

---

* Copies of several letters, written by Mr. Hale to his relatives in England, and also to his agents in London, are in the archives of the Antiquarian Society, at Worcester. They contain no local information, and relate chiefly to matters in which the public would not feel interested.

ried Lucy, daughter of Benjamin Herrick, by whom he had two daughters, Hannah and Lucy. He succeeded Dr. Jones in business, and practised to some extent in the neighboring towns. He was a member of the second church, and his life appears to have been that of an exemplary Christian. Shortly before his decease, which occurred in 1797, at the age of 83, he remarked, "If I were to live my life over again, I could not serve mankind more faithfully than I have done."

DR. SPOFFORD came to this town from Rowley, and married for his second wife Ruth, the second daughter of Col. Larkin Thorndike. He was reputed skilful in his profession, and was also much devoted to music. He died June 14th, 1786, aged 35. His remains lie in the first burying-ground. His gravestone bears masonic emblems, above which is the following inscription: " Orphani Viduæ Musæ Medicinaque Lugent." Beneath the date of his decease is the following : " Candidus insuetum miratur limen Olimpi sub pedibusque videt nubes et fidera Daphnis."

DR. THORNDIKE, son of Col. Larkin Thorndike, was born in this town, and graduated at Harvard College in 1782. During the difficulties with France, under the administration of the elder Adams, he entered the navy as surgeon, on board the sloop of war Herald, from which he was transferred to the Congress frigate. He died at Norfolk, Va., in 1798.

DR. LAKEMAN came to this town from Hamilton, but did not live long to pursue his profession.

14

Dr. Tucker was born in Newbury, of which town his father was clergyman. He graduated at Cambridge in 1779, and practised here several years. He subsequently removed to Wenham, and thence to his native place. He possessed a kind heart, and is remembered for gentleness of disposition and simplicity of manners. He was a proficient in the French and Spanish languages, and was much employed as an instructer in the former.

Dr. Orne was born in Salem, in 1749. In his childhood he was remarkable for the precocity of his understanding. At the age of twelve years he entered Harvard University, where he received the degree of A. B. in 1765. He began his medical studies under the direction of Dr. E. A. Holyoke. In 1770, he removed to Beverly and established himself in medical practice, with a fair reputation and increasing fame. In 1777, he returned to Salem, under auspicious circumstances, where he continued till his death. He possessed a sound and discriminating judgment. His ardor for the improvement of medicine, and in enriching his own mind with scientific knowledge, was evinced by his importing from Europe the most recent valuable publications, and dedicating all his leisure to the investigation of new subjects. Dr. O. possessed not only a taste for poetry, painting, and the belles lettres, but also for natural philosophy; and had his short sojourn in life been protracted, his talents would probably have been devoted to the most useful purposes. But insatiate consumption seized him as its victim, and terminated his earthly career July 28, 1786, in the 37th year of his age. Several of his papers have appeared in the

Massachusetts Medical Communications. He was one of the original members of the American Academy of Science.*

DR. ELISHA WHITNEY was born in Watertown, March 11th, 1747, old style, and graduated at Harvard College in 1766. He pursued his medical studies with Dr. Russell, of Groton, and commenced practice in Ipswich, Mass. He made several voyages as surgeon on board privateers commanded by Captains Giles and Hill. The first exercise of his surgical skill was in the amputation of Capt. G's leg; and Capt. H., as a mark of esteem, presented him with a chaise manufactured for the governor of Barbadoes, found on board a prize. While resident in Ipswich, Dr. W. volunteered in the regiment commanded by Col. Wade, which marched to suppress Shays' rebellion. He married Miss Eunice Farley, of Ipswich, by whom he had ten children, viz: Elisha, Michael (who died in infancy), Elizabeth, Susan, Michael, Dorothy, Lucy, Israel (who died young), Israel and Lucy Ann.

In 1792, Dr. Whitney removed to Beverly, where for fifteen years he pursued a laborious and extensive practice. His social nature drew around him a numerous circle of friends, while the kindness of his address relieved the timid and humble of the restraints imposed by stately reserve. No physician was more welcome in the chamber of sickness, as no one better understood the importance of cheerfulness in combating disease. He always had a word in season, and possessed a happy faculty of saying the

* See "Thacher's Medical Biography." "The Massachusetts Gazette" for Feb. 6, 1786.

best thing in the best way. The elasticity of his spirits imparted to his conversation an influence eminently calculated to dissipate the gloom incident to protracted illness, and the hopefulness of his tone inspired his patients with a confidence scarcely less serviceable than medical prescriptions. His benevolence, of which the poor, in his practice, enjoyed a large share, and his professional skill, gave him a deserved popularity; and his decease, which occurred Feb. 22, 1807, at the age of 60, was universally lamented.

DR. JOSHUA FISHER was born in Dedham, May, 1749. His ancestors were respected and wealthy farmers. He was second cousin to Fisher Ames. He graduated at Harvard College in 1766, at the age of 17. His parents designed him for the ministry; but after teaching a school in Rowley for two years, he was seized with disease of the lungs, which led him to relinquish this purpose, and in 1770 he began the study of medicine under the direction of Dr. Lincoln, of Hingham, brother of Gen. Lincoln. He always spoke of his preceptor as a man of rare talent, and much in advance of his profession. He practised for a time in Ipswich and then in Salem, but soon removed to Beverly, where he passed the remainder of his life. The times in which Dr. Fisher entered on his professional career possessed extraordinary interest. The great question of the future government of the country had begun deeply to agitate the whole land. It addressed itself to every individual, and profound interest was felt by each and all in the decision. It was this fact in the history of the revolution, which gave to it character and ultimate success. Dr. Fisher was not insensible to the patriotic spirit which then prevailed; and we find him leaving the quiet of village practice and entering a private armed vessel as surgeon. He sailed from Marblehead: a valuable prize was captured and sent into Salem. We next find him in the British channel, where, after cruising some time, the vessel was surrounded by English ships of war. Escape being impossible, the privateer was run ashore, those on board hoping to secrete themselves on land. They were, however, soon discovered and pursued, and all but Dr. Fisher secured as prisoners. He was seized by two strong men; but suddenly, with a desperate effort, he threw them to the ground and escaped. Through a series of most perilous and romantic adventures, in which he displayed great adroitness and energy, he made his way over a considerable part of England, and finally got to France, where he entered another privateer. After a successful cruise in this, he took passage in a letter of marque for Boston, and arrived there after a most dangerous voyage. His public and enterprizing spirit next led him to take an active part in establishing a cotton factory, which was situated in Upper Beverly, and of which he was superintendent. This project, the first of the kind in New England, was unsuccessful, and after much loss was abandoned. He therefore early returned to his practice as a physician. The professional character of Dr. Fisher presents points of great interest. He was largely gifted with those moral and intellectual qualities which give honor and usefulness to the medical profession. He brought to every case his whole mind. He possessed extraordinary powers of observation and reflection, and seized with wonderful tact on

14*

what was most worthy of consideration. He employed but few remedies, and those were selected
from the most powerful. His treatment of inflamma-
tion, whether of the serous, mucous, or other tissues,
differed from that of many of his brethren. He
rarely or never bled, but attempted to relieve pain
by opium; and then by large quantities of calomel
to subdue the morbid processes on which the existence of the disease depended. "When driving a
nail, (he would say) why strike it a timid and use-
less blow? Nothing is to be gained by that: use at
once the force required, and the object is accomplished." Such was the kind and the illustration of his
practice. The independence and originality discovered
in it, belonged to his mind after a manner which distinguished all he did. He could not be seduced by
the mere pretension of novelty from what he had
ascertained to be true in principle and correct in
practice; and his respect for authority never so far
blinded him as to disturb his confidence in what, as
he believed, his own sound and accurate observation
had established.

Dr. Fisher was, from native constitution and habit,
a retiring man. But this was true only of his intercourse with the many: with the few he was unre-
served. He was singularly acute in discerning character; and he delighted in studying it. It was the
individual case which had to him the greatest interest in his study of disease, and the same was true of
his intercourse with men; he loved to study the
individual. He took great pleasure in receiving from
those with whom he thus familiarly associated all
they could impart, and he communicated in turn
what the occasion required, being always anxious to

be useful. It was natural, therefore, that he should be regarded ever as the agreeable and instructive companion. Few, more than he, have exerted a more powerful and enduring influence on individual minds. He was truly honored and beloved by his patients. His reputation was great; and this brought him forward as a consulting physician over a wide circuit. A moral and intellectual quality of his character, which is especially remembered by those who best knew him, is purity—purity of mind and heart. This it was that gave to his intellectual nature its greatest beauty, power and attractiveness. It constituted the tone of his mind—it was the atmosphere in which it expanded, and by which it was invigorated. It caused him to shrink with horror from moral taint, and to love the good wherever it existed. While it made him most sensible to vice, his native kindliness led him to pity what he could not but condemn. The moral dignity of such a character, if we may not attain to, we may love; and so diffusive is it, that the mere contemplation of it must make the observer better. Such a mind was admirably fitted for the study of nature, and few have felt a deeper interest in natural history. His strong powers of comparing, observing and remembering, singularly qualified him for pursuing this branch of science; and he devoted himself to it whenever and wherever opportunity offered. He had a genuine love of nature. He felt its beauty in its truth and whole amount, and derived perpetual pleasure from the perception of it. Had his means originally allowed his so doing, he would have chosen natural science as his profession, and his success would have been great. A standing testimony of his zeal in this cause is furnished by his munificent endowment of the Fisher Professorship of Natural History in Harvord University, to which by his will he gave $20,000. He has, in a sense, thus perpetuated his own mind among us. He has at least provided the means by which one of his most cherished objects shall be perpetually promoted.

He was twice married, and was highly favored in both connexions—having been thus united to two most amiable and excellent women. Without children of his own, he was yet surrounded by those whom he regarded as such, and who, with not less than filial affection, contributed to the happiness of his advancing years. His home was the abode of true hospitality; and it was there he found most constant and pure enjoyment, as well as the retire-ment congenial to his inclinations. But though he shrunk from general society, he never did from public duty. He was in an important sense a public man. He took an active part in politics, and was the intimate associate and friend of George Cabot. His connexion with Fisher Ames, and the harmony of their political views, established similar re-lations between them. It were sufficient praise to have been the associate and friend of these two of the most honored men of our State. He sustained important public offices. He was president of the Massachusetts Medical Society, a senator of the Commonwealth, and president of the Beverly Bank and the Beverly Charitable Society. He was the project-or of the latter; and having largely added to its funds during his life, left it a munificent bequest in his will. Connected with his donation at its com-mencement, was this peculiar condition—that $100 of it should be set aside to accumulate (in the shape of loans, on undoubted security, to deserving young men—or at least, preference being given to such) for a hundred years, when it would amount, in available funds for the society, to many thousands of dollars. He was a very liberal benefactor, in his lifetime and by bequest, to other public objects—particularly the first parish in Beverly, and the west parish in Dedham—his native parish. The whole amount of his legacies to such objects was upwards of $30,000.

He retained his intellectual energy remarkably to the close of life,—though, for many of his latter years, he withdrew from general practice. He loved knowledge from his youth, and he loved it to the last. His interest continued unabated in all the true sources of information, and of intellectual and moral gratification. He kept pace with the current literature, and took constant interest and pleasure in it to the latest period of his long life. But he was not unobservant of the effect of time on some of his faculties—memory in particular. How strange is this power of the human intellect, looking on its own faculties as its instruments, and discovering at once, with a distinctness none else can, where the machinery is wearing away, while it feels how powerless it is to repair it. There are few things more interesting in the contemtemplation of a really vigorous mind, than this single fact. Such a mind was Dr. Fisher's. This was acknowledged by all who came within its reach, and could apprehend its power. His affections were strong. His moral faculties were vigorous and in continual exercise. His religious sentiment was pure and elevated and enlightened. He looked on death as " an event in life"—the appointment of a perfect Father, as were all other events; and he submitted to it humbly, but with a bright hope and full trust.

He died in Beverly, on the 15th of March, 1833, at the advanced age of 84.

DR. ABNER HOWE was born in Jaffrey, N. H. in 1781. His father was an eminent and much-respected physician of that place. He graduated at Dartmouth College in 1801. Having an early predilection for the medical profession, he devoted himself with ardor to its study, under the distinguished Professor Smith, at Dartmouth. He also, for several months, attended the hospitals of Philadelphia, and the lectures for which that city was then, as it is now, noted,—enjoying, at the same time, the private instruction of the celebrated Dr. Rush. He commenced practice in his native town, as a surgeon and consulting physician, but soon removed to Beverly, where he passed the remainder of his life, and died, after a gradual decline, May 15, 1826, leaving behind him the well-earned reputation of an enlightened, devoted, successful physician, an upright and useful citizen, and a true Christian. "This excellent physician (says the author of the Memoir referred to below,* than whom none knew him better) was removed from life at the meridian, in the full vigor of his powers, enriched by the experience of twenty years of successful practice, endeared to the community, and a blessing above estimation to a young and numerous family. To amiable views of

---

* Memoir of Dr. Abner Howe, by Rev. Dr. Abbot, published in the Christian Visitant, vol. 1, No. 5, pp. 201—215.

religion, his life was happily conformed. He was an humble and devotional man at home, as well as in the house of God. He was the kindest of husbands and best of fathers. But his well-principled and enlightened mind was not confined to personal and domestic views; his notion of charity was much more expansive. In the best sense of the word, and according to his means and opportunities, he was a public man. He sought to advance the general interest by promoting the peace of the town, and christian affection among the churches, by a word spoken in season to soften prejudices and to rectify misunderstandings. For this christian office his opportunities were great, and they were discreetly improved. Dr. Howe felt a lively interest in the young. Amid his pressing professional duties, he secured time to watch over the schools, to give encouragement to the teachers, and his affectionate countenance to the youth,—his best advice to improve the plans of education, and when necessary, his liberal contribution. He was a friend of charitable institutions, whether for the relief of the indigent, or the promotion of christian knowledge and piety; and in several of them he gave his time and attention, as an officer, to advance their funds and extend their influence. In his professional course, his charity was most remarkable. Here, he was the poor man's friend; in numerous cases giving attendance and medicine to the sick, and often relief to the distressed family, without the hope of earthly reward. No man was ever distressed or made uneasy by his claims upon him. His brief and fleeting life passed without any of those remarkable incidents which tell in story. Without special pretensions to genius or striking talents, without being known to fame in a wide circle, the very respectable powers of his practical mind were cultivated with great care, and intensely applied in his immediate sphere. In that sphere, the effect was admirable. To be a good and useful man was his chastened and holy ambition, and to a high degree it was gratified. He was warmly esteemed as an enlightened and faithful, a humane and pious physician. As the sweet odor of precious ointment poured forth, his name will be long cherished."

MILITARY.

MILITARY defence was early found necessary in this town, both against savage and other foes, though the peaceful terms on which the Naumkeag territory was obtained, and the honorable manner in which the claims subsequently set up by the heirs of the Sagamore of Agawam, were liquidated, secured this place from the Indian depredations which many other New England settlements suffered. In 1662, there was a " foot company " in Beverly, commanded by Capt. Thomas Lothrop.

After his death the General Court appointed Mr. John Hathorne of Salem, to the command. The appointment was strongly objected to by the citizens of this town, and a petition was immediately forwarded to "the much honored General Court," praying for the substitution of a nomination made by themselves. The petitioners say, " though the gentleman may be worthy to lead a far more honor-

able company than ours, yet in regard of his distance of place, and as great an inconvenience of the
ferry, he is wholly in a manner uncapable to be serviceable unto us, especially in times of war, either
by impressing soldiers, ordering us in arms, regulat-
ing our trainings, especially upon disappointments
of weather, or appointing times of meeting; wherefore our humble request is, that your honors will be
pleased to settle our whole militia within our town."
The prayer of the petitioners was granted, and
Lieut. William Dixy received the appointment of
captain. In 1689, he was succeeded in command
by Paul Thorndike.*

Previous to 1689, a company of horse was organized in this town, of which William Rayment, sen.
was captain, William Dodge lieutenant, John Dodge
jr. cornet, Thomas West quartermaster. In 1690,
for reasons not apparent, the General Court medi-
tated the disbanding of this association, and merging
its members in the "foot company." Against this
procedure the cavalry strongly remonstrated. They
declared, "First, we are already provided for and
fitted with furniture and arms, fit for the service of
a troop. Secondly, we are and have been always
trained up in the exercise of a troop. Thirdly, our
inability at the present to serve the country in any
other way of service besides what belongs to a
troop. We are unfit in respect of arms and practice." They concluded by saying that if their petition to remain in their existing organization is
granted, they will "with all readiness and willingness serve God and the country to the utmost abili-

* Provincial Records.

ty." The Court, after considering the subject, consented to their request provided they made up "a number of forty able-bodied troopers," furnished and equipped according to law, within a specified time. The terms were eagerly assented to, and two days before the expiration of the term, a list embracing the requisite number was forwarded, and an accompanying nomination of officers confirmed.*

In 1641, all the companies in Essex county constituted a single regiment. In 1680, this regiment was divided, and a second formed, comprising the companies in Beverly, Salem, Marblehead, Wenham, Ipswich, Gloucester and Lynn. A new organization of the military within the bounds of these regiments took place in 1690, when three regiments were formed, one of which consisted of the companies in Beverly, Salem, Marblehead, Lynn and Manchester. In 1723, the Beverly companies were attached to the Salem regiment, and afterwards were enrolled in the Danvers regiment. They were subsequently united with the Manchester companies, and formed the Beverly regiment, of which John Francis was the first colonel. This regiment was disbanded in 1831, and two companies of infantry, with the light infantry, were attached to the first regiment, composed of four companies from Marblehead and six from Salem. In 1834, the volunteer companies were taken from this regiment, and the sixth regiment of light infantry formed from Beverly, Salem, Marblehead, Lynn, Danvers, Manchester and Rockport.

At what time more than one foot company was

* Provincial Records.

formed in this town is unknown, but in 1775 mention is made, in the records, of three. These companies met for military parade at the first and second parish meeting-houses, and at the Cove.

After the revolutionary war broke out, an independent company of grenadiers was raised, consisting of the tallest men in town. It was commanded by Henry Herrick, son of Col. Henry Herrick, and marched to Rhode Island to reinforce the troops there. At what time it was disbanded is not known.

After the peace of 1783, the military declined, but revived again before the war of 1812. During this last contest with Great Britain, a volunteer company of artillery was formed, under the command of Capt. Nicholas Thorndike, and the militia were kept in constant readiness for service.

The first light infantry company commenced by a voluntary association of individuals, at a meeting held October 17th, 1800, but was not established by law until June 2d, 1801, when, under an order from Lt. Col. James Burnham of the third regiment, they were regularly enlisted. On the 15th of the same month, a meeting was held for the choice of officers. Jonathan H. Lovett was chosen captain, Josiah Gould lieutenant, and Robert Rantoul ensign. Mr. Gould declined, and at a subsequent meeting Mr. Rantoul was chosen in his stead. The vacancy made by this promotion was filled by the choice of Samuel Stickney for ensign. Capt. Lovett having been chosen major, Mr. Rantoul was chosen captain and Timothy Wyer lieutenant. In 1809, Captain Rantoul was discharged by his own request. His successor was T. Wyer, who was succeeded by Robert Tuck. On the fourth of July, 1807, an elegant standard was presented to this company by the ladies of Beverly. The ceremony of presentation was performed by Miss Susan Whitney, accompanied with an appropriate address. The colors were received by Ensign Stickney, who made a brief and pertinent reply. The company was finally disbanded.

The present light infantry company was organized about 1815. The first commander was William Thorndike. His successors have been Cotton Bennett, Samuel P. Lovett, Stephen Nourse, Charles Stevens, and Josiah Woodberry. On the 23d September, 1836, the company paraded in an entire new uniform, under the command of Capt. Charles Stevens, accompanied by the Boston Brass Band, on which occasion a beautiful standard was presented them by Miss B. L. Chapman, in the name of the ladies of Beverly. This company holds a high rank as a well-disciplined and efficient corps.

From the close of the revolutionary war until quite recently, an organized and well-disciplined militia has been considered vitally important to the safety of the State; and within twenty years, "May training," and the autumnal regimental or brigade muster, was anticipated by young and old with an interest surpassed only, if at all, by that felt in "election" and "thanksgiving" days. On these occasions the people poured in from adjacent towns to witness the pageant, and the "tented field" displayed a heterogeneous collection of omnivorous beings, biped and quadruped. Here were sires leaning on the staff of age, and youths alarming the timid with the mimic musketry of "India crackers," or imitating their elders in copious potations of punch and "egg pop." Here were modest swains paying faithful devoir to bashful maidens, "flaunting in silks," or decked in habiliments of rainbow hue; and there groups of urchins, exchanging their silver and copper for the merchandize of venders of ginger-bread and candied sweets. Here, the athletic exhibited their skill in "wrestling;" and there, "the ring" was formed for the mysteries of "pawpaw," "hustling," "wheel of fortune," and other forms of popular gaming. The "nodding plume," the "flashing sword," and "bristling bayonet," were gazed upon by the young with unsuppressed admiration, while the shrill fife and rattling drum rekindled in the breasts of revolutionary patriarchs the fire of "times that tried men's souls;" and seated in the "booth," or beneath a friendly shade, they recounted for the hundredth time the deeds of daring at Trenton, Yorktown and Stony Point, and with the vigor of former days, "fought all their battles o'er again."

But this "right arm of defence" was not without its enemies. With such, the Washingtonian doctrine of preparing for war in time of peace had become obsolete, and the whole system was assailed at every vulnerable point. To frequent and disastrous legislation was united the powerful auxiliary of ridicule. The burlesque regimental review at Philadelphia, under the redoubtable Col. Pluck, was the signal for similar fantastical parades throughout the country. Before the omnipotence of ridicule the system could not stand. The glory departed; subordination ceased, resignation of officers multiplied, a rapid decline followed, and in 1840 the militia organization of this State expired, leaving the guardianship of public safety to the volunteer companies.

15*

SOLDIERS.

FROM the settlement of Beverly until the close of the revolutionary war, there was hardly an expedition against the Indians or French, or a battle of any moment, in which the town was not represented. The following list of soldiers, in addition to the names mentioned elsewhere, has been compiled with great labor from the muster-rolls in the State archives, orderly books, and other sources, though it probably presents but a part of the number actually engaged in service.

1676. In a company stationed at Wells, on the eastern frontier, under the command of Capt. Frost, John Ellingwood, Thomas Parlor and Samuel Collins. Ellingwood was wounded, having the fore-finger of the right hand shot away ; in consideration of which the General Court granted him, in 1720-1, £5 for his present relief, and £3 per annum during life.

1696. In Capt. John Hill's company, at fort St. Mary, near Saco, John Burt, Benjamin Carrill, John Pickworth, and Israel Wood.

1756. Enlisted in Capt. Andrew Fuller's company, for the Crown Point expedition, Benjamin Balch, William Eborn, Daniel Gloyd, Corp. John Simonds, William Moneys, Azor Roundy, Joseph Baker, Eliezer Ellingwood, John Clark, Peter Stokes, Daniel Butman, (enlisted again in 1759,) Robert Matthews, George Spence, (enlisted again in 1759 and 1761,) Andrew Woodberry.

1757. In Capt. Israel Herrick's company of Eastern Rangers, Osman Baker, Bartholomew Peart, John Simonds, John Trask, (enlisted again 1758,) Josiah Trow, Robert Baker (Canada expedition, 1759).

1758. In Capt. John Tapley's company. Wells Standley, William Herrick, Bartholomew Taylor, John Clark (at the capture of fort William Henry).

In various other companies. 1756. Moses Dodge (at fort Edward). 1758. John Smith, Samuel Tuck, Jonathan Thorndike, Samuel Woodberry. Josiah Woodberry, James Woodberry, Jonathan Corning, (seaman,) Zebulon Butman, David Hill, (drummer,) Jonathan Dodge, Nathaniel Woodberry, John Hubbard, Abraham Hix, (enlisted again in 1761,) William Dodge (again in 1761). 1759. Robert Elliot, James Giles, Jonathan Larcom, Corp. Andrew Woodberry, Benjamin Brown, William Presson, Richard Standley, John Wallis, Barebeel Woodberry, Samuel Bean, Josiah Creesy, Aaron Crowell, Andrew Elliot, Amos Hilton, William Morgan, Robert Pickett, Nicholas Standley. 1761. Benjamin Presson, Ralph Tuck, Wilks West, Robert Standley, Joseph Williams, Benjamin Dike, Jonathan Dodge, Timothy Howard, Jacob Poland, Nathaniel Butman, Samuel Stickney.

A roll of the officers and soldiers of a company enlisted in Beverly, for the expedition against Louisburg, 1744.

Benjamin Ives, jr. captain; George Herrick lieutenant, Josiah Bachelder ensign, Job Cressy and Samuel Woodberry, sergeants; Benjamin Cleaves, jr. clerk, Barth. Brown and John Picket, corporals; Joseph Raymond, drummer. Privates: Benjamin Smith, Benjamin Clark, Samuel Harris, John Roundy, Israel Byles, Elias Picket, Ebenezer Cox, Jonathan Byles, Andrew Herrick, Benjamin Hervey, Samuel Cole, Richard Ober, Thomas Butman, William James, Jonathan Harris, Edmund Clark, John Grover, John Morgan, Eleazer Giles, Ezra Trask,

John Presson, Francis Elliot, Benjamin Dike, Samuel Stone, Israel Ellwell, Israel Woodberry, Josiah Woodberry, Jonathan Morgan, Joshua Rea, William Badcock, Benjamin Trask, Edward Cox, James Trask, Joseph Elliott, William Leach, Benjamin Howard, Christopher Bartlett, Ebenezer Hadley, Daniel Stephens, Caleb Page, Samuel Chute. Total 50.

The following is a list of the privates in Capt. Moses Brown's company, raised in this town for the war of the revolution, August, 1776.

Richard Ober, Jonathan Harris, Freeborn Thorndike, Jonathan Foster, Samuel Stone, William Crowther, Cornelius Woodberry, Luke Woodberry, Andrew Woodberry, John Cressy, Amos Cressy, Robert Lovett, Thomas Parker, Bartholomew Smith, Mihill Woodberry, Thomas Cox, Nathan Batchelder, Nathaniel Ober, Joseph Ober, James Ober, William Cook, Abner Stone, Benjamin Foster, James Patch, Henry Pierce, James Goldthwait (Salem), John Darby (Salem), Asa Larcom (Salem), Robert Stone, Esop Hale, Herbert Standley, John Biles, Josiah Woodberry, Jacob Poland, Andrew Elliot, William Herrick, Ebenezer Rogers, John Stone, William Cressy, Israel Greene, Benjamin Porter, Thomas Morse, Joseph Hall, William Kimball, Daniel Carleton, William Gage, Jonathan Gage, Caleb Wallis, Ebenezer Messer, Joseph Cross, Elisha Webber, William Harriman, John Berry, Joseph Foster, John Swain. The officers were William Groves, first lieutenant; John Wallis, second lieutenant; John Clark, ensign; Samuel Foster, William Bowles, Richard Ober and Samuel Cressy, sergeants; William Dike, Joshua Ellingwood, Francis

Ober and Ezra Ober, corporals; Jonathan Grover drummer, and John Leach fifer, both of Marblehead. Total, 69.

The following persons belonging to this town were enlisted in Capt. Billy Porter's company, and were in Col. Tupper's regiment at West Point, 1779.

Thomas Francis, lieut.; William Burley, lieut.; Benjamin Shaw, ensign; John Pickett, sergeant; Jeremiah Woodberry, corporal; Benjamin B. Wood, drummer. The privates were Asa Batchelder, Jonathan Conant, Benjamin Corning, Mathias Claxton, Alexander Carrico, Samuel Dodge, Simeon Dodge, George Grose, Andrew Herrick, Claton Jones, Nathan Jones, John Kennady, Abner Raymond, Benjamin Woodberry, Benjamin Woodberry, jr. Israel Woodberry, Nathaniel Woodberry, William Woodberry. Total, 24.

The company commanded by Capt. Page of Danvers, enlisted the following persons from Beverly.

Samuel Goodridge, 1st lieut.; Joseph Raymond, sergeant. Privates, Robert Edwards, Scipio Bartlett, James Hurley, Joseph Poland, Primas Green. Total, 7.

Jonathan Conant, sen. was paymaster in Col. Francis' regiment, and afterwards under Col. Benjamin Tupper. He was in the battle of Monmouth. Joshua Twist was in Gates' army at the taking of Burgoyne. William and Samuel Cressy were in the battle of Trenton. Luke Roundy was a lieutenant in Capt. Low's company. He was wounded at Saratoga, and died at Albany. Nathaniel Cleaves was in the same engagement. William Goodridge, Robert Goodridge, Israel Trask,

Benjamin Ellingwood, Thomas Lovett, Benjamin Bickford, Benjamin Bickford, jr. John Bickford, Nathaniel Friend, Isaac Smith, Jonathan Woodberry, Zachariah Morgan and Benjamin Spriggs, were also in the service.

TEMPERANCE.

On the subject of temperance, this town has kept in the van of enlightened public sentiment. While mistaken hospitality required the decanter to grace the sideboard, and the "social glass" constituted an essential element of friendly intercourse, spirituous liquors were here, as in other places, freely used. To neglect to offer, or to refuse to partake, would, according to prevailing opinions, have been regarded as a violation of etiquette on the one hand, and as indicative of austerity or displeasure on the other; and though a general sobriety prevailed, and gross instances of intoxication were less frequent than in most other towns, still there were here many victims to the inebriating cup. The idea prevailed here as elsewhere, that, aside from convivial occasions and social greetings, a necessity existed for the use of alcoholic drinks by laboring men. This idea was encouraged by municipal action. In repairing the highways, or in executing any public work, the town made a liberal provision of rum, and a half-pint per man of this beverage was frequently added to daily pay. The practice of "treating" on being inducted into a town or parish office, and of providing selectmen and assessors with dinners, wine, punch, toddy, flip, etc., at the tavern in which they held their meetings, also prevailed, though with no sensible advantage to the public interest. But as temperance principles became better understood, these customs were abandoned.* In 1821, two innholders and twenty-one retailers were licensed to sell ardent spirits; but for several years past, no licenses have been granted to taverns or stores, and the sale of distilled liquors and wines has been restricted to medical prescriptions. This reform has been promoted by judicious individuals, who early appreciated the evils of intemperance. It has been of gradual growth, and effected with but little excitement,—an evidence of its purity, and a pledge of its permanency.

In the progress of temperance, the appointment of a "committee of inspection" in 1675, to prevent "private tippling and drunkenness," may be considered a primary measure.† Though much was probably done intermediately, the second act of the town worthy of remembrance was the vote of March 8th, 1790, by which the practice of "giving drink" to public officers on being qualified, was abolished. A third step was a vote of March 9th, 1807, by which

---

* About 40 gallons of rum were consumed annually at the expense of the town, in repairing the highways. Parish tavern bills were about $30 per annum, and town tavern expenses were considerably more. Between Aug. 1, 1789, and Feb. 1, 1790, excise was paid on 2,037 1-2 gallons N. E. rum and other distilled spirits, 420 1-2 gallons foreign rum, 119 1-4 gallons other foreign distilled spirits, and 52 1-2 gallons of wine.

† This committee was chosen in obedience to a law of the General Court, and consisted of William Dodge, sen., Humphrey Woodberry, Josiah Roots, Exercise Conant, John Hill, Robert Hibbert, Nathaniel Hayward, Richard Ober and John Dodge, sen. Each member of the committee had the supervision of ten families.

the selectmen were requested "not to approbate or
recommend for the renewal of their license any person in future as an innholder," who was not provided with accommodations for entertaining travellers.
Both Dr. Abbot and Mr. Emerson early gave their
public testimony against the evils of intemperance,
and contributed essentially in awakening a more
general attention to the subject. These, with other
acts of a less public character, opened the way for
the consummating measure of concentrating and
consolidating public opinion through the agency of
temperance societies.

The first movement towards obtaining pledges to
total abstinence from distilled liquors, except as a
medicine, was about 1830, and a society was soon
after formed.

The BEVERLY BAPTIST TEMPERANCE SOCIETY was organized in 1832. In 1835, these societies were united, under the name of THE BEVERLY TEMPERANCE So-
CIETY.

The VILLAGE TEMPERANCE SOCIETY, at the Farms,
was instituted April 2d, 1832. The constitution dis-
countenances traffic in distilled liquors, and prohibits
their use as a common beverage.

In 1833, a TEMPERANCE ASSOCIATION was formed
in the Second Parish, the members of which pledged
themselves not to use distilled spirit, nor provide it
for others, except as a medicine, and in all proper
ways to discountenance its use in the community.

The UNION TEMPERANCE SOCIETY was formed April
6th, 1835.

The TOTAL ABSTINENCE SOCIETY was organized in April, 1838. Its motto is "total abstinence from all that can intoxicate."

Between two and three thousand persons have united with these several associations, and through the agency of lectures and efficient committees, as well as individual example, each organization has effected much for the general cause. In 1840, the "Washingtonian reformation" commenced, and gave a new impulse to the temperance movement throughout the country. Of this influence, Beverly has partaken. Lectures by reformed inebriates have been delivered before numerous and interested assemblies, and a large number of pledges taken. It is deserving of honorable mention, that no fishing vessels sailing from this port, take ardent spirits as a part of their regular supplies.*

CHARITABLE AND OTHER ASSOCIATIONS.

THE benevolent virtues are not the least among the characteristics of Beverly. Several associations exist, having for their object the alleviation of misfortune and distress. March 1, 1807, a society was incorporated by the name of the BEVERLY CHARITABLE SOCIETY, for the purpose of raising a fund to relieve any inhabitant of the town who from sickness or misfortune may require assistance†. It also pro-

---

* The temperance reform has materially reduced the number of persons supported by the town.

† The corporate name of this society has since been changed to the "Fisher Charitable Society."

posed to aid the destitute widow, provide for the
helpless orphan, and generally to perform such acts of
charity and benevolence as its funds would from
time to time allow, excluding from its good offices such as were idle, prodigal, intemperate, or to
whom relief should more properly come from the
overseers of the poor. This society, from the distinguished liberality of several gentlemen, has a
considerable fund. The late Dr. Fisher may be
considered as its founder. He left a legacy of
$1000, in addition to $200 presented it in his life-
time. The society has distributed large sums in
charity since its foundation.

The BEVERLY FEMALE CHARITABLE SOCIETY was
incorporated April 5th, 1836. The members of this
society have been the active distributors of a large
amount of property in money, clothing, and other
necessaries and comforts. Formerly, an annual public address was delivered before the society, and a
collection taken up in aid of its funds; but these
have for several years past been discontinued. The
personal labors of several of the ladies of this institution, in visiting, counselling and relieving the needy,
have been in the true spirit of that christian philan-
thropy which is never weary in well-doing.

The FEMALE SEAMEN'S FRIEND SOCIETY was organized in September, 1832, and consists of about one
hundred members. The object of this society is the
laudable one of promoting the comfort and improving
the moral and religious condition of seamen. The
means for promoting this design are derived from the
annual subscription of members and the avails of

the society's labor at its semi-monthly meetings. Bibles and tracts are purchased for distribution on board of vessels sailing out of this port, and all monies remaining on hand are annually paid over to the Seamen's Friend Society at New York, for the diffusion of religious knowledge among seamen. This society may be regarded as among the many approved agencies for hastening the fulfilment of the divine prediction that "the abundance of the sea shall be converted unto" the Most High.

The HOME SEAMEN'S FRIEND SOCIETY was organized March 18th, 1833, and numbers eighty-four members. The object of this institution is to relieve destitute seamen and their families, the funds for which are derived from the annual subscription of members and the proceeds of work performed at semi-monthly meetings. For several years past an annual address has been delivered before the society, and in some instances a collection taken for its benefit. At the time of its organization, the society consisted exclusively of ladies of the Baptist denomination, and was called the Baptist Seamen's Friend Society; but as ladies from other denominations subsequently united with it, the expediency of changing its name was suggested, which was effected at the annual meeting, Nov. 5th, 1839. This society has rendered valuable service to the families of those for whose relief it was instituted. Other societies for the relief of the poor exist, whose labors of love and works of charity have gladdened many a desolate heart. Of the private charities we can only speak generally. There is abundant reason to believe that this mode of bestowing alms is practised to as great an extent as can be reasonably expected. A wealthy individual of this town, now resident in the metropolis, has at several different times made liberal donations that are gratefully remembered ; and gifts by other individuals are registered in the recollections of numbers.

The BEVERLY MECHANIC ASSOCIATION was formed in 1836. The design of this institution is "the moral and intellectual improvement of its members, and their relief in distress." As yet, drafts upon its funds for the last mentioned object, have been found necessary in two instances only. Its library is gradually enlarging. The funds of the association amount to $450. The present number of members is ninety-two. Three dollars are required as the fee of membership, subject to an annual assessment of one dollar. Seven dollars will constitute a life membership exempt from assessments. Quarterly meetings of the association are held, at which subjects for discussion are presented.

A MASONIC LODGE was established here during the revolutionary war. This was dissolved, and another established under a charter from the Grand Lodge of Massachusetts, in 1824.

The BEVERLY ANTI-SLAVERY SOCIETY was formed Feb. 21st, 1834, at which time a constitution was reported and adopted. The society consists of one hundred and twelve members.

The UPPER BEVERLY ANTI-SLAVERY SOCIETY was organized in 1837. According to the second article of the constitution, "The objects of this society shall be, 1st, the emancipation of the people of color from legal slavery; 2d, the emancipation of the same people, bond and free, from the despotism of a corrupt public sentiment."

Though slavery existed in Massachusetts until 1780, it never assumed the objectionable features exhibited in the southern section of the United States. As a system, American slavery is an unqualified evil, and its perpetuity can in no way be reconciled with the principles of a republican government. The voice of humanity and the law of God demand its abrogation, and the day is approaching when every yoke will be broken and the bond go free.

The BEVERLY BANK was incorporated July 23, 1802, the charter to expire in 1812. It has since been twice renewed. The capital stock was originally $160,000. In 1815, it was reduced to $100,000, and increased again, in 1836, to $125,000. Its presidents have been Israel Thorndike, Moses Brown, Joshua Fisher, William Leach and Pyam Lovett, the last of whom now fills the office. It has had but two cashiers, Josiah Gould and the present incumbent, Albert Thorndike. This institution is of convenience to trade, and affords a safe investment of capital to those who do not wish to manage private loans. Through all the financial changes and pressures of the last eight years, it has maintained its integrity unimpaired, and its affairs are conducted with great exactness and skill.

The BEVERLY MARINE INSURANCE COMPANY was incorporated in June, 1809, with a capital of $100,000.

16*

The charter was for twenty years, and the company expired with the limitation, part of the stockholders being opposed to its renewal.

FIRE DEPARTMENT.

THE usual precautions against fire have been adopted by this town. At a town meeting, Nov. 17, 1774, it was voted, that if any number of men, not exceeding thirty-two, shall enter into agreement to purchase a good fire-engine and the necessary apparatus, and contract to improve the same for extinguishing fires as is customary in other towns, then in such case they shall be excused from serving in any town office or as juryman. It appears that this vote was availed of, and a fire company formed which purchased an engine and the necessary apparatus. The proprietors, however, in 1795, gave up their engine, engine-house, hooks, ladders, etc. to the town, and also a sum of money in hand, on condition that the town should purchase one of the best engines that could be procured. May 16th, 1805, it was voted to raise $1000 for the purchase of a new fire-engine, and in 1828, it was voted to procure another.

The fire apparatus now belonging to the town consists of three engines, managed by efficient companies, with the necessary appendages of hose, buckets, axes, etc. One of these is in the second parish and the other two in the first. Fire-hooks and ladders are placed at several convenient points. In addition to these, the Union Fire Society, formed in 1804 for the purpose of aiding each other in case of fire, have ladders, fire-hooks, axes and sails, and each member is provided with two leather buckets, a large cloth bag, a bed-key and screw-driver. This company has a fund of about $1400, in addition to their apparatus.

Four cisterns have been built to furnish water in cases of fire.

The principal fires that have occurred in this town, and which have put in requisition the important services of the various fire associations, are: one that took place in 1828, which consumed the brick factory in the second parish; one on the 20th April, 1829, which destroyed the barns of Robert Currey and Michael Whitney, and damaged more or less the dwellings of Messrs. Whitney and Jeremiah Lovett, and also a barn near the store of S. P. Lovett; one on 29th May following, which consumed the dwelling of Robert Currey, the barn and store of Samuel P. Lovett, with part of the goods, and the dwellings of Michael Whitney and Josiah Raymond; one Dec. 8th, 1832, which burned to the ground the Dane-street meeting-house,—the three last of which were supposed to be the work of incendiaries,—and one, May 20th, 1841, which consumed a large store and most of its contents on Foster's wharf.

STREETS.

THE public streets, courts and squares, forty-three in number, were named by order of the town in 1838. They are as follows: Cabot, Congress, Water, Davis, Front, Union, Bartlett, Central, Lovett, Franklin, Washington, Hale, Ellingwood, Charity, Cox, School, Burley Court, Lafayette, Elm, Wallis, Federal, Essex, Briscoe, Church, Winter, Knowlton, Dane, Charnock, Colon, Elliott, Mill, Conant, Liberty, Dodge, Ober, Lothrop, Howard, Thorndike, Brown, Endicott, Abbot, Burley, and May.

BURIAL GROUNDS.

THE burial grounds in this town are eight in number, viz., three in the first parish, two near the second parish meeting-house, one in Dodge's row, one at Rial-side, and one at the Farms. A traditionary account is, that the first burying place was at Woodberry's Point; but the oldest of which there is any record is that near the vestry of the first parish, in which repose the remains of the first three settled ministers, Hale, Blowers and Champney. The earliest dates decyphered on any of the stones are 1686, 1678 and 1683, the last of which is over the grave of Mrs. Rebecca, wife of John Hale. This burying ground was the only one used within the limits of the first parish until Jan. 1790, a period of more than one hundred years. In 1684, John Green, of Rial-side, obtained liberty to bury his dead in this ground, on condition that he contributed towards the expense of the same. At the same time, measures were adopted to enclose the ground. The earliest date that can be found in the burying ground at Rial-side is 1730. In 1788, the first parish purchased of Daniel Adams a piece of land, near the Common, for burial purposes; and Jan. 17, 1790, the remains of

Widow Mary Allen, aged 71, were deposited there, in the first grave. The town burying ground on Hale street, and adjoining the former, was laid out at a still later period, and is now most used. The burying ground at the Farms was laid out in 1840, and, on the 24th of August, the same year, it received for its first deposit the remains of Deacon David Larcom.

The first burial place in the second parish was opened about 1715, and the remains of Eleanour, child of John Dodge, Jr., and Elizabeth, wife of John Trask, were among the first, if not the first, it received. The most ancient stone is at the grave of Joseph Herrick, and bears date Feb. 14, 1717–18. The graves of Mr. Chipman, his two wives and his daughter Sarah, are in the south-western corner, shaded by a beautiful oak; but time has been busy with the grave-stones, and unless some " Old Mortality" soon exercises his friendly office, few inscriptions that can be decyphered will remain. The second ground, adjoining the second parish meeting-house, was laid out in 1803, and now contains upwards of three hundred graves. A tomb was built here in 1806, by Joseph Chipman, son of the first minister, and another in 1836, by William Friend. The wife of the Rev. Mr. Fairfield was the first person buried in this ground. In the burial grounds of the south parish are several tombs and handsome monuments.

Among the places of painful interest, the village grave-yard will always be conspicuous. It speaks in solemn tones of man's mortality,—of withered hopes, and of plans unfinished. Here lies the infant pledge of love, "plucked like a bud from its parent stem, to bloom a sweeter flower in a fairer clime;"

and close by its side, the child of many prayers,
whose early promise death has prematurely blasted,
piercing the parental heart with sorrows which only
parents know.   Here repose the ashes of lover and
friend, of simple and lettered, of poverty and wealth,
alike to rise in the resurrection morn.   It is instructive to walk amidst the congregation of the dead,
and meditate on life's mutations and ambition's end.

"The very turf beneath our feet seems bent in silent prayer,
The trees to lift their green boughs up, and ask a father's care ;
And though the flowers may fade and fall, we mourn them not in vain,
They tell us that thus we must die, and thus shall live again."

Here, too, the chord that binds the soul to kindred
and home, is drawn still closer round the affections.
We sadden at the thought of dying among strangers,
with no friendly voice to speak to us the consolations
of religion, nor friendly hand to close our eyes and
perform the last offices of the living to our lifeless
clay.   And when the possibility of such an event is
suggested by busy fancy, our prayer ascends to the
Author of being that our grave may be made in the
midst of kindred and friends, by whom our memory
will be cherished when our dust is blended with the
earth whence it sprang.

It is consonant with pious sentiment and pure affection, to build the mausoleum and erect the column
over the remains of departed worth ; and even the
simple head-stone, with its brief epitaph, is a memen-
to of friendship that speaks favorably for civilized
man.   Other methods, however, than these may be
adopted for giving utterance to affection's language.
At trifling cost, trees may be planted in every village

grave-yard, which in a few years will become beautiful groves; and though these may be less attractive than a Pére la Chaise or a Mount Auburn, they will, nevertheless, increase the sacredness of the "field of graves," and impart a chastened cheerfulness to places so fruitful of melancholy associations.

COMMON LANDS.

"BEVERLY COMMONS" consisted of eighteen hundred and fifty acres, in seven distinct tracts. The largest of these tracts was that known as the Sheeppasture, containing 1013 acres. The others are designated as Mackerel Cove, Rubly Hill, Cedar Swamp, Burnt Hill, Snake Hill and Bald Hill pastures.

In 1670, the town "voted that there shall not be any of the town's land lying in common, disposed of upon any account, but by consent of the whole at a general town meeting, legally warned; and it was also voted, for preventing the dividing of the same, that they shall abide in common as they now are, and not be divided without the consent of the whole, by general town meeting legally warned. If six considerable men in the town oppose the division, it shall not be granted."

It appears that the town and "commoners," or proprietors of grants, held a divided jurisdiction over these lands, which it is now difficult to reconcile. These latter held separate meetings, the records of which, from 1698-9 to 1750, are in the town clerk's office. The town having disposed of several parcels of the common lands by grants and exchange, the

commoners, at a meeting, May 4, 1714, confirmed
the titles to prevent " disturbance amongst friends."
In 1716, the common lands were divided into stints
or rights of six acres each ; ten of which were set
apart for the use of the poor—two for the ministry in
the first, and one for the ministry in the second parish.   An assignment of rights was also made to
individuals on the following principles, viz : One
right each to freeholders of a cottage or house erected
in or before 1661, and standing and inhabited in June,
1715 ; to freeholders whose house was erected or
standing and inhabited in 1668; and to freeholders
of all other dwellings standing in 1699, erected subsequent to 1661, and not in succession to any of the
former between 1668 and 1699.   Other rights were
granted upon distinct grounds, but the rocks were to
remain free for the use of all the inhabitants of the
town forever.   The separate pastures into which the
commons were divided, were afterwards managed as
separate fields by the proprietors of each.   The
records of Snake-hill propriety, commencing in 1728
and continued about sixty years, are extant.   Most
of the common lands are now private property.

REPRESENTATIVES.

The following is a list of the representatives from
this town in General Court, from 1672 till 1842.
Until 1693 they were styled " deputies."

Thomas Lothrop (4 years), John Dodge, John
West, Paul Thorndike, William Dodge, Exercise
Conant (2 y.), William Rayment, Thomas West,

Andrew Elliot (5 y.), Peter Woodberry, John Dodge
(3 y.), Samuel Balch (14 y.), Isaac Woodberry (2 y.),
Robert Hale, sen., John Balch (3 y.), Joseph Herrick
(4 y.), Robert Briscoe, John Thorndike, Jonathan
Rayment (2 y.), Robert Woodberry (2 y.), Andrew
Dodge (2 y.), Henry Herrick (24 y.), Robert Hale,
jr. (16 y.), Daniel Conant (2 y.), John Leach, Josiah
Batchelder, jr. (6 y.), Jonathan Conant (2 y.), Nich-
olas Thorndike, Larkin Thorndike (7 y.), Nathan
Dane (4 y.), Joseph Wood (17 y.), Israel Thorn-
dike (6 y.), John Cabot, Moses Brown (3 y.), John
Stephens (2 y.), James Burnham (2 y.), Abner Chap-
man (11 y.), Thomas Davis (15 y.), Thomas Ste-
phens (4 y.), Robert Rantoul (20 y.), Isaac Rea (5 y.),
Nathaniel Goodwin (7 y.), Nicholas Thorndike (4 y.).
Josiah Lovett (3 y.), Oliver Obear (4 y.), William
Thorndike (2 y.), Henry Larcom (4 y.), Amos Shel-
den (2 y.), John Safford (4 y.), Jesse Shelden, Nehe-
miah Roundy (3 y.), Cotton Bennett (3 y.), John
Conant (2 y.), Stephen Nourse (2 y.), Pyam Lovett,
David Larcom, Ezra Dodge, Daniel Cross, Jonathan
Batchelder, Edwin M. Stone (2 y.), Thomas B.
Smith (2 y.), William Lamson (2 y.), John I. Baker,
Edward Stone, John Pickett.

STOCKS.

In the early period of the colony, stocks and the
whipping-post were considered as essential appurte-
nances of a village as the schoolhouse and tavern;
and to dignify them in the eyes of peaceable citizens,
probably, (for no other reason is readily suggested,)
17

and to give a sacred character, perhaps, to the torture inflicted, they were usually set up in the vicinity of the meeting-house. Here, offenders were exposed to the jeers and rude assaults of a thoughtless rabble, or subjected to a discipline peculiar now to the army and navy, and eminently calculated to harden the transgressor and extinguish the last emotion of manliness glowing in his breast. Such were the spirit and practice of the times; and it is no reflection upon the natural kindness of the inhabitants to say that, in harmony with common opinion and common custom, which is common law, Beverly was very early furnished with these ancient auxiliaries to justice, which was sometimes summarily administered. In those times a magistrate might, upon view of an offence, proceed at once to convict and punish, —an exercise of power not always tempered with mercy. An anecdote is related of a good justice of the peace, which shows, that tenacity for every "jot and tittle" of the law did not necessarily banish from the heart the spirit of hospitality. "On a severe cold night in winter, a traveller came to his house for shelter and refreshment. The ready hospitality of the justice was about being displayed, when the traveller unluckily uttered a word which his host considered profane. Upon this he informed his guest that he was a magistrate, pointed out the nature of the offence, and explained the necessity of its being expiated by sitting an hour in the stocks! Remonstrance was unavailing. Cold as it was, the justice, aided by his son, conducted the traveller to the place of punishment. Here he was confined in the usual mode, the benevolent executor of the law remaining with him to beguile the time of its tedium by edifying conversation. At the expiration of the hour, he was re-conducted to the house, and hospitably entertained till the next morning, when he departed with a determination, doubtless, to consider his words more carefully before giving them utterance in the hearing of a conscientious magistrate." It is hardly necessary to add, that these relics of a barbarous age have long since disappeared.

DISEASES, DEATHS, MARRIAGES.

THE diseases most prevalent in this town, are consumption, fevers and dysentery.

The average number of deaths, annually, is about one in 70 of the population. From 1772 to 1781, a period of nine years, the number of deaths recorded by Mr. Willard, in the first parish, was 390, averaging 43 and a fraction annually, for that part of the town. But this included most of the revolutionary war, and was a period of extraordinary destruction of human life. The deaths recorded by Mr. McKean, from 1782 to 1801, a period of twenty years, were 956, or 47 15-20 per year, for the first parish. In this estimate are included 149 occasioned by an epidemic in 1795 and 1796. The average number of deaths in the first society for twenty years preceding Jan. 1, 1824, was 42 per year.

The deaths in the second parish, recorded by Mr. Chipman, from 1715 to 1769 inclusive, a period of nearly fifty-five years, are 631, averaging a fraction over eleven per year. The annual deaths during Mr. Chipman's ministry, varied from six, the small-

est number, to thirty-eight, the largest, which occurred in 1737, when the scarlet fever and throat distemper prevailed. From 1801 to 1812, inclusive, the
deaths were 137, or 11 5-12 per year. Of this number, 16 were between the ages of 60 and 70, eight
between 70 and 80, nine between 80 and 90, one
aged 92, and one 99 1-4. The number of deaths for
ten years ending Jan. 1, 1840, is 92, averaging 9 2-10
per year, showing a decrease of more than two per
cent. This improvement in the health of the second
parish, is to be attributed in part to a more strict
regard to the laws of the physical constitution, and
the improvement of low, wet lands.

The deaths in the whole town in 1818 and '19,
exclusive of deaths abroad, were 127, of which 30
were fever, 26 consumption, and 19 dysentery. In
1820 the deaths were 60, of which 11 were consumption and 9 fever. In 1827 the deaths were 67
at home, and 9 abroad. Few towns in the Commonwealth, of the same population, can exhibit
more numerous instances of longevity. The whole
number of deaths in the first parish for the ten years
ending Jan. 27th, 1840, was 213, of which 124, or
nearly one half, were persons between 50 and 97
years. Mr. James Woodberry, of Beverly Farms,
who died in 1842, aged 88 years and 8 months, was
the oldest man in town at his decease, and of a family remarkable for longevity. Two sisters survived
him, one aged 85 and the other 87. Both his father
and mother died at 86. His widow is 72; and her
mother, Mrs. Appleton, is still living at the advanced
age of 102. Mrs. W.'s father, at his death, was 90,
and her grandmother 92. The united age of ten of

the family amount to 866 years, and their average is 86.

The average number of marriages in this town per annum, for the last twenty years, is 33—births, 132.

POPULATION, &C.

It is impossible to ascertain with entire accuracy, the population of this town at early periods of its settlement. Still, from careful calculations that have been made, the number of inhabitants at the time the town was incorporated in 1668, may be estimated at six hundred. The population in 1708, was one thousand six hundred eighty, and in 1753, it had increased to two thousand and twenty-three. The following census, taken by authority, exhibits with exactness the population at subsequent periods :

1765, including 80 blacks,	2163,
1790,	3290,
1800,	3881,
1810, including 61 negroes,	4333,
1820,	4283,
1830,	4231, excess of females, 213.

By the census of 1840, the entire population, including twenty-three colored persons, is four thousand six hundred eighty-nine. White males two thousand two hundred forty-seven—females two thousand four hundred nineteen. Excess of females one hundred seventy-two. Number of families, one thousand sixty-six. Average number in a family, a fraction less than five. Number of polls, one

17*

thousand one hundred sixty-nine, of which seventy-six are not taxable. Number of revolutionary pensioners, ten, four of whom are females.

Persons under 5 years,	323 males—	285 females,
5 and under 10 "	284 "	272 "
10 " " 15 "	240 "	197 "
15 " " 20 "	204 "	250 "
20 " " 30 "	394 "	409 "
30 " " 40 "	326 "	333 "
40 " " 50 "	182 "	222 "
50 " " 60 "	140 "	183 "
60 " " 70 "	94 "	150 "
70 " " 80 "	42 "	82 "
80 " " 90 "	18 "	33 "
90 " " 100 "	00 "	2 "
100	00 "	1 "

The population in the second parish is about seven hundred and thirty. The number of dwellings in the town at different periods is shown by the following table :

In 1753 there were 289,
   1765 " " 307,
   1786 " " 308,—shops 51—barns 235,
   1790 " " 422,
   1800 " " 460,
   1811 " " 476,—shops and warehouses 80,
   1831 " " 519,—shops, warehouses and stores 146—
   1840 " " 585   barns 345.

AGRICULTURE.

A CONSIDERABLE portion of this town is essentially agricultural. There are many excellent farms, producing abundant crops of hay, corn, rye, oats, barley, potatoes, beans and other vegetables. Much swamp land has been reclaimed and rendered valuable, by draining and other processes. The events of the few past years, illustrating the superior safety of investments in real estate, have not been lost upon this community, as is manifested by an increased attention to this vitally important branch of industry.

The whole number of acres of land in this town, is between nine and ten thousand.

Of stock and products, the valuation of 1767 returned 164 horses, 143 oxen, 741 cows, 1099 sheep, 37 swine, 586¾ tons English hay, 367¼ tons meadow hay, 93 tons salt do., 10,728 bushels grain, 821 barrels cider.

The valuation of 1786 returned 164 horses, 164 oxen, 639 cows, 900 sheep, 260 swine, 261 barrels cider. It also returned 674¼ acres of tillage, 1170 acres English mowing, 696 do. fresh meadow, 102 do. salt marsh, 3746½ do. pasturage, 156 do. woodland, 355 do. unimproved, 1009 do. unimprovable.

The valuation of 1840 returned 217 horses, 440 oxen, 512 cows, 41 steers and heifers, 180 sheep, 900 swine, 754¾ acres tillage, 2014 do. English mowing, 302½ do. fresh meadow, 55 do. salt marsh, 3271 do. pasturage, 64 cow rights, 728 acres woodland, 814 do. unimproved, 5 do. owned by the town, to which may be added, 560 do. unimprovable, 227 do. used for roads, and 306 do. covered with water.

There were raised the same year, 20,560 bushels potatoes, 10,427 bushels corn, 2666 bushels barley, 1240 bushels oats, 821 bushels rye, and 100 bushels wheat. Of hay, 4050 tons were cut. The value of dairy products was $20,000, orchards $3000, market gardens $2800, poultry $1000. Five hundred cords of wood were cut and sold.

An increasing attention is paid to horticulture and the cultivation of fruits.

VALUATION, MANUFACTURES, COMMERCE, &C.

THE valuation of Beverly in 1811, was $822,908 66; in 1821, $853,079 33; in 1831, $973,029 06; in 1840, $1,306,509.

The manufactures amount annually in value to about $120,000, from a capital invested of about $40,000, and giving employment to nearly five hundred persons. They consist of boots, shoes, cabinet ware and chairs, Britannia* and tin ware, bricks, hair, mustard, soap and candles.

The foreign and domestic imports for 1787 were £13,667.7.1¾; for 1788, £13,663.7.8¾ Among the exports for 1787, were 1517 tierces fish, 1364 quintals do., 696 hhds. do., 32 boxes do., 68 bbls. pickled do., 112 bbls. mackerel, 700 bushels corn, 116 bbls. potatoes, 370 bushels do., 8000 bunches onions, 1000 lbs. cheese, 17 bbls. cranberries.

The vessels employed in 1786 were sixty in number, with 492 men. Of these, nineteen were in the West India trade. In 1787, sixty-nine vessels, with 408 men were employed, viz: 1 ship, 5 brigs, 5 sloops, 31 fishing schooners, and 17 trading do. In 1788, there were thirty-two fishing vessels, employing 271

* The manufacture of Britannia ware in this country was commenced in this town, in 1812, by Mr. Israel Trask.

men. The whole number of vessels at present employed in the fishing, coasting, freighting and foreign trade, is 78, investing a capital of $160,000, and employing between four and five hundred men.

From the commencement of the war in Europe, consequent upon the French revolution of 1789, until 1807, the cod-fishery was prosecuted with great success and large pecuniary profit. The embargo which began in December of the year 1807, and closed in the spring of 1809, entirely prostrated this business. It was resumed in a degree in the course of the year last named, and continued till the war of 1812, when it was again interrupted for the space of three whole seasons. After the peace of 1815, the business revived, and has been continued with a success depending on the discounts of the " Grand " and other banks of the Atlantic.

Much of the fish cured in this town was formerly shipped to Spain and other catholic countries of Europe. At present, they find their way mostly to South America, the West Indies, and the valley of the Mississippi. Throughout the State, fish has in times past been a standing dish for Saturdays. The custom of dining on fish on Saturday rather than on Friday, originated in a desire of our ancestors to avoid the remotest approximation to the observances of the catholics, who, during lent and other fasts, substituted this article of food for meat.

The wharves are twelve in number, which, with sixteen stores thereon, are valued at $30,000 to $40,000. The annual importation and sale of eastern wood amounts to about 3000 cords ; coal, 250 tons ; and lumber, 700,000 feet, forming an aggregate value of $27,500.

There are, in the first parish, ten groceries, six dry goods stores,—in two of which drugs and medicines are sold,—five tailors, two milliners, three hardware stores, three shoe stores, one public-house, three block-tin manufacturers, one lawyer's office, one watchmaker, one barber, three wheelwrights, three blacksmith's and two cooper's shops, three hair manufactories, two sailmakers, one ropewalk, one pump and block maker, one mustard factory, one hatter, one tinplate worker, two cabinet-makers, one steam saw-mill, one soap and candle factory, three painters and glaziers, one trunk and harness maker, one provision store, and several carpenter's shops. There is also a patent balance for weighing hay and other heavy loads, the property of the Fisher Charitable Society, and a post-office, at which several mails are daily received.

In the second parish are two stores, two blacksmith's and three wheelwright's shops, five slaughter-houses, three grist-mills, one saw-mill, one carding-machine, and three brick-yards. The tanning business was early commenced in this part of the town, but was many years since abandoned.

The facilities for communicating with Boston have been greatly increased by the opening of the Eastern rail-road. By an existing arrangement, the metropolis may be visited at six different hours daily, and four trains pass through town daily to and from the east. Beverly is favored with one of the safest and most commodious harbors in New England, with a depth of water sufficient to bring vessels of the largest class directly to the wharves. During the residence of the late William Gray, Esq., in Salem, many of his vessels, engaged in the indirect European trade, were unloaded here. The natural advantages of this town for the prosecution of commerce and manufactures, are not surpassed by any coast town in the Commonwealth.

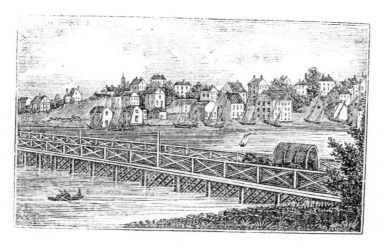

VIEW OF PART OF THE HARBOR AND TOWN OF BEVERLY.

(From a point near the south end of Essex Bridge.)

ECCLESIASTICAL HISTORY.

THE FIRST PARISH.

FROM the settlement of Beverly until 1649, the inhabitants worshipped with the first church in Salem. As population increased, the inconvenience of crossing the river in boats suggested the expediency of establishing a separate church. A request to that effect was made to the Salem church—but for various reasons the plan did not meet with favorable attention. On the 22d of the seventh month (September,) 1650, the request was renewed, and on the second day of the month following, an answer was returned authorizing the brethren on "Bass-river-side" to procure the service of an able and approved teacher— still retaining their connexion with the church in Salem. With this liberty they successively employed Messrs. Josiah and Jeremiah Hubbard* and Mr. John Hale.

---

* In the town records this name is uniformly written *Hubbard*. The catalogue of Harvard College has it *Hobart*. A note in Mass. Hist. Coll. says it should be so written. Joshua and Jeremiah Hobart were sons of Rev. Peter Hobart, of Hingham. Joshua settled in the ministry at Southhold, L. I. Jeremiah was minister of Topsfield, and afterwards of Haddam, Conn. He was grandfather to Rev. David Brainard, the distinguished missionary.

In 1656, the first meeting-house was erected near the north-west corner of the old burial-ground. Of this building there is no account other than that, in addition to religious services it was used for the transaction of public business and for a school-room. A church organization was still wanting to give stability to the pastoral relation, and in the winter of 1666, the following petition was presented to the church in Salem:

"We, whose names are underwritten, the brethren and sisters on Bass-river-side, do present our desires to the rest of the church in Salem, that with their consent, we and our children may be a church of ourselves, which we also present unto Mr. Hale, desiring him to join with us and to be our pastor, with the approbation of the rest of the church." Signed by Roger Conant and forty-eight church members, to which were added the names of twenty-four others not in full communion, but desiring to be dismissed with their parents. This petition was received with the deliberation its importance demanded, "and the last of the 12th month, by the consent of the brethren both on that side of the river and here at the town, was publicly observed as a day of solemn fasting and prayer, to seek unto God for his direction and presence in such a weighty matter."* On the 4th of July, 1667, the subject of the petition was again considered; "when there was a unanimous consent of the brethren present unto their desire, only it was left to the sacrament day after [July 21st] when in the fullest church assembly the consent of the rest of the church was signified by their vote,—

* Salem Church Records.

18

lifting up their hands,—and so they have their liberty to be a church of themselves, only they continue members until their being a church." This permission closes with the benediction : "The Lord grant his gracious presence with them."

With this unanimous consent, the brethren, on the 28th August following, renewed their call to Mr. Hale to become their pastor, to which he made the following reply :

"When I look at the weight of the work which you call me unto, of which Paul cried out, Who is sufficient unto these things ? I then looking upon my manifold infirmities and indisposition of spirit, then unto so many discouragements; but when I duly consider the Lord's sovereignty over me, and all-sufficiency for my support, I desire, when I see his work and call, to say with Isaiah, 'Here I am, send me.' And in particular when I observe the remarkable providences of God in bringing me hither and paving out our way hitherto, and the room the Lord hath made for me in your hearts, (which I acknowledge with thankfulness to God and yourselves,) I also look at the call of God in the present call, as a call to me ; being the more confirmed herein by the concurrence of our apprehensions which hath appeared in those things we had occasion to confer about, concerning our entering into and proceeding with church affairs, which I hope the Lord will enable me to practise accordingly ; wherefore, while you walk according to God's order of the gospel and in the steadfastness of the faith of Christ, and I see that with a good conscience and freedom of spirit, I can carry on my work, and discharge my duty to God and man, and these that are under my care, according to the respective relation I may bear unto them, so long as the Lord is calling me to labor in this part of his vineyard, I desire to give up myself to the Lord and his service in the work of the ministry in this place; requesting you to strive together with me in your prayers for me, that it may redound to his glory, the edifying of every soul that shall dwell amongst us, and for our joyful account in the day of Christ's appearance.

By me. JOHN HALE."

The 20th September was set apart for the interesting and impressive service of ordination, an event, the infrequency of which, at that early period, must have rendered it peculiarly attractive. Invitations were sent to the churches of Salem, Ipswich and Wenham, to assist, by their pastors and messengers, on the occasion, which were cordially accepted. The Salem church, in the free spirit that granted unanimous leave for separate organization, was largely represented. "In regard," the records say, " to our nearness, and that they are a church issuing out of ourselves, it was thought meet for as many to be present as could, so when the day came, divers of the brethren were present." Previously to the solemnities of ordination, the church was organized. Mr. Hale "propounded and read a confession of faith and covenant which they had often considered amongst themselves, and did then (all that had been in full communion in the church of Salem,) express their consent unto that confession and covenant, and so were owned as a particular and distinct church of themselves, by the messengers of the churches pres-

ent." The names of those who were formed into a
church on this occasion, are as follows : John Hale,
Richard Dodge, sen. William Woodberry, sen. Richard Brackenbury, John Stone, sen. John Dodge, sen.
Roger Conant, William Dodge, sen. Humphrey
Woodberry, sen. Hugh Woodberry, Nicholas Patch,
John Hill, Thomas Lothrop, Samuel Corning, Robert Morgan, John Black, sen. Lot Conant, Ralph Ellingwood, William Dixey, Henry Herrick, sen. Peter
Woolfe, Josiah Rootes, sen. Exercise Conant, Edward Bishop, Elizabeth Dodge, Mary Lovett, Elizabeth Haskell, Mary Woodberry, Sarah Leach, Free-
grace Black, Elizabeth Corning, Elizabeth Woodberry, Ellen Brackenbury, Hannah Woodberry,
Elizabeth Patch, Hannah Sallows, Bethiah Lothrop,
Anna Dixey, Anna Woodberry, sen. Elizabeth Woodberry, Martha Woolfe, Hannah Baker, Mary Herrick, Bridget Luff, Mary Dodge, sen. Anna Woodberry, jr. Ede Herrick, Mary Dodge, jr. Abigail Hill,
Lydia Herrick.

The services of induction to the sacred office of
the ministry then proceeded, " by the laying on of
hands of the Rev. Mr. John Higginson, of the church
of Salem, of Mr. Thomas Cobbett, pastor at Ipswich,
and of Mr. Antipas Newman, of Wenham ;" and
thus Mr. Hale received fellowship, and was publicly
recognized as pastor of " the church of Christ at
Bass river, in Salem."

On the 22d September, Mrs. Rebeckah Hale was
received to the church, on letters of dismission from
the church at Salisbury ; and on the 29th of the same
month, the sacrament of the Lord's supper was for
the first time administered, on which occasion Mr.
Hale explained the requisitions for admission to the

ordinance. It was, doubtless, a season of uncommon delight to all who participated in this beautiful and affecting service. After a delay of several years, mingled with fear and hope, they had obtained the desire of their hearts. They were now peacefully established as an independent church "in the congregational way," relieved from the inconveniences attending their earlier worship, and with a devoted and beloved pastor were happy in sustaining an institution recognized as "the pillar and ground of truth," and whose existence is vitally connected with the moral condition of the world. Oct. 23, the same year, Humphrey Woodberry and Sarah, his wife, John Clark, jr. Humphrey Woodberry, jr. Remember Stone and Sarah Conant, were received to full communion, being the first persons admitted on their "profession of faith and repentance." The first child baptized, after the formation of the church, was Abigail, daughter of John and Hannah Sallows, Oct. 13, 1667. The next person receiving the rite, Dec. 1 following, was Richard Patch, a young man about nineteen years of age, who, "pleading a covenant interest in the covenant engagement of his mother, and making, also, confession of his own faith and repentance, having the testimony of a blameless life," was at the same time received into the church.

At the time of Mr. Hale's call to the pastoral care of the church, provision was made by the society for his support. They agreed to pay him £70 per annum, and to furnish thirty cords of fire-wood, according to an existing custom. They further agreed to give him the use of a house they had built, two acres of land to be fenced in by them, as much

18*

meadow as bare "about four loads of hay," and the
"benefit of pasturing," during the time he remained
with them in the ministry. "Yet because," said
they, "it is *his* duty to provide for wife and children
that he may leave behind him, and *our* duty to have
a care of him in that respect, we do therefore promise and engage, that in case he die in the ministry
with us, that either the house and two-acre home-lot
shall be his, or that which is equivalent—to be paid,
(according to his last will and testament) within the
compass of one year after his decease."   The first
persons chosen to make rates for Mr. Hale's mainte-
nance, in 1665, were Capt. Lothrop, Mr. Thorndike,
Roger Conant, Samuel Corning and Joseph Rootes.
At a subsequent meeting, measures were adopted "to
build a house for Mr. Hale's cattle," eighteen feet
long, ten feet wide and seven or eight feet stud.   It
was also agreed to pay "Farmer Dodge" for his
ground, bought for the ministry, "either two cows
or ten pounds," and to pay Humphrey Woodberry
twenty shillings an acre for his ground, he having
"free liberty to pass through with a cart when he
hath occasion." Various measures were adopted, from
1667 to 1684, for the supply of Mr. Hale's wood, at
which latter date, his salary was fixed at £64 in
money, instead of £70, payable in produce at a regulated price, called *rate pay*, and which was not more
valuable than the former sum.   About the time of
his marriage, £10 were added to his salary, and from
thence to his decease he continued to receive £74 per
annum.

In 1674, the church advised in a difficulty originated in the church in Salem, by a movement to
form a church at Lynn, which was amicably ad-

justed, and in February, 1675, Mr. Hale assisted at the ordination of Mr. Joseph Gerrish, in Wenham.

Mr. Hale was born at Charlestown, June 3, 1636, and was the son of Robert and Rebeckah Hale. His father emigrated from England, and became a member of the church in Charlestown between July and October, 1632, of which he was subsequently chosen deacon. He was made a freeman in 1634, was member of an artillery company in 1644, and in 1659 held the office of ensign. Of the mother of John Hale but little is known, but when we consider the characters of those who descended from her for three successive generations, without other means of judging, we are led to very favorable inferences.

Where Mr. John Hale pursued his preparatory studies is not known, but he graduated at Harvard College in 1657, at the age of twenty-one, and in 1664, three years before his ordination, came to Beverly as a religious teacher. Previously to his settlement in the ministry, he was married to Rebeckah Byles, daughter of Henry Byles of Sarum, England, who emigrated to this country and settled in Salisbury, Mass. as early as 1640.* She was the mother of two children—Rebeckah, who was born April 28, 1666, and died May 7, 1681, aged 15 years, and Robert, born Nov. 3, 1668. Mrs. Hale died April

---

* The mother of Rebeckah Byles, previous to her marriage with Henry Byles, was the widow of John Hall. After the death of Mr. Byles, she married Rev. William Worcester of Salisbury, Mass. She married for her fourth husband, Deputy Governor Samuel Symonds of Ipswich, and died July 21st, 1695, aged 78. She distributed £100 to persons who lost by the great fire in Boston, and who suffered in the Indian wars about 1682.

13, 1683, aged 45 years.   Mr. Hale was again married March 3, 1684, to Mrs. Sarah Noyes, of Newbury, from the church in which place her relation was removed to the church in Beverly, the following October.   By this marriage there were four children, viz. James, born Oct. 14, 1685 ; Samuel, born Aug. 13, 1687 ; Joanna, born June 15, 1689, and John, born Dec. 24, 1692.

James graduated at Harvard College in 1703, and was ordained to the ministry at Ashford, Conn. Nov. 26, 1718, where he died in Oct. 1742, at the age of 57.   Samuel settled in Newbury, where he married Sophia Moody, May 2, 1714.   He had three sons, Richard, John and Samuel, the former of whom settled in Coventry, Conn. and was the father of Nathan Hale, who was inhumanly executed by the British in the revolutionary war.   John, the third son of Rev. Mr. Hale by the second marriage, settled at Gloucester.   His mother died May 20, 1695, aged forty-one.

Mr. Hale was a third time married in 1698, to Mrs. Elizabeth Clark of Newbury, who was received into the church in Beverly, by dismission and recommendation from the church in Newbury, Sept. 17, 1699.   He did not, however, continue long to enjoy her society.

In 1690, when the expedition against Canada had been determined on, the General Court invited Mr. Hale to join it as chaplain.   This invitation was submitted to his people, and though doubtless gratified with such evidence of the public estimate of their pastor, they withheld their assent, and appointed Samuel Corning, John Hill, Peter Woodberry, Thomas West, Nehemiah Grover and Andrew

Elliot, " as a committee in behalf of the church and town of Beverly," to assign their reasons " to the honored court and council." These were: first, that by their pastor's absence they would " be as sheep without a shepherd." Second, they did not think his bodily strength adequate to such an expedition. Third, that being " thin of men, and men of conduct " at that time, owing to the number engaged in " the present essay," and " liable to suffer by enemies," they desired the presence of their pastor " as a comforter and encourager in such a case." These objections do not appear to have had much weight with the Court, as the next day after their presentation, it was " ordered, that the Rev. John Hale, Mr. John Wise, Mr. Grindal Rawson, and Mr. John Emerson, ministers of God's Word, be desired to accompany the General and forces, in the expedition against Canada, to carry on the worship of God in that expedition."*

What induced Mr. Hale to accept this invitation, contrary to the strongly expressed wish of his flock, is unknown. It is not improbable, that as a large number of his people were engaged in this enterprize, he was anxious to accompany them that he might watch over their morals. In 1734 the General Court, in consideration of the time and service rendered, granted his heirs three hundred acres of land.

In 1692 the witchcraft delusion broke out. It commenced in Salem Village, in the family of Rev. Mr. Parris, whose child a physician declared to be under an evil hand—and spread with rapidity to several of

* Provincial Records.

the adjacent towns. During this period the most
extravagant fanaticism prevailed. Individuals free
from any moral stain were accused on the most friv-
olous pretences. Persons under infatuation, or to
gain notoriety, or, as was not unfrequently the case,
to gratify revenge, suddenly cried out as in pain,
and declared themselves tormented by unseen agents
in distant places. Children eight years of age were
encouraged to testify against their parents, and wives
gave evidence against their husbands. If a poor,
decrepid old woman could not weep when accused,
through alarm or indignation, the fact was assumed
as evidence of guilt. Rev. George Burroughs, a
graduate of Harvard College, and for some time a
minister in Salem Village, having exhibited feats of
unusual strength, was accused of being aided by the
prince of darkness, and was condemned and executed. He died with christian composure; and while
on the ladder made a speech, and offered a prayer
with such fervor as to affect many to tears. But
this was charged upon him, by the procurers of his
death, as proof of his intimacy with the devil; and
when cut down, his body was thrust into a hole with
two others, and but partially covered. Giles Cory,
at the age of eighty, was accused, and refusing to
plead to the indictment, was condemned and crushed
to death. Such was the general feeling, on the side
of prosecutions, that accusation was almost the sure
precursor of condemnation. Some of the judges, to
increase their popularity, resorted to arts to entrap
their unwary victims. And whenever the magistrates were inclined to mercy, or acquitted one whom
the popular voice had consigned to the scaffold, an
indignant clamor burst forth.

Among the persons in this town, accused and condemned, though not executed, were Dorcas Hoar,
Sarah Morey, Susanna Rootes, and Job Tuckey.
Sarah Morey was the daughter of Peter and Mary
Morey. She was accused in May, 1692, and thrown
into prison, where she remained until January following, supported by her parents. Dorcas Hoar lay
in prison eleven months, the charges of which were
defrayed by herself. Tuckey was a laborer, and
probably was fond of exciting wonder by marvellous
speeches. On the 4th June depositions were filed
against him at Salem, by John Landers, Samuel and
Daniel Bacon, John Stacy, and John Pudney, Jr.
The charges were—first, that Tuckey declared that
he could " as freely discourse with the devil" as
with him, the said Landers; second, that the accused
" said he would take Mr. Burroughs' part;" third,
that the accused had " afflicted" Mary Warren, Mary Walcot, and others. On the 7th June he was
examined before Maj. Gedney, Mr. Hathorne, and
Mr. Corwin, when two more accusers appeared, viz:
Elizabeth Booth and Susanna Shelden. They confirmed the testimony of Stacy and Pudney, concerning Tuckey's afflicting Mary Warren. They further
charged him with bewitching Betsey Hews, and with
causing the death of Andrew Woodberry; and also
testified, that on a certain occasion they saw the
apparitions of three men, three women and two children, " who all cried out for vengeance against
Tuckey." *

To this delusion, Mr. Hale, in common with the
clergy and the principal public men of the day, ap-

---

* Witchcraft papers, State archives.

pears to have committed himself, so far at least as to attend the examinations and trials of accused persons, and participate in the religious services of those occasions. It is possible, that possessing, as Higginson observes, a mind of "singular prudence and sagacity, in searching into the narrows of things," he might have been present at these assemblies from a desire to investigate the merits of the various accusations, rather than with an intention to endorse the prevailing opinions.

In October, 1692, a person in Wenham accused Mrs. Hale of witchcraft. This was giving the subject an aspect he had not anticipated. But it effectually broke the spell. He knew her worth too well to believe for a moment that she could be in league with the "powers of darkness." He was at once satisfied of her innocence ; and he could not but perceive that the reasons which, on maturer reflection, weighed with him in her case, lost none of their force when applied to others. And when convinced of the error into which he had fallen, he resolved, with an independence highly honorable to his character, to discard the prejudices of early education, and in the face of popular opinion, exert his powers to extinguish a fanaticism that had already consigned twenty human beings to the scaffold.

" The whole community was convinced that the accusers, in crying out upon Mrs. Hale, had perjured themselves ; and from that moment their power was destroyed ; the awful delusion ceased ; the curtain fell, and a close was put to one of the most tremendous tragedies in the history of real life. The wildest storm, perhaps, that ever raged in the moral world, instantly became a calm ; the tide that had threatened to overwhelm every thing in its fury, sunk back in a moment to its peaceful bed." *

In 1697, Mr. Hale wrote a work entitled "A modest inquiry into the nature of witchcraft, and how persons guilty of that crime may be convicted; and the means used for their discovery discussed, both negatively and affirmatively, according to scripture and experience." † In his preface he says, in a commendable spirit of acknowledgment, "I have had a deep sense of the sad consequences of mistakes in matters capital, and their impossibility of recovering when completed; and what grief of heart it brings to a tender conscience, to have been unwittingly encouraging of the sufferings of the innocent. And I hope a zeal to prevent, for the future, such sufferings, is pardonable, although there should be much weakness, and some errors, in the pursuit thereof. I have special reasons moving me to bear my testimony about these matters, *before I go hence and be no more;* the which I have here done, and I hope with some assistance of his spirit, to whom I commit myself and this my labor, even that God *whose I am and whom I serve,* desiring his mercy in Jesus Christ to pardon all the errors of his people in the day of darkness."

* Upham's Lectures on Witchcraft, p. 23.

† Referring to this work, Cotton Mather makes the following remarks : "I will assure the reader that he hath now to do with a writer who would not for a world be guilty of overdoing the truth in an history of this importance." "None can suspect a gentleman so full of dissatisfaction at the proceedings then used against supposed witchcrafts, as now that reverend person is, to be a superstitious writer on that subject." *Magnalia, vol. ii. pp.* 408, 537.

Mr. Hale discusses the subject of witchcraft through 179 pages 18mo., and in his closing chapter, after saying, " We have cause to be humbled for the mistakes and errors which have been in these colonies, in their proceedings against persons for this crime, above forty years ago and downwards," he adds, " but I would come yet nearer to our own times, and bewail the errors and mistakes that have been in the year 1692; in the apprehending too many we may believe were innocent, and executing of some, I fear, not to have been condemned; by following such traditions of our fathers, maxim of the common law, and precedents and principles, which now we may see, weighed in the balance of the sanctuary, are found too light. . . . . In the prosecution of witchcraft, we sought not the Lord after the due order; but have proceeded after the methods used in former times and other places, until the Lord in this tremendous way made a breach upon us.   And hereby we are made sensible, that the methods formerly made use of are not sufficient to prove the guilt of such a crime."   Mr. Hale palliates the conduct of those who acted conspicuously in the transactions that gave rise to his volume.   "I am," he says, " abundantly satisfied, that those who were most concerned to act and judge in those matters, did not willingly depart from the rules of righteousness.   But such was the darkness of that day, the tortures and lamentations of the afflicted, and the power of former precedents, that we walked in the clouds, and could not see our way."   This is a decision at which a charitable judgment, after the lapse of a century and a half, would naturally arrive. That all who participated in the witchcraft delusion, or that even the most intelligent of them, were actuated by bad motives, is not to be supposed. Something is to be allowed for the habits of thought and the tendencies to excessive superstition then prevalent; and when we say "learned men are not always wise," and that good men sometimes err, we but repeat the utterings of all past experience. And while the excesses of error and fanaticism in that awful drama are deplored, we should not lose sight of the redeeming traits in the character of the actors, nor should the palliating circumstances which charity suggests, be disallowed.

To the little work of Mr. Hale's, from which the preceding extracts have been taken, is prefixed "an epistle to the reader," by Rev. John Higginson, of Salem, then at the advanced age of 82, recommending it as a work which, from the "pious and modest manner" of the author, would "be generally acceptable to all the lovers of truth and peace." The only other production of Mr. Hale's pen, known to have been published, is an election sermon, preached in 1684, before the State authorities. The text was, Haggai, ii. 4.

Mr. Hale appears to have possessed an enlarged mind and a generous public spirit. In 1676, he directed the selectmen to appropriate £6 of his salary—nearly a twelfth part of the whole—to public uses, such as fortifications, ammunition, and country rates on account of the war. In 1683, he gave £5 towards erecting a house of worship; and in 1690, he loaned the town £3 of the £48 borrowed of nineteen different persons, to purchase "great guns" and ammunition, and to pay for building a fort. Nothing appears to have occurred to affect materially the prosperity of the church, during his protracted ministry of forty-seven years; and that his worth was appreciated by his parishioners, the interest they manifested for his temporal comfort is conclusive evidence. He died May 15, 1700, aged 64. His grave-stone bears the following inscription. "Here lies the body of the Reverend Mr. John Hale, a pious and faithful minister of the gospel, and pastor of the first church of Christ in this town of Beverly, who rested from his labors on the 15th day of May, anno domini, 1700, in the 64th year of his age."

On the 24th Feb. 1668, five months subsequent to Mr. Hale's settlement, the church made choice of Humphrey Woodberry to fill the office of deacon, from which time to the present, nineteen persons have served in that capacity. As early as 1665, Henry Bailey filled the office of sexton, and his compensation was fixed at one peck of corn per annum from each householder. Of his fidelity, the best evidence is found in the fact, that when succeeded twenty years afterwards, 1680, by William Hoar, it was stipulated, that he should "do in all respects as Goodman Bailey had done,"—the highest panegyrick that could have been pronounced on Mr. Bailey's character. At this time was commenced the practice of ringing the bell at 9 o'clock, for which additional duty Goodman Hoar found compensation in additional pecks of corn, derived from an increased number of families. The office of sexton, always indispensable, was peculiarly important at this period. Besides keeping the key of the meeting-house, ringing the bell, &c., it was made his particular duty to keep, and on the sabbath, *turn the glass.* The hour-glass, which the more convenient clock has displaced, was

turned by him at the naming of the text in full view
of the minister. If he completed his discourse "before the sands had all run out, he was admonished
that he had not complied with the reasonable expectations of his hearers, whether sleeping or waking,—
both classes having tacitly contracted for an hour's
enjoyment in their own peculiar way. If his zeal
inclined him to go beyond the standard measure, the
turning of the glass by the faithful sexton reminded
him that he was asking more of the patience of his
hearers than they had tacitly agreed to give." But
instances were not rare, in those days, when long
sermons were less alarming than in this age of despatch; in which, as has been facetiously remarked,
both preachers and hearers were well contented to
take the second, and even the third glass together.
Sexton Hoar was succeeded by Josiah Woodberry,
1748, who served with fidelity forty-one years, and
died in Dec. 1789. Wells Standley was appointed
in 1790, and continued in office about seven years,
when he died suddenly, 1797. Joshua Wallis, who
succeeded him, fell down while ringing the bell for
nine o'clock, and died immediately, of apoplexy, a
month or two after his appointment. The present
incumbent, Thomas Barrett, was appointed to office
in June, 1797, forty-five years ago, and will long be
remembered for the faithful traits which marked the
character of Goodman Bailey. In March, 1842,
Ezra Woodberry was associated with him as colleague.

After the death of Mr. Hale, some difficulty appears to have arisen in the church, the nature of
which is not defined, but which was amicably adjusted through the intervention of Rev. Nicholas

19*

Noyes and Rev. Joseph Gerrish.   Immediately, however, on the decease of Mr. Hale, measures were
taken for " procuring a suitable and meet person to
labor in the ministry."   An invitation to settle, as
pastor, was given to Mr. Thomas Blowers, of Cambridge, which being accepted, he was ordained
Oct. 29th, 1701.   The sermon was preached by Mr.
Clarke, of Salem Village (now Danvers); Mr. Noyes,
of Salem, gave the charge, and Mr. Cheever, of Marblehead, gave the right hand of fellowship.

The salary of Mr. Blowers was £80, and £100
settlement, and besides the ordinary services of the
sabbath, he was required to preach a monthly lecture and "catechise" the children.   Owing to the
depreciation of bills of credit, additions were made
to his salary, to save him from loss, and in 1728, it
was fixed permanently at £140.   In addition to this,
he had the use of rights granted him in Bunker's
meadow, in Topsfield, and in Snake Hill pasture.

There are but few incidents recorded, to diversify
the ministerial life of Mr. Blowers.   At the time of
his settlement, a public relation of religious experience was required by the church; but at a church-
meeting, Jan. 11, 1727–8, it was unanimously voted
to dispense with this practice, and to receive from the
pastor some statement concerning the individuals
propounded, before asking a vote for their admission.
It does not appear that the relation of experiences in
public was required during Mr. Hale's ministry, and
it is conjectured that the agitation of this subject
after his death was the occasion of the difficulty before referred to, which delayed Mr. Blowers' settlement some time after his election by the parish.

Aug. 21, 1705, Mr. Blowers attended a meeting of

ministers at Salem, to consider the following question : " What further steps are to be taken, that the councils may have due constitution and efficacy in supporting, preserving and well ordering the interests of the church in the country." The meeting took up the question by recommendation of the convention in Boston the May preceding, and deputed Messrs. Gerrish and Cheever to present their result to the general convention, to meet in Boston on the 13th September following. The proposals of a convention of ministers at Boston, for the consociation of the congregational churches, in 1705, is recorded at length, by Mr. Blowers, in the church record, with the names of the signers, though nothing appears to show that he favored the project. These proposals are the more interesting from the movement of the Massachusetts General Association, in 1814, to revive them, as the basis of another attempt to consociate the churches, and which, like that of 1705, met with so much opposition as to induce the projectors to abandon it.

In 1707, objections being made to the appointment of Mr. Leverett to the presidency of Harvard College on the ground of his being a layman, Mr. Blowers, with thirty-eight other clergymen, who were not influenced by professional partiality, united in an address to Gov. Dudley, advocating the appointment.*

Sept. 27, 1716, Mr. Blowers and Mr. Chipman, minister of the second parish, united with others in forming an association of clergymen in Salem, which has continued to this day.

Mr. Blowers was the son of Pyam and Elizabeth

* Quincy's Hist. Harv. Col. vol. i. p. 505.

Blowers, his mother being sister of the Hon. Andrew Belcher. He was born at Cambridge, Aug. 1, 1677, and graduated at Harvard College 1695. The year subsequent to his settlement in the ministry, he was married to Emma Woodberry, of Beverly. His children were Pyam, Emma, Thomas, John, Elizabeth and Andrew. One of his grandchildren, Hon. Sampson Salter Blowers, of Halifax, N. S. died in October, 1842, at the advanced age of one hundred years,—having, for a considerable period, been the senior surviving graduate of Harvard University.

The term of Mr. Blowers' ministry was nearly twenty-eight years, and was closed by death, June 17, 1729, in the fifty-second year of his age, after an illness of a few days. A notice of his decease, written on the day of his interment, says: " He had frequently, of late, expressed an expectation of dying very speedily, though his state of health seemed much the same as for some time before, and without any extraordinary symptoms upon him. It is worthy of remark that, on the last Sabbath he was abroad (June 8), one of his sermons was on those words of Neh. x. 39, ' We will not forsake the house of our God,' and the other on Psalms x. 14, ' The poor committeth himself unto thee : thou art the helper of the fatherless.' On Friday following, he appeared more than commonly intent on his preparations for the sabbath, studying upon those words, Acts xi. 33, ' And exhorted them all, that with purpose of heart they would cleave unto the Lord ;' but still under an apprehension that he should never preach the discourse. ' The thought,' (he said) ' was strangely impressed upon him at every head he came to, that he should not live to preach it. And, alas !

it happened accordingly, for on the next morning he
fell sick of the sickness whereof he died ; and though,
after the first sudden shock of his distemper, which
laid him in a dying posture, he had some revival for
about two hours, yet he was, for the most part, in a
manner wholly speechless, and scarce able, but by
signs, to explain his inward peace and good hope
through grace. He has left behind him a good name,
better than precious ointment and preferable to great
riches ; the character of a very valuable man, a good
scholar and excellent minister. He was a distinguished example of warm devotion, of extensive
goodness, meekness and sweetness of temper; of
great stability in his principles and steadiness in his
conduct ; a very faithful friend and obliging neigh-
bor ; a most tender and kind husband and father ; a
vigilant, prudent pastor and close, pathetic preacher ;
had in great veneration among the associated pastors
in the vicinity ; highly esteemed by all his acquaintance, and universally beloved by his flock, who much
lament their great loss."

The parish appropriated £50 to defray funeral
charges and erect a monument over his remains. In
1818, a solid block of hammered granite was placed
over his grave, covered with a slab of freestone
bearing the following inscription : "In memory of
Rev. Thomas Blowers, obt. June 17th, 1729, in the
28th year of his ministry." On removing the earth,
to lay the foundation of this block, the bones were
found perfect, but the coffin and grave-clothes were
entirely decayed and mingled with the surrounding
earth.

The only publication from the pen of Mr. Blowers,
of which information has been obtained, was a ser-

mon on the death of Rev. Joseph Green, of Salem
Village, 1715. He left, as a legacy to the church, a
silver cup inscribed with his name, which is the oldest piece of plate, save one, now belonging to it. His
dwelling-house was destroyed by fire in 1782.

Mr. Blowers was succeeded by Mr. Joseph Champney, who received and accepted a call within six
months of his predecessor's decease. The first Thursday in December, 1729, was set apart as a season of
humiliation and prayer for the divine blessing on the
proceedings, and John Balch, Robert Woodberry,
Dea. William Dodge, Dea. Benjamin Balch, John
Thorndike, Israel Wood and Henry Herrick, were
appointed a committee to invite the churches to assist
at the ordination of Mr. Champney. Twenty pounds
were also voted to defray the expense of the ordination, and a committee was chosen to make provision
for the clergy and others who were to assist on the
occasion. December 10th, the ordination took place.
Mr. Fisk offered the introductory prayer. Mr. Appleton preached the sermon. Mr. Barnard gave the
charge, and Mr. Chipman the right hand of fellowship.

Mr. Champney's salary was fixed at £140 in province bills of credit—the sum to rise or fall as the
bills might fluctuate from time to time. A free contribution was also to be kept up for him during his
continuance in the work of the ministry. His settlement was £200 in province bills of credit, one half
to be paid in one year and the remainder in two
years. As in the case of Mr. Blowers, it became
a part of his duty to preach a monthly lecture and
catechise the children.

The difficulties which existed in the first church

in Salem for several years after the settlement of Mr. Champney, excited considerable interest in the church under his pastoral care. These difficulties began in the ministry of Mr. Fisk, between him and a respectable minority of his church and congregation. Mr. Fisk maintained the independency of each church, and denied the right of other churches to interfere by council or otherwise, unless solicited by the church to be counselled or advised. In this position he was sustained by a majority of his people, and set at defiance council after council gathered from the whole colony, and holding their imposing meetings on the spot. The excitement in Salem led to debates and discussions here; and taking the records for evidence, no subject, from the organization of the church, ever engaged more attention. For reasons connected with this controversy, probably, the church in 1736 declined assisting at the ordination of John Sparhawk.

These discussions in Mr. Champney's church led to the consideration of the principles of its own ecclesiastical government, and a meeting was called " to look into the church covenant and the ancient foundation of the church." At this meeting, March 31, 1734–5, after considerable debate, the church voted, by a very small majority, to acknowledge the platform as the rule of government and discipline. At an adjourned meeting the 14th April following, that vote was unanimously reconsidered, and a committee chosen " to peruse and examine the platform, and to report such explanations of any part of it as they might think proper." This committee consisted of Robert Hale, chairman, and ten others, and on the 9th of June, 1735, they reported that the church should accept the platform, reserving the lib-

erty of receiving certain articles in *their own sense,*
which report was accepted.   From these proceedings,
it appears that the Cambridge platform, so often
referred to by Congregational churches as an authority in matters of ecclesiastical government, was not
in any sense received by the first church in this town,
until about sixty-eight years after its formation, and
then only with modifications and exceptions—a fact
of considerable importance in the history of the
churches in Massachusetts.

In 1736, unsuccessful attempts were made to choose
ruling elders according to the provisions of the platform, and the subject was finally abandoned.   In
1737, the church by its pastor and messengers, assisted at the ordination of Mr. James Diman over the
second church and parish in Salem; and again in
1745, assisted in a council held in Salem, to consider
some new difficulty in the first church.   In 1740, and
again in 1770, the celebrated George Whitefield
passed through the country, and excited a great
deal of unpleasant feeling (for which he afterward
expressed his regret) by the rudeness with which he
assailed the clergy.   The usefulness of his itinerant
labors were variously estimated, and Mr. Champney
is understood to have concurred with those who were
opposed to the course pursued by him.   Between
1735 and 1749, the bills of credit in which Mr.
Champney's salary was paid, became less valuable,
and various sums were added, besides several special
grants.   In 1749, the last year of paper-money, the
parish voted him £660 old tenor; and in 1750, they
voted him £90 lawful money, which sum he received annually, with few exceptions, to the time of
his death.

In 1772, Mr. Joseph Willard received and accepted a call to settle as colleague with Mr. Champney. £200 settlement was voted him, and a salary of £100, to be increased to £120 after Mr. Champney's decease. The ordination took place Nov. 25th. The churches invited, were the first and second churches in Cambridge, the three churches in Boston, of which Dr. Elliot, Dr. Cooper, and Mr. Howard were pastors, the second church in Scarborough, the church in Stafford, the first and second churches in Salem, the second church in Danvers, the churches in Wenham and Manchester, and the second church in Beverly. The Rev. Samuel Cook of Cambridge, offered the introductory prayer; Rev. Andrew Elliot of Boston, preached the sermon from 2 Tim. iv. 2, "Preach the word;" Rev. Nathaniel Appleton of Cambridge, offered the prayer of ordination, and gave the charge; Rev. James Diman prayed after the charge, and Rev. Nathan Holt of Danvers, gave the right hand of fellowship.

Mr. Champney died Feb. 23, 1773, less than three months after the settlement of Mr. Willard, in the 69th year of his age, and the forty-fourth of his ministry. The parish voted to defray the expenses of his funeral, to erect a monument over his grave, and to pay his widow the whole of his salary for the current year. In 1818, the monument over his grave was repaired by direction of the first parish. Mr. Champney was born in Cambridge. He was early sent to Harvard College, where he was classmate of Col. Robert Hale. He took his degree in 1721 and 1724, and devoted himself to the study of divinity. He served the people of his charge without interruption till the last year of his life, when

20

his labors were suspended by a general decay. An affectionate regard for the people, which manifested itself both in their prosperity and adversity; a readiness to serve them upon all occasions; a peaceable temper and behavior, and a steady, prudent conduct, distinguished his ministry, and gained him the love and esteem of all. His life appeared to be that of a sincere Christian, and its close was serene. He was a kind and affectionate husband, and a tender and faithful father. He was of medium stature, light complexion, of social habits, and, as was customary with clergymen of his time, wore a wig and cocked hat.

Mr. Champney was married Oct. 1, 1730, to Elizabeth, daughter of his predecessor, Mr. Blowers. She survived the birth of her son Joseph but a short time, and died Jan. 13, 1731, aged 19 years 3 months. His second wife was Thankful Pickens of Lynn, to whom he was married in 1733. She survived him, and died July 31, 1777, aged 71. The children by this marriage were—Richard, who died young, Richard, Israel, Sarah, Elizabeth and Thomas. Elizabeth is well remembered as the faithful and exemplary schoolmistress. She was for many years without a rival, the best female teacher in the town, and three successive generations partook of her care. Under her guidance, many of the ladies who now move in the important spheres of wives and mothers, in this town and elsewhere, commenced their education. She died unmarried, April 23, 1806, aged about 66.

The first person admitted to the church by Mr. Champney was William Ellingwood, Aug. 9, 1730. The first baptism was Anna, daughter of Robert and Precilla Woodberry, Dec. 14, 1729.

The call of Mr. Willard was not entirely unanimous, and after his settlement the minority petitioned to be set off as a distinct parish, but the reasons appearing insufficient, the request was not granted. At this time a strong feeling existed concerning what is known as the Arminian controversy. Mr. Willard was supposed to lean to the Arminian view, and with many, supposition was equivalent to proof. One of his parishioners, not minutely versed in polemics or skilled in technical theology, alarmed at his apprehended unsoundness of opinions, came to him one day, and among other things informed him that he was reported to be a musk-melon, meaning probably Arminian! Mr. Willard facetiously replied, that the report could not be true, for if it were, he should have been eaten up a long time before. Some serious explanations followed, and the conversation resulted in making a firm friend of one who was on the point of being settled in opposition.

Mr. Willard, like his predecessors, experienced the evils of a fluctuating currency. From £420 to £3000, were at various times voted in payment of his salary of £120, and yet his losses by depreciation were not fully repaired. In 1779, he memorialized the parish on the subject, showing that the extra grants had not equalled the depreciation, and in consequence he had been obliged to expend a part of his settlement for his support. On the 7th Aug. 1780, he presented a statement to the parish meeting, which, as it affords a practical view of the monetary condition of the times, is presented entire.

"Brethren : I present to you some calculations to save you trouble, and help your minds in determining what is just, this afternoon. In these calcula-ions I have compared the prices of some of the most necessary articles of living, through June and July last past, with what they were before the war, by which it will appear how much the articles have multiplied in their prices. Before the present war, corn, per bushel, 3s. 4d.; veal, in the summer, per lb., 3d.; butter, per lb., 8d.; wood, per cord, at the wharves in summer, highest, 13s. 4d. The cost of a bushel of corn, a pound of veal, a pound of butter, and a cord of wood, 17s. 7d. June and July, 1780, corn, $60 per bushel, is £18; veal, $5 per lb., is £1, 10s. 0d.; butter, $15 per lb., is £4. 10s. 0d.; wood, the very lowest, $300 per cord, is £90. The cost of a bushel of corn, a pound of veal, a pound of butter, and a cord of wood, £114. By this it appears that the price of the necessaries of living are a little more than 129 for 1. That is, $129 would not purchase, through June and July past, more than $1 would before the war. Leaving out the article of wood, and making the calculation upon the three others, it will make almost 113 for 1. If we take the necessary articles of clothing into the account, we shall find an estimate surpassing the first. But even if the lowest estimate is taken, it will be found I have not had in value quite £27 of the last half year's salary, which should be £60, so that it has fallen short more than half. The parish voted me but 50 for 1, which not being assessed till the latter part of May, it has been gathered, received and made use of, when money has been of the above low value. What, therefore, may be reasonably expected, is, that the parish, at their meeting, should vote a sum to make up the deficiency of the past half year's salary, as well as to determine what may be just to raise for the half year of which between two and three months are past." The next year, Mr. Willard requested the parish to fix his salary upon the necessaries of life, to be regulated according to prices every three months, which was complied with, as was also a request to hire him a house.

After a peaceful ministry of nine years, marked by mutual confidence and affection, Mr. Willard was called, by a unanimous vote of the overseers, to the presidency of Harvard University. This election, after "prayerful consideration, weighing things on every side, and consulting the most judicious persons," he felt it his duty to accept. Nov. 19, 1781, he addressed a communication to the parish on the subject, and requested their consent to his dismissal from the pastoral office. The same request had been previously made of the church, which "concluded not to act as a separate body, but as a part of the parish." This communication was referred to a committee, who reported as follows: "That it is with the greatest reluctance that we think of consenting to our pastor's leaving us, with whom we have lived happily for so long a season; and when we think of the difficulties that may attend a re-settlement among us, should he go from us, our minds cannot but be much affected. Yet, when we consider that our pastor is invited to a station of very great importance, and where he may be much more extensively useful to the churches of Christ than if he were to continue to minister to a single church and parish, we fear to withhold our consent, lest we should be found to be contending against Providence. We therefore, though with pain, give him up for the sake of the public, and ardently wish, when invested with the president's office, that he may be a rich blessing to the world." This report was accepted:

20*

and Dec. 30, 1781, Mr. Willard publicly took leave of the first church and congregation, in a discourse from Acts xx. 32. " And now, brethren, I commend you to God, and to the word of his grace, which is able to build you up, and to give you an inheritance among all them which are sanctified." Subsequently, on petition, as it appears was customary in such cases, the parish received £100 from the treasury of the Commonwealth, to aid in defraying the expense of settling another pastor.

Mr. Willard was born at Biddeford, Me., Dec. 29, 1738, and was son of Rev. Samuel Willard, and grandson of Vice President Willard. He was graduated at Harvard College in 1765, in which he was subsequently a tutor about six years. Soon after his ordination, he was married to Miss Mary Sheafe, an accomplished lady, and of a distinguished family in Portsmouth, N. H. His children, born in this town, were Sophia, Augustus, Mary, and Sidney, who was a professor in Harvard College for many years. He continued to preside over the college for nearly twenty-three years, and died at New Bedford, Sept. 25th, 1804, in the 66th year of his age. He was particularly distinguished for his acquaintance with classical literature, and with astronomical and mathematical science. His attainments in Greek learning have been equalled by few. At the head of the university, he mingled paternal tenderness with strict authority; and by his dignified person and deportment, united with candor, generosity and benevolence, he secured at the same time respect and affection. " His unbending integrity," says one who knew him intimately, and who was associated in college government with him, " his patience and fidelity in duty, his claims to professional and literary respect and confidence, gave him a high rank among the worthies, guardians and guides of that generation." *

As a minister of the gospel, he was less anxious to display his critical learning than to impart the most useful instruction. He made doing good the great object of his sacred office; and his piety, which was equally remote from superstition or overwrought enthusiasm, was manifested by his resignation to the will of God under pains and afflictions, and by his constant exertions to promote the interests of religion. His publications were: a thanksgiving sermon, 1783, a sermon at the ordination of Joseph McKean, 1785, a sermon on the death of Timothy Hilliard, 1790, a sermon at the ordination of Hezekiah Packard, 1793, a Latin address on the death of George Washington, 1800, and several mathematical and astronomical communications in the Memoirs of the American Academy of Arts and Sciences.

After the removal of Mr. Willard, the pulpit remained vacant more than three years, during which time it was supplied by Rev. Messrs. Bentley, Motee, Mellen, Dwight, Story, Lockwood and White. Mr. Story received an invitation to settle, which he declined; and Dec. 6th, 1784, a unanimous call was given to Mr. Joseph McKean, which he accepted, and his ordination took place May 11th, 1785. On this occasion, Rev. Phillips Payson made the introductory prayer; Rev. Joseph Willard preached the sermon, from 2 Tim. i. 7, "For God hath not given us the spirit of fear, but of power, and of love, and of a sound mind;" Rev. Joseph Swain, of Wenham,

---

* Rev. Dr. Thayer, in his published sermon at the ordination of his son, Rev. C. T. Thayer.

made the ordaining prayer and gave the charge; Rev. Thomas Barnard, of Salem, gave the right hand of fellowship, and Rev. Nathan Holt, of Danvers, made the concluding prayer.

Mr. McKean's salary was £200, and his settlement £300. In 1801, an addition of $200 was made to the former. In 1802, he received, and after mature consideration, accepted an invitation to become the first president of Bowdoin College, at Brunswick, Me. Previously to his acceptance, he laid the subject before the parish and church, and requested a dismission from the pastoral office. This request, after serious deliberation, was granted, though the greatest reluctance was expressed to part with a pastor and teacher, with whom they had so long lived in harmony, love and friendship.

Rev. Joseph McKean was born in Londonderry, N. H., Oct. 15, 1757. His immediate ancestors were from the north of Ireland, though of Scotch descent. He was graduated at Dartmouth College, in 1774, and in the summer of 1780, resided at Cambridge, pursuing the studies of astronomy and mathematics, for which he had a decided predilection. For several years he taught a school in his native town, and was for some time an assistant in Phillips' Academy, at Andover. He early directed his attention to the ministry, in which profession he continued about seventeen years, when he was called to the presidency of Bowdoin College. He continued in this office until his death, which occurred July 15, 1807, in the 50th year of his age, leaving the seminary over which he presided, in a very flourishing condition.

From his early youth Mr. McKean was strong and

athletic, able to support fatigue and endure hardship;
and in his youth and long after, excelled in all the
manly exercises to which the active and hardy yeo-
manry of our country were then accustomed. In
the year succeeding his settlement in the ministry
here, he was married to Alice Anderson, of Londonderry, N. H.   The children by this marriage, were
Joseph, Nancy, John, Mary, Alice, Margaret, James
and Alice. Mr. McKean was of cheerful temperament,
and devoted himself with unwearied industry to the
promotion of science and religion, while his talents
and unostentatious piety gave him an honorable
rank among the distinguished men of the day. "He
had, from his youth," says an intimate friend, "a
respect for the genuine simplicity and unassuming
worth that distinguished other times. A puritan in
heart, he was, however, the gentleman in manners.
His knowledge of the world, and the peculiar sweetness of his disposition, rendered him accommodating
to all.   Though naturally reserved, perhaps, he was
yet communicative in confidential intercourse and
in the exercise of his office. A stranger to deceit,
his language was ever the expression of his feelings,
sincere though guarded, warm and animated, but
never extravagant. . . . . . His peculiar excellency
seemed to be a sound, discriminating judgment. . . . .
He was a humble pupil of the Redeemer, and his
life will rank among the most consistent, simple and
impressive examples of the efficacy of his faith." *
Besides some papers in the Transactions of the
American Academy of Arts and Sciences, Mr. Mc
Kean published an election sermon, in 1801, a sermon
at the ordination of Rev. Rufus Anderson, at North

* Eulogy on Rev. Joseph McKean, by William Jenks, D.D.

Yarmouth, a sermon at the ordination of Rev. Mr. Moore, at Newbury, three sermons on occasions of public fasting and prayer, and the address delivered by him at his inauguration. The fast sermon of April 9th, 1801, is remembered by many now living. Its subject was, speaking evil of rulers; and though suggested by the political events of the time, and delivered at a period of strong political feeling, the discourse was generally well received, extensively read, and doubt- less exerted a favorable influence on the public mind.

After hearing several candidates, a call was given to and accepted by Rev. Abiel Abbot, who was in- stalled Dec. 13, 1803. On this occasion, the intro- ductory prayer was offered by Rev. Ezra Ripley, of Concord; sermon by Rev. T. M. Harris, of Dorches- ter; installing prayer by Rev. Mr. Fuller, of Glou- cester; charge by Rev. Mr. Clark, of Lexington; right hand of fellowship by Rev. Moses Dow, of Beverly; concluding prayer by Rev. Dr. Barnard, of Salem.

Dr. Abbot was born in Andover, Mass., August 17th, 1770, and from a pious mother early received religious principles and impressions, which in subse- quent life imparted increasing lustre to his piety. His preparatory studies were pursued at Phillips' Academy, under the direction of the celebrated Dr. Pemberton, during which time he occupied the first rank in his class. He entered Harvard University in 1788, and graduated in 1792, with distinguished honors. His literary reputation procured for him the appointment to deliver the oration before the society of Phi Beta Kappa, in 1800, when he chose for his subject, "A review of the 18th century."

Soon after leaving college, he was employed as an

assistant in Phillips' Academy, Exeter, N. H., and afterwards as principal of Phillips' Academy, Andover, during which time he pursued his theological studies with Rev. Jonathan French. In 1794, he commenced preaching at Haverhill, and having accepted a unanimous call, was ordained June 3, 1795. His ministry here was harmonious and successful; and when, in 1803, he felt it his duty to ask a dismission, he received from the church and society the most ample testimonials of unabated love and respect. Previous to his settlement in this town, he was solicited to preach as a candidate in the Brattlestreet society, Boston, and proposals were also made to him from a society in Providence, both of which he declined. His ministry in Beverly was commenced under the disadvantage of debility, and his introductory sermon, from the words "We all do fade as a leaf," was delivered under the consciousness that it might be his last. His health was never firm, having sustained a shock at the age of fourteen, by inconsiderately thrusting his arm into a cold spring in the heat of a summer's day. But with an ardent mind, bent on high degrees of usefulness, the effects of his labors were early visible in the increased seriousness of his congregation. In 1804, he writes, "My labors have been apparently blest more than in any former period. The serious of the society have expressed to me their joy and gratulation; the whole assembly appears more solemn and attentive and full than formerly." In 1805, he writes, "The additions to the church in less than a year have been nearly fifty, and they seem to adorn their profession." His style of preaching was practical, close of application to the heart and conduct, and was eminently successful, because often founded on circumstances in the experience of those whom he addressed.

In 1806, he commenced delivering a course of expository lectures, in the town-hall, on the history and doctrines of Christ, which were so numerously attended as to render it necessary to repair to the church. In 1809, he delivered the annual discourse at Plymouth in commemoration of the landing of the Pilgrims, which was published. The summer of 1810 was marked as a season of religious interest in his society, and his acknowledged ardor in the cause of practical religion procured for him at this time the expressions of affection and tenders of ministerial exchanges from those from whom he differed materially in many speculative points of religion. His health becoming seriously affected in 1818, he yielded to medical advice, and sought its renovation in the more genial clime of the south. He sailed for Charleston, October 28th, at which port he arrived November 9th, after a tempestuous passage, and was cordially received by many friends who were waiting his arrival. The winter and succeeding spring were spent in South Carolina, Georgia and Virginia, where he formed numerous acquaintances, from whom he received the kindest attentions, and returned home with hopes of health realized.

The season of ministerial life which followed his return, is to be considered, perhaps, the most laborious and successful of his life. His preaching was much enforced by considerations peculiar to Christianity. A partiality for authors of the class of Baxter and Doddridge, produced a tinge of thought and expression which gave interest to his sermons, and led to what he deemed a more useful impression, without the adoption of those peculiarities which he might not approve. Whenever he deviated from the accustomed manner of his preaching, and assumed topics bordering on the region of controversial discussion, it was with the fixed design rather of " preaching up his own sentiments, than of preaching down the sentiments of other men." The principal aim of his discourses, however, was to produce serious impressions on the minds of his hearers, and to lead them to self-inspection rather than to investigating the errors and censuring the motives of others.

In 1818, he preached the Dudlian lecture at Cambridge, and received the degree of Doctor in Divinity in 1821. After several years of unremitting labor, he found himself obliged in 1827 to leave his charge and resort once more to the south for the recovery of his health. He sailed from Boston October 28th, and arrived at Charleston November 6th, from which place he addressed an interesting and affectionate letter to his church and congregation. He does not appear to have been sanguine of the favorable results of this voyage. On a visit made to him at his request by a ministering brother, a few days before his departure, " at a time when the heart has no disguise, and the soul is anxious to utter all that it deems true and kind, important and useful, he thus addressed him; (evidently with a wish that it should be remembered and at a fit time communicated.)—' I believe the hour of my departure is at hand; how near I cannot say, but not far distant is the time when I shall be in the immediate presence of my Maker. This impression leads me to look back upon my life and inwardly upon my present state. In the review

21

I find many things to be humbled and penitent for,
and many things to fill me with gratitude and praise.
I have, I trust, the testimony of my heart, that my
life, my best powers, my time, and my efforts, have
in the main been sincerely given to God and to mankind.   Of all the years of my life, the present, in the
review, gives me most pleasure.   You know my
recent plans and labors, and the design of them : [al-
luding to discourses delivered before the convention
of ministers, and at the ordination of Rev. A. Abbot,
and to certain contributions to a religious publication,
the Christian Visitant, whose object coincided with
his views, and to extend the circulation of which he
was making great efforts.]   In these, 1 have endeavored to check the spirit of contention among Christians, and, as a disciple of the Prince of Peace, to
diffuse the spirit of love and peace, to inspire Christians with a warmer zeal for the great object of
religion.   The efforts were great.   My health and
perhaps my life are the sacrifice.   If the Lord will,
be it so.   If ever I faithfully served him, it was in
these services.   If ever I felt prepared for death, it
was when they were finished.   If ever I knew and
felt the delightful import of that passage,—*I am now
ready to be offered and the time of my departure is at
hand ; I have fought a good fight, I have finished my
course, I have kept the faith, &c.,* it was then, and it
is now.   In my bosom there is peace.   Whether life
or death be before me, all is well.   I can say, *the will
of the Lord be done.*   With the greatest serenity he
alluded to the expected issue of his disorder, and
seemed filled with *a good hope through grace* of
eternal life."

The forebodings of death were soon realized, yet

not without some encouraging symptoms of returning health. Failing to realize the hopes of anxious
friends, he sailed in February for the still milder
climate of Cuba, from which place he wrote a series
of interesting letters that have since been published.
During his residence here his health apparently improved, and he indulged a hope that he might be
spared to labor a little longer in the vineyard of his
master. Anxious to return home, he embarked for
Charleston, where he arrived Saturday morning,
May 31st, and spent the day in calling on numerous
friends. On Sunday morning he attended Rev. Mr.
Gilman's church, and partook of the sacrament. In
the afternoon, though complaining of the weariness
produced by the exertions of the day before, he
preached with great animation from the words,
"God said let there be light," and fixed the attention of his audience by contrasting the spiritual
darkness of the region he had just left behind, with
the light with which our own country is favored.

On Monday he embarked in the Othello for New
York. A few days out he showed signs of illness,
unattended by any alarming symptoms. On Saturday morning, though still languid, he rose early,
dressed himself, and went on deck. After reclining
in the cabin a short time, he went on deck again
with assistance, where a cloak and pillows had been
spread for him. After resting a few moments, he
walked supported by the arm of a friend, twelve
times across the deck. His respiration was observed
to be burdened and difficult, which was at the time
ascribed to the bracing effect of the fresh air. But
immediately on sitting down, he was attacked with
bleeding. He begged his friends not to be alarmed,

said he was aware that his old spring complaints had returned with violence, and requested that his wife and family might be prepared to see him return in still feebler health than that in which he left them. He afterwards expressed the hope that he should be able to write himself. As he grew gradually fainter from the loss of blood, he was asked by one of the passengers, if he felt alarmed ? " No," he replied, " I am in the hands of God, and I trust he will take care of me." The hemorrhage increasing, he said no more, but raising his eyes to heaven, and breathing the intense language of mental devotion, the pure spirit freed itself of the body, the countenance as serene and peaceful as when he had that morning been seen asleep in his birth. His remains were interred on Staten Island, and an appropriate funeral service was performed by Rev. Mr. Miller. Thus, in the twenty-fourth year of his ministry in this town, and in the 57th year of his age, was taken to his rest an eloquent, learned, affectionate and faithful minister of the gospel. On the intelligence of his death at Beverly, the bells were tolled, a mournful silence pervaded the streets, customary business was in many instances suspended, and the pulpit and church clothed in black for forty days. Appropriate public services were performed at the request of the parish, and a discourse delivered by Rev. Dr. Flint of Salem, in which the characteristic qualities of the deceased were portrayed with a discriminating and affecting power.

Dr. Abbot was married in 1796, to Miss Eunice, eldest daughter of Ebenezer Wales, Esq. of Dorchester. In the commencement of his ministry he entertained a belief in the Trinity, but on this sub-

ject his views altered, and the fundamental principles of Unitarian belief became the objects of his
decided conviction. His publications consist of eight
sermons preached on particular occasions, an eulogy
on the character of Washington, a discourse at
Plymouth on the 188th anniversary of the landing
of our forefathers, a temperance address, discourses
on Baptism, a volume of sermons to mariners, the
Parent's Assistant and Sunday-school book, an address before the Berry street conference, and a volume of letters from Cuba. After his decease a volume of his sermons was published, to which is prefixed a memoir of the author. From that memoir,
the preceding notice has been principally compiled.

Dr. Abbot was succeeded by the present minister,
Rev. Christopher T. Thayer, of Lancaster, a graduate of Harvard University, who was ordained Jan.
27, 1830. The services of his ordination were as
follows : introductory prayer and reading the scriptures,* by Rev. Mr. Loring ; sermon by Rev. Dr.
Thayer, father of the pastor elect ; ordaining prayer
by Rev. Dr. Lowell; charge by Rev. Dr. Bancroft ;
right hand of fellowship by Rev. Mr. Lothrop ; address to the society by Rev. Dr. Flint; concluding
prayer by Rev. Mr. Bartlett.

Having thus completed the history of the several
former ministers in the first parish, we return to no-

---

* The scriptures were first publicly read in the first church, May
2d, 1773, about which time the copy now in use was purchased. It
is a folio volume, and was printed in London by Thomas Baskett,
1759. It contains, besides the canonical books of the old and new
Testament, the apocrypha, the liturgy of the Church of England,
including the Psalter, the whole of Psalms set to metre by Sternhold
& Hopkins, a copious index, and a concordance by John Downan.

21*

tice its houses of worship. The first was erected in
1656, near the old burial-ground, and not far from
the site of the first parish vestry. Of its dimensions
there is no account. This house was variously
altered from time to time, for the accommodation of
an increasing congregation. In 1671, liberty was
granted to certain females wanting seats, to build
three at their own charge. Richard Brackenbury
and Samuel Corning, sen. "had leave to make a
seat at the north end of the pulpit," and Mrs. Hale,
the pastor's wife, had "liberty to make a seat where
she now sitteth, it not being prejudicial to the rest."
A gallery was also authorized to be built on the east
side of the meeting-house, and Humphrey Woodberry, John West and John Raiment, who undertook
the work, were "to have each of them a seat in the
fore-seat for their trouble." In 1672, "it was agreed
that the meeting-house be ceiled up to the wall-
plates, rabbitted, and the windows glazed." Mrs.
Lothrop likewise "had liberty to make a seat convenient by the chief pillar."

This house continued to be used about twenty-five
years, when the parish having so increased in numbers as to render it inadequate for their accommodation, it was sold with the exception of the pulpit,
for £7.10s, and in 1682 a new house was erected,
fifty feet in length and forty feet in width. It stood
on the site occupied by the first parish meeting-house
at the present time, and the terms of contract for
building were " £370 in silver, the one half to be paid
at the raising, and the other half at the delivery of
the key; otherwise £550, the one half in Indian
corn, and the other half in pork at prices current,
the one half to be paid at the next May day, and

the other at Michelmas." This house, like the first, was used for the transaction of public business, and besides the alterations and improvements made at various times, a powder room was built in it in 1727, for the safe-keeping of the ammunition belonging to the town.*

SECOND MEETING-HOUSE—BUILT 1682.

In 1753, the population of the parish was about 1300 souls, and a necessity was felt for the enlargement of the meeting-house, or the building of another. The house was examined by a committee, who made a report adverse to enlarging, and recommended building. This question was agitated about nine years; and June 27, 1770, the house was taken down to make room for the third, having stood nearly eighty-nine years. While destitute of a house of worship, divine service was attended under a large mulberry tree in front of Mr. Champney's house, at

---

* As fires at this time were never kindled in the meeting-house, it was considered the safest place to deposit powder. The sacredness of the place did not, however, allay the fears of the congregation, who left the house whenever a thunder-shower occurred.

the north-east corner of the common, near the burial-
ground.

The third meeting-house was erected under the
superintendence of Henry Herrick, James Woodberry, Joseph Corning, Samuel Goodridge, and Larkin Thorndike. It was 70 feet long, 53 feet wide,
and 28 feet stud. The tower at the westerly end
was 15 feet square, and the porch at the eastern end
14 feet square. Two rows of pews, sixty in number,
were built round the wall, on the floor of the house ;
and the area, separated in the centre by an aisle running from the front door to the pulpit, was filled with
free seats, for the accommodation of those who did
not choose to sit in pews. The pulpit was on the
north side of the house, opposite " the great door;"
beneath it was the elders' seat, and lower still the
deacons' seat. The gallery contained twenty-seven
wall pews, and seats were appropriated for the accommodation of colored persons. The cost of the
house was about £1300, or $4,333,33. Pews were
subsequently built, from time to time, until 1795,
when the house was enlarged, by dividing it through
the centre and inserting twenty feet. On the area
thus formed, twenty-seven pews were built, and eight
additional pews in the gallery. The deacons' seat
was removed, and the elders' seat contrived for their
accommodation. An additional front door was opened, and a portico of 30 feet front, supported by four
pillars, and covering both entrances, was built. The
whole cost of enlarging, painting and repairing the
house, was $3,428,15, and the work was executed
under the superintendence of Joseph Wood, John
Stephens, and Josiah Gould.

In 1835, the house was remodelled, to conform to

the improved taste displayed in public buildings, at an expense of $10,000. The whole interior was removed; the steeple, with its gilded chanticleer, was severed from the main body, and fell with a tremendous crash; the eastern porch was taken away, and converted into a shop for mechanical purposes; and the stout oak frame, which had borne the storms of more than sixty years, was alone retained. The style of architecture is Grecian. The front presents a handsome portico, sustained by large fluted columns. The entrance is by three doors, opening into a spacious porch, from which the gallery is reached by two flights of stairs. The pulpit, at the eastern end, is finely proportioned, and built of mahogany. The orchestra is furnished with an excellent-toned organ; and the cupola with a clock of Willard's manufacture, and a bell weighing 1244 lbs.* The improvements reflect much credit on the taste and the public spirit of the parish.

In 1842, the interior of the house was painted in fresco, by Mr. Thomas Coleman. The walls are ornamented with pilasters and panels, and the ceiling with oblong panels, terminating in the centre, which gives a pleasing effect. Behind the pulpit is a painting emblematic of the light of Christianity breaking upon the darkness of the world, and scattering the clouds of ignorance, superstition, suffering and sin. Altogether, for beauty and convenience, this church is not surpassed by any in the county; and by few, if any, in this country.

The structure of the first and second houses of worship must have been exceedingly plain, and would have rudely contrasted with the architecture

* This clock was procured in 1796, at the charge of the parish.

of the present day. The whole frame-work was visible to the very "ridge-pole," for it was not until forty-four years after the second house was erected, (1726,) that measures were taken to lay a floor "upon the beams with boards and joist." A coat of whitewash served as a substitute for paint; "laths and plaster" were dispensed with, as superfluous; and the introduction of a stove, for the purpose of rendering the house comfortable during the winter months, would probably have been regarded as an imputation upon the piety of the congregation. Indeed, warming the meeting-house is quite a modern innovation; and within twenty-five years past, the little "foot-stove" was considered as essential an element of a lady's sabbath paraphernalia as the muff and hymn-book.

The first departure from the primitive simplicity of long seats, in the occupancy of which the sexes were not permitted to mingle, appeared in the erection of the square pew, with its open-work top, through which graceless urchins played at "bo-peep" with others graceless as themselves, and its "leaning-board" and "hinge-seats," whose "slam down," at the close of each prayer, produced reports not dissimilar to the irregular musketry of undisciplined militia. In these enclosures favored individuals gathered their families around them, to the scandal, doubtless, of many envious spirits. But time and fashion have changed, and these "chief seats" have given place to the more convenient slip-pew.

Of bells, including the one already mentioned, there have been five. The first, as before stated, was obtained by Capt. Lothrop, from a Catholic friary at Port Royal, in the expedition of 1656, and presented by him to the parish. The second was purchased by the parish, in 1685-6. It weighed 109 lbs., and cost £13. 12s. 6d. The third, weighing 267 lbs., was the gift of Robert Briscoe, in 1712, which, as was probably the case with its predecessors, was hung over the centre of the house, so that the bell-rope came down into the broad aisle. The fourth, weighing 1387 lbs., was imported from London, but was soon cracked, and gave place to the fifth and present one in 1803, weighing 1244 lbs., of the manufacture of Paul Revere & Son, of Boston.

Among the municipal regulations of the parish, those for *seating the meeting* were not the least important. The first record relating to this subject is in 1671, when Roger Conant, Wm. Dixey and Richard Brackenbury were "joined with the selectmen to seat all the married persons in the meeting-house." Committees were chosen for this purpose from time to time, who probably were governed by various rules until after the second house of worship was erected, when a regular system was drawn up by Col. Hale and adopted. This system provided—

"That every male be allowed one degree for every complete year of age he exceeds twenty-one.

"That he be allowed for a captain's commission twelve degrees; for a lieutenant's, eight degrees, and for an ensign's, four degrees.

"That he be allowed three degrees for every shilling for real estate in the last parish tax, and one degree for every shilling for personal estate and faculty.

"Every six degrees for estate and faculty of a parent alive, to make one degree among his sons, or where there is none, among the daughters that are seated.

" Every generation of predecessors heretofore living in this town, to make one degree for every male descendant that is seated. That parentage be regarded no farther otherwise than to turn the scale between competition for the same seat.

" That taxes for polls of sons and servants shall give no advancement for masters or fathers, because such sons or servants have seats.

" That no degree be allowed on account of any one's predecessors having paid towards building the meeting-house, because it had fallen down before now, but for the repairs since made.

" That some suitable abatement in degrees be made, where it is well known the person is greatly in debt.

" That the tenant of a freehold for term of years shall be allowed as many degrees as half the real estate entitles him to, and the landlord the other half.

" That the proprietor of land in any other parish shall be (if under his own improvement) allowed as much as he would be if they lay in the parish; but if rented out, only half as much.

" Married women to be seated agreeable to the rank of their husbands, and widows in the same degree as though their husbands were yet living.

" That the foremost magistrate seat (so called) shall be the highest in rank, and the other three in successive order.

" That the next in rank shall be in the foremost of the front seats below, then the fore-seat in the front-gallery, then the fore-seat in the side-gallery.

" That the side-seat below shall be for elderly

men, the foremost first or highest, and the others in order.

" 'That the seats behind the fore-front seat below, shall be for middle-aged men, according to their degree.

" That the second or third seats in the front and side galleries shall be for younger men, to rank alternately the second from before first, and the third next."

The women were seated separately from the men.

Upon these principles, three hundred and thirty-two men and three hundred and twenty-one women were seated, and their names recorded,—at the head of which stands the name of Col. Robert Hale, who, with Robert Haskell, Joshua Herrick, Robert Morgan, James Woodberry, Benj. Cleaves and Henry Herrick, occupied the first seat.

Those who are disposed to ridicule a practice which imperfectly accords with later ideas of republican equality, should remember that it was in unison with public sentiment at the time, and that when seats were free, some system for assigning them, sanctioned by the parish, was necessary to preserve harmony among their occupants. Nor is the assignment of the first seat to Col. Robert Hale, who drafted the plan, to be regarded as an assumption or the result of design, as, under any previous rule, his office, wealth and service would have commanded it.

The unsocial method of seating the meeting necessarily separated the heads of families from their children, who were placed on benches in the aisles, or required to sit on the pulpit stairs. As might be expected, this arrangement was fruitful of disturbance alike annoying to the minister and scandalous

22

in the eyes of the devout. To remedy the evil, Feb. 9, 1676, it was " ordered by the selectmen, that the hinder seats of the elders' gallery is to be altered, and the boys are to set there, and Robert Hubbard, sen. to have an eye-out for them, and for the first offence to acquaint their parents or masters of it, and if they do offend again, to acquaint the selectmen with it, who shall deal with them according to law." And again, Jan. 11, 1698–9, it was "voted by the town, that the selectmen make such orders as convenient for the prevention of boys and idle persons from setting in such places, in our meeting-house, wherein they are out of public view, and so in time of public worship to spend much of their time in play and disorder."

Displays of juvenile irreverence were not peculiar to Beverly. In Salem, April 20th, 1676, it was "ordered, that all ye boys of ye towne are and shall bee appointed to sitt upon ye three paire of staires in ye meeting-house on ye Lord's day, and Wm. Lord is appointed to look to ye boyes yt sitt upon ye pulpit staires, and for ye other staires Reuben Guppy is to look to and order soe many of ye boyes as may be convenient, and if any are unruly, to present their names as ye law directs." *

In some places, at a still earlier period, it was customary, during the public service, for a person to go about the meeting-house to wake the sleepers. He bore a long wand, on one end of which was a ball, and on the other a fox-tail. When he observed the men asleep, he rapped them on the head with the knob; and roused the slumbering sensibilities of the

* Annals of Salem.

ladies by drawing the brush slightly across their faces.*

The musical exercises of the sanctuary, according to the custom of the times, were conducted by one of the deacons, who officiated as chorister to the congregation. He read the hymn line by line and "set the tune," in which each member joined "by rote," in key and measure not always the most exact or harmonious. Probably, as musical taste improved, this desultory practice fell into disrepute ; as, by a vote in 1764, the deacons were authorized to select singers, and seats were appropriated to their use, "that the spirit of singing psalms might be revived, and that part of worship conducted with more regularity." This arrangement continued until 1774, when a choir was regularly installed in "the front seats of the south gallery," and authorized, "by vote of the parish, to pitch the tune and take the lead in singing." In 1766, an improvement was attempted by the introduction of Watts' psalms and hymns, but not, however, without strong expression of dissatisfaction from those attached to the old version then in use. In the course of the succeeding fourteen years several ineffectual attempts were made to abolish the practice of "deaconing" the psalm; but, in 1780, the spirit of compromise led to the vote "that the psalms be sung in the congregation in the forenoon, by reading line by line, and in the afternoon without such reading." This compromise was of short duration. The friends of the ancient order, in yielding a part, paved the way for the loss of the whole, and, sustained by the current opinion, the entire service soon devolved on the choir, as now constituted.

* Lewis' Hist. Lynn.

THE SECOND PARISH.

THE second or north parish, known as " *The Pre-cinct of Salem and Beverly*," was incorporated by act of the General Court, in October, 1713. Previously to this, in 1711, the town of Salem, which then included the whole of Rial-side and Conant-street, or in other words, the entire territory west of the brook near the residence of Major John Conant, " voted, that the inhabitants of Rial-side be allowed, with some of their neighbors of the Village, and also of Beverly, to build a meeting-house near Horse-bridge, on the line between Salem and Beverly."

The formation of a second parish did not receive the unanimous approbation of the town, and at a meeting held Dec. 19 following, it was " voted, that Deacon Samuel Balch, Joseph Herrick and Robert Woodberry are chosen as agents for the town, to make objections against the prayer of the petition of some of the inhabitants of the northerly part of Beverly and the inhabitants of Rial-side, in Salem, and some of the inhabitants of Salem Village ; said petition bearing date Oct. 23, 1712, and preferred by them before the Great and General Court, Oct. 25, 1712, the town being now served with a copy of said petition, by order of said Court." One objection offered to granting the prayer of the petitioners, was, that some living within the limits of the proposed parish, were unwilling to leave their minister, Mr. Blowers. The remonstrance failed of its object, and the decision of the General Court was acquiesced in.

On the 13th Nov. 1713, a meeting was held by the inhabitants of the new precinct, to take preliminary steps for erecting a house of worship. A committee, consisting of Nathaniel Hayward, Joseph Herrick, Thomas Rayment, John Trask, Jonathan Rayment, Edward Rayment, John Rea, Jonathan Dodge, and Andrew Dodge, was chosen to carry the vote of the meeting into effect; and at a subsequent meeting, £350 were voted to be raised, " to be improved for building a house for the public worship of God, and to purchase land for the use of the people of said precinct."

The dimensions of the house were ordered to be fifty feet in length and forty in width, if the timber which had been procured would admit of it. The largest sums paid towards building it were by Dea. Jonathan Conant, who paid £25 13s. 3d., and Captain Thomas Rayment, who paid £20 10s. In the course of the season the house was erected, and fitted for public worship. Its interior partook of primitive simplicity. Long rows of substantial seats filled the area, but in progress of time they were displaced by " square pews," a few of which at an early day were built against the wall. The oaken pulpit was in excellent keeping with the massive frame-work that economy left naked, and the " deacons' seat " was of such ample dimensions as became the dignity of its occupants. At first, there was no steeple or bell, but simply a turret at the west end. A porch at the east end was built about the year 1771, by Caleb Dodge, at his own expense, for which the parish granted him a pew privilege in the south-east corner of the house. Previously to the erection of this porch, the women's entrance to the gallery was by a flight of stairs in the corner. In 1751, it was voted

22*

to build a steeple, and purchase a bell of about 400 cwt.

In 1715, after a season of fasting and prayer, a call to settle in the ministry was voted to Mr. John Chipman. The call was secured by the vote of Mrs. Mary Woodberry, who owned considerable property in the parish, and had probably contributed towards defraying the expenses of erecting the meeting-house. Her interest in the result was doubtless the cause of her being present at the meeting; and her exercise of a franchise, novel in that day, settled for more than half a century a question of vital moment to the church and society.

Mr. Chipman's salary was fixed at £60 per annum, to be increased, in event of marriage, £5 annually, till it amounted to £80. He was to receive £100 settlement, besides one acre of land in fee simple, and the " stranger's money " as a perquisite.*

This call, Mr. Chipman accepted, in the following note :

BEVERLY, Nov. 8, 1715. Whereas my answer relating to ye votes passed by you for ye encouragement of my settlement was conditional, and the conditions on your part being performed (as by record appears) to my acceptance,—these are to signifie to you that I do accept thereof, and engage to settle with you, and (by divine assistance) to serve you in ye ministry of ye Gospel, officiating in all ye service that shall be incumbent on me, as preaching, catechising the youth, &c.

To the Clerk of the Precinct of Salem and ⎰ JOHN CHIPMAN.
Beverly, to be communicated to said Precinct. ⎱

* " *Stranger's money.*" It was customary for a box to be placed near the door of the meeting-house, into which strangers put money on the sabbath, on the principle, it is presumed, that every person was morally obligated to contribute to the support of public worship. The sum thus obtained was usually paid over to the minister, in addition to his salary.

On the 28th Dec. 1715, Mr. Chipman was ordained to the work of the ministry, previously to which, a day of fasting and prayer was observed. Before proceeding to ordination, a church was organized and publicly acknowledged, and the covenant signed by the following persons :—John Chipman, Edward Dodge, Jonathan Rayment, Joseph Dodge, Jonathan Dodge, Josiah Woodberry, Elisha Dodge, Nehemiah Wood, John Dodge, sen., John Leach, Joseph Herrick, John Cresey, Jacob Griggs, John Brown and Moses Fluant. The covenant was drawn up by Mr. Chipman, and continued in use for seventy years, until the ministry of Rev. Daniel Oliver, when it was superseded by one framed by him. In 1831, the church unanimously agreed, " that the church may hereafter be built up upon the platform drawn up by Rev. John Chipman, at its organization, Dec. 28, 1715 "; and accordingly the formulary prepared by Mr. Oliver from that time ceased to be used.

In the services of ordination, the charge was given by Rev. Joseph Gerrish, of Wenham; the right hand of fellowship by Rev. Thomas Blowers, of the first parish in Beverly, who, together with Rev. Geo. Curwan, of the first church in Salem, and Rev. Benj. Prescott, of the third church in Salem, laid on hands.

On the 11th Jan. 1716, the church held its first meeting,—at which John Cresey was chosen the first deacon. At the same meeting " it was voted, that a relation of experiences shall be made in public, by such persons as shall be admitted to communion with us at the table of the Lord," and that in admitting persons to full communion, the " brethren may signify their consent by the vote of the hand." The vote

in relation to experiences (though not designed,)
seems after a series of years to have been construed
as part of the covenant and consequently constitut-
ing a term of communion,—and as such, evidently
conflicting with the clause in the covenant which
sets forth faith and repentance and an unblamable
walk and conversation, as the *only* test of fitness for
christian fellowship. This misapprehension led to
a meeting in 1755, to " explain and settle the terms
of communion."

It was considered that one article of the solemn
covenant which this church entered into with God,
and with each other, at their first embodying, on the
28th Dec. 1715, stands recorded in these words, viz :
" We promise also to admit to our communion such
as shall desire to join themselves to us, if by a profession of their faith and repentance, and unblamable
walk and conversation, they may in charitable discretion be accounted qualified for it." It being also
considered, that there was a " vote passed by this
church, Jan. 11, 1715-16, in these words, viz : ' That
a relation of experiences shall be made in public, by
such persons as shall be admitted to the table of the
Lord,' which vote seems to be dissonant from said
article, and carries a face on it as though we required
some further term of communion with us than what
is expressed in said article in our covenant : This
church therefore thinks it expedient to declare, that
we have from our very first beginning, which is more
than thirty-nine years past, insisted on no other terms
of communion with us than what are expressed in
the said article in our covenant, but have received
many persons to our communion at the table of the
Lord, who have made no relation of their experiences

in public, but only a profession of their faith and repentance :—Wherefore voted,

" 1st. That as this church has ever interpreted the vote aforesaid as *permissive*, and not as *compulsive*, so we do not now, nor will we for the future, insist on any other terms of communion with us than those expressed in said article in our covenant; and yet, that any person who upon his coming into communion with us, shall be desirous of making a relation of his experience in public, shall have liberty so to do.

"2dly. Voted, that any person desirous to join himself to this church, shall have liberty to manifest his faith and repentance either orally before the church, or by writing, to be read to the church, or privately to the pastor, to be by him communicated to the church in the substance of it, the person owning before the church that which shall be read or communicated by the pastor." This liberal course the church never deviated from until the ministry of Rev. Daniel Oliver.

The first person received to the church after its organization, was Jonathan Dodge, jr. The first adult baptized, was John Frost, and the second was Joseph Reed, a negro freeman, who was at the same time admitted to full communion. April 22, 1716, twenty persons were received from the first church in Beverly, and three from the church in Wenham. The names of the persons received from the first church were

Nathaniel Hayward and his wife Elizabeth; Nehemiah Hayward and Bethiah his wife; Sarah, wife of Deacon John Cresey; Mary, wife of Lt. Rayment; Sarah Woodberry; Mary, wife of Edward Dodge; Eleanour, wife of Jacob Griggs; Mary, wife of Elisha Dodge; Mary, wife of Moses Fluant; Elizabeth, wife of John Dodge; Sarah, wife of Jonathan Rayment; Mary Woodberry, Alice Woodberry; Jerusha, wife of Jonathan Dodge sen.; Lydia, wife of Josiah Woodberry; Mary, wife of Roger Conant; Susanna, wife of Nehemiah Wood; and Patience Woodberry. From Wenham, Sarah, wife of Jonah Dodge; Eliza, wife of Jonathan Dodge, jr., and Abigail Trillmore.

At a meeting of the church, April 26, 1722, Jonathan Rayment was chosen deacon. At the same meeting it was voted, that " whereas there are divers members of other churches cohabiting with us, and every way appertaining and belonging to us, saving that they yet neglect to put themselves under the watch and care of this church by coming in fully into the covenant and communion with us as a particular church of Christ: Wherefore, voted, that the deacons of the church be desired to discourse (with) those members of other churches, and to endeavor to persuade them to come up fully to their duty in this article, that their communion with us may be more fully stated and regular."

In 1727, twenty-five were added to the church; and on the last day of the year Mr. Chipman writes, " Soli Deo Laus qui et terram violenter exagitavit et super populum suum spiritum suum effudit." " Praise to God alone, who has both shaken violently the earth, and poured out his spirit on his people."

In 1725, the parish, through a committee, applied to the town for an enlargement of territory. The application was unsuccessful, and the next year a movement was made to procure the incorporation of the precinct as a separate town. At a meeting held July 1, 1726, " after a debate of an hour and a half, the people were of opinion that it was most likely, to do their duty as aforesaid, for this precinct to be incorporated into a township, and it being put to vote by the moderator, it was voted for a township by a great majority." From this decision eighteen dissented. This subject was agitated about thirteen years, when the parish concluded to settle down quietly as they were.

Very soon after the house of worship was erected, a committee was chosen to *seat the meeting*. The rule adopted was : "to show respect to ye aged people amongst vs, as allso to have a speciall regard unto persons that have don service for ye benefit of ye precinct, and have contributed high in building of ye hous for ye publick worship of God, and purchasing land for ye use of ye people of sd. precinct, and are Likely to pay considerable in ye Charge of ye ministry amongst us :—as allso not to seat above two-thirds so many persons in any seat, as ye seats will comfortably hold." This last provision indicates that their numbers at that time, were not equal to their room. At a meeting, March 19, 1715-16, it was voted that " ye Committee that was chosen to seate ye meeting-house heretofore, are now chosen, and desired to seate all such persons as are inhabitants amongst us, and pay rates with us, and are not as yet seated." To prevent the young females from pressing in and incommoding the married women who sat in the gallery, it was voted at a meeting, March 29, 1715, that the front seat in the east gallery "be parted in ye middle." In 1730, the committee, in performing the duty assigned them, were directed " first to have a regard to old age, and second to what men pay for their real estates ;" and in 1755, it was voted to have "special regard to age, rates and commission."

The musical exercises in public worship were conducted in a manner similar to the practice of the first church, already described. The deacon "lined" the psalm, and "set the tune," in which the congregation joined. The first attempt to improve this method was by the introduction of music-books, and probably the formation of a choir. This movement produced a strong sensation. The deacon felt that his prerogative was usurped, the congregation were disturbed by the introduction of tunes with which they were unacquainted, and by many worthy people it was viewed as a dangerous innovation. The uneasiness thus created, led to a church meeting in 1730, to devise a plan for the restoration of harmony. The importance the subject assumed may be best estimated by the following record of proceedings.

"Whereas there has been some difference of opinion in some of the members of this church, relating to the way or method of our psalmody, some thinking that the way or method of singing the psalm tunes which has heretofore been in common use among us, should still be retained by us; but others, that the way or method of singing the tunes by note, as has been of late years introduced into many other churches and congregations in the land, should be promoted and established in this society: for the accommodation of which affair the church is now met. And having first considered, that it is our indispensable duty to harmonize in the way or method of our singing the praises of God, and to use our utmost endeavors to prevent all manner of discord therein, so that we may not only with one mind, but also with

one mouth, glorifie God according to that precept,
Rom. xv. 6. It was then voted, that considering
our present circumstances, the church does judge it
to be most conducive to the peace of this people to
sing the psalm tunes in the way and method which
has heretofore been in common use among us, and accordingly does determine yet to sing them in that
way and method."

At a subsequent meeting this vote was reconsidered, and " the church having first considered several inconveniences which had arisen from said vote
of April 16th, 1730, which were likely to continue
and increase, if the said vote should be strictly ad-
hered to for the future, then agreed and voted, That
this church does determine to sing the psalm tunes
regularly by note, once upon every Lord's day, and
once upon fast days, viz. at the first time of singing
in the afternoon, and once upon every thanksgiving
day also. Voted likewise at the same meeting, That
Mr. Joseph Cresey be desired to set the tune, or lead
the song, at all such times as the church has agreed
to sing regularly by note. Moreover, seeing that an
inconvenience and disorder hath happened by the
introduction of a psalm tune which the people of
this church and congregation are mostly unacquainted with : wherefore it was agreed and voted,
that no psalm tune which has not been in common
use among us, shall be speedily introduced, set or
sung in this congregation, excepting the tune called
St. Marie's or Hackney, and the tune called Com-
mandment tune." This course of compromise was
continued little more than a year, until Oct. 28,
1731, when at a church meeting it was " voted that
they would for the future time, sing (at all times of

23

singing in the public worship) the psalm tunes by
rule, according to the notes pricked in our psalm
books." A relative of Mr. Cresey above mentioned.
was for many years an efficient leader of the choir.

Another disturbing movement was the introduction of Watts' Psalms and Hymns, in 1770. The
dread of innovation seems to have neutralized in
many minds the spirit of improvement, and on this
occasion an elderly gentleman rose in the midst of
divine service greatly excited, and declared that had
Solomon been witness to what his eyes had that day
seen, he never would have written " there is nothing
new under the sun." These prejudices gradually
subsided as the people became familiarized with the
change, and at a later period veneration for Watts
became general.

Among the early friends and benefactors of the
parish, was Robert Hooper jr. of Marblehead, who
owned the farm at Rial-side, the property of the late
Rufus Putnam.   ·

In 1753 he presented the parish with a bell.
which was gratefully received; and besides making
him a free grant of a pew, it was voted, as a further
mark of respect, " to lath and plaster over-head,
over the above said pew, upon the parish's cost ;"
and six years after, the parish " voted that the Hon
Robert Hooper, Esq. be desired when he occasionally attends divine worship with us, to take the up-
permost end of the fore-seat on the floor before the
pulpit." Col. Robert Hale and Lieut. Henry Herrick, also receive honorable notice, the former of
whom is styled a " generous benefactor" and owned
a pew in the house.

In 1759, it was " voted that Lieut. Henry Herrick

be desired, when he attends divine worship with us, to take the second seat on the floor before the pulpit,"—and in 1764, a vote was passed desiring Mrs. Herrick to take a seat in the women's fore pew.

In 1760, legacies having been left to this church by Ebenezer Raymond, Hannah Woodberry, and Dea. John Conant, amounting to £7.1.4, a contribution was taken which increased the sum to £13.13.5 with which a silver tankard for the communion was purchased. Sept. 29, 1769, Mr. Chipman confirmed the gift of a silver cup, made by his wife Hannah to the church in her last illness. In 1809, Josiah Batchelder jr. bequeathed a silver tankard. In June 1832, the late William Friend presented a silver cup to the church, and in 1838, Elizabeth Friend, his widow, presented a copy of the scriptures for the use of the pulpit.

In the course of a few years after Mr. Chipman's settlement, the currency became greatly disordered, and to secure him against loss from paper depreciation, £20, £80 and £120, were added to his salary. In 1735, in consequence of the expenses arising from sickness in his family, the parish voted to take a quarterly contribution for his benefit. In 1740 a precinct meeting was held, to ascertain why Mr. Chipman had not receipted in full for his salary,—whereupon he gave a receipt in full for all the time since his settlement, specifying that he did it partly for considerations other than value received. The continual depreciation of bills of credit not having been fully made up to him by the precinct, was the reason why, although he was willing to give them a discharge in full, he would not acknowledge he had been paid in full. In 1748 an attempt was made to regulate his salary by the current value of silver, but it did not succeed, and £600 old tenor were voted for his salary of £80. In 1750, when paper-money ceased to circulate, the precinct voted him £80 lawful money. In subsequent years his salary was increased to £85, £88, and finally to £90.

July 22, 1757, letters signed Oliver Carter, &c. in behalf of about eighteen or nineteen brethren of the church in Leominster, Mass. were received and complied with, requesting the pastor, with delegates, to assist at a council convened for the purpose of examining a complaint entered against their pastor, Rev. John Rogers. The letters set forth that he had denied the doctrine of original sin, and had " rendered himself suspected of unsoundness, even in some of the fundamental doctrines of Christianity ; more particularly of the Deity of the Lord Jesus Christ." Deacon Joshua Dodge and Joseph Cresey were chosen delegates to accompany the pastor.

Until 1770, Mr. Chipman discharged his ministerial duties without assistance, but being now disabled by age and infirmity, Mr. Enos Hitchcock was employed to supply the pulpit ; and in 1771, after several consultations through a committee with Mr. Chipman, the church and society gave a call to Mr. Hitchcock to settle as colleague-pastor, which was accepted. His settlement was fixed at £133.6.8, and his salary during Mr. Chipman's life, at £60, to be increased after his decease to £95.

On the 21st March, 1771, Mr. Hitchcock was received into this church by letters of dismission and recommendation from the church in Truro. The first day of May following was appointed for his ordination, and a committee chosen to procure two suitable persons to provide for the council, and for the scholars and gentlemen who might attend. The churches in Salem of which Rev. Messrs. Barnard and Diman were pastors,—the first church in Beverly, the second church in Pembroke, the second and third churches in Brookfield, and the churches in Danvers, Manchester, Wenham and Middleton, assisted on the occasion. The services commenced with an anthem. Prayer by Rev. Mr. Forbes, of Brookfield. Sermon by Rev. Gad Hitchcock, of Pembroke, from 1 Cor. ix. 19 : " For though I be free from all men, yet have I made myself servant unto all, that I might gain the more." Mr. Diman, of Salem, gave the charge; Mr. Swain, of Wenham, gave the fellowship; Mr. Smith, of Middleton, made the concluding prayer ; after which, was an anthem.

The sermon, which was published, was a clear exhibition of the gospel plan as understood by the author, and of the duties of the ministry, affirming that " a slavish submission to human creeds and formularies, and a trembling concern to make them the basis of our discourses to the people, is degrading to the sacred character, an affront to the scriptures of truth, and a contradiction of the fundamental principles of protestantism."

Mr. Chipman survived the ordination of Mr. Hitchcock about four years, and died March 23, 1775, at the advanced age of eighty-five. The parish voted £14 to defray funeral charges. The solemnities of the occasion were such as became the venerable age and estimable character of the deceased. The corpse was carried into the meeting-house, when a prayer was offered by Mr. Hitchcock, and an appropriate ad-

23*

dress delivered by another clergyman present.* On his grave-stone in the old burying-ground of the precinct is the following epitaph in latin, conjectured to have been written by Mr. Hitchcock :

" *To this grave are committed the remains of the reverend and truly venerable John Chipman, A. M. ; a graduate of Harvard College, and for more than fifty-nine years the faithful pastor of the second parish in Beverly ;—a man eminent for solid powers of mind and useful learning, and particularly distinguished by his acquaintance with the Scriptures ; serious and pungent in preaching the word ; penetrated with love of the religion of Jesus, and by his own example teaching others its precepts ; in presiding over the church, vigilant and upright ; to all the flock, benevolent and just; embracing from his soul the good of all sects; remarkable for the performance of mutual and social offices ; in his family an example of every christian virtue ; far from being inflated by prosperity ; most patient in adversity. Having attained an advanced age, and in the firmest hope of a happy immortality, he expired on the 23d day of March, A. D. 1775, aged 85.*"

---

* It was customary at that period, as it is in some places now, to present mourning rings, gloves, &c. to the near friends of the deceased. In consequence of the scarcity of money during the revolutionary war, the provincial government recommended the discontinuance of this practice. Tradition states that some little delay occurred in the burial of Mr. Chipman, from a strong desire on the part of the executors or nearest relatives, to *revive* the custom at this time. A proviso in the parish grant of the £14 would seem to confirm the tradition.

Mr. Chipman was a native of Barnstable, Mass. and graduated at Harvard College in 1711. He was twice married—first to Rebeckah, sister of Col. Robert Hale, and second, to Hannah Warren, who died without issue, June 24, 1769. By his first wife he had fifteen children, viz. : Elizabeth, Sarah (died in infancy), John, Sarah, Samuel, Rebeckah, Robert (died young), Henry, Biley, Robert Hale, Joseph, Mary, Hannah, Abigail and Benjamin. John, the eldest son, graduated at Harvard College, and engaged in the practice of law. He died suddenly, at Falmouth, Me. of apoplexy, with which he was seized while arguing a cause before the Superior Court, July 1, 1768. He was highly esteemed, and his brethren of the bar erected a monument " to the remembrance of his great learning, uniform integrity, and singular humanity and benevolence." His son, Ward Chipman, graduated at Harvard College, and was distinguished as a judge of the Supreme Court of New Brunswick, and for his great influence with the government at home. Ward Chipman, jr. and grandson of John, also graduated at Harvard College with the highest honors of his class, and was afterwards appointed Chief Justice of New Brunswick. Samuel, second son of Rev. John Chipman, died at St. Martin's, Sept. 19, 1761. He had a son John, who was the father of Rev. Richard Manning Chipman, of Athol.

Mr. Chipman's life and the period of his ministry exceeded that of all the other clergymen in Beverly, and he probably outlived nearly all those who were of age at the time of his settlement. In person he was about five feet eight inches, and of full habit. His pulpit efforts were devout and energetic, and he

appears to have been held in the highest esteem and
reverence by his people, over whom he exercised
an uncontrolled influence to the termination of life.
This influence upon the vicious, oftentimes supplied
the want of correct moral principle, in restraining
them from sinful courses: with the virtuous, it was
a powerful incentive to the diligent performance of
every duty. The manners of the time in which he
lived, allowed him to command that obedience,
which is now only to be sought by the more mild,
though not less effectual means of persuasion. His
influence abroad was commensurate with that exerted at home. He was frequently called to assist in
ordinations, and in the settlement of difficulties that
arose in the neighboring churches. His virtues, though
of the sterner sort, were not the less real. In 1746,
with Mr. Wigglesworth, of Ipswich, he published a
controversial pamphlet, directed against Rev. Wm.
Balch of Bradford, who was accused of propagating
Arminian tenets.* This, with a thanksgiving discourse and a sermon on the close of the year, are the
only writings of Mr. Chipman, so far as is ascertained, that were ever published. The joint production of Messrs. Wigglesworth and Chipman is a pam-

---

* The Rev. Wm. Balch was the son of Mr. Freeborn Balch, who
became a member of the second parish in 1715. He was born in
Beverly, in 1704, admitted to the second church in 1722, graduated
at Harvard College 1724,—was ordained at Bradford, Mass. June 7,
1727 (upon which occasion Mr. Chipman assisted) and died 1792, in
the 88th year of his age. He is said to have possessed strong powers of mind, was mild and conciliating in his manners, and was universally beloved by his flock. He was fond of agriculture, and the
fruit of his orchard was said to be the best in the county of Essex.
His cider, which bore the best price in the market, was called "Arminian cider."

phlet of forty-four pages. It is written in a temperate spirit, and dedicated "To the Ministers and Churches of our Lord Jesus Christ in New England." Mr. Balch's reply occupies ninety-two pages, and displays perspicuity and independence. "It is the grief of my soul (he says) to see the Bible so much neglected, and other books so much made the standard;" and he cannot "help miserably bewailing the state of the reformed churches who stick" where they were left by the reformation.

Mr. Chipman is understood to have been partial to the science of medical astrology. His seventh son, Joseph, came in possession of the parsonage estate, and during a long life of persevering industry and enterprize, did much to improve and beautify its appearance. His widow has in her possession a portrait of Rev. John Chipman. It was taken several years before his death, and is pronounced, by an aged lady now living, who frequently watched with him in his last sickness, an excellent likeness.

Mr. Chipman was pastor of the second parish for nearly 60 years; during which period he received 384 persons into the church, administered the ordinance of baptism to 834 children and 34 adults, united in wedlock 303 couples, and attended 631 funerals. The first couple united in wedlock by him, was Samuel Smith and Elizabeth Hayward, both of Beverly, Jan. 19. 1716; the last, John Dodge 3d. and Mehitable Batcheller, both of this town, Dec. 1, 1768. The first death recorded by him, is Eleanor, child of John Dodge, Jr., Oct. 13, 1715; the last, a daughter of Jonathan Cresey, 1769.

Mr. Chipman solemnized the marriages of six clergymen, viz: Dec. 12, 1727, Rev. Pain Wingate of

Amesbury, to Mary Balch of Beverly. March 12, 1728, Rev. Wm. Balch of Bradford, to Rebecca Stone of Beverly. Oct. 1, 1730, Rev. Joseph Champney to Elizabeth Blowers, both of Beverly. April 21, 1737, Rev. John Warren of Wenham, to Elizabeth Chipman of Beverly. Feb. 14, 1749, Rev. Nehemiah Porter, of Ipswich, to Rebecca Chipman of Beverly. July 3, 1751, Rev. Joseph Swain to Eliza Warren, both of Wenham.

Soon after Mr. Chipman's decease, Mr. Hitchcock's salary was increased to £95. But in consequence of the depreciation of the paper-money then in circulation, it was raised in 1778 to £400 ; in 1779 to £800 ; and in 1780 to £4275, being at the rate of £45 for £1 of his original salary. Some idea of the wretched state of the currency at this period may be formed from the fact, that in 1781 the parish pasture, of a few acres, was rented for £145, and £10,000 were raised to defray the current expenses of the parish for the year.

Mr. Hitchcock was a native of Springfield, Mass., and graduated at Harvard College in 1767. In the first year of his ministry he married Miss Achsah Jordan of Truro. In common with the clergy of his times, he warmly espoused the cause of his country. In 1777 he entered the army as chaplain, though he was not dismissed until 1780. The following letters, addressed, while in the public service, to his intimate friend, Josiah Batchelder, Jr., are here preserved as interesting memoranda of that important period :

VALLEY FORGE, May 15, 1778.

DEAR SIR:—I most heartily congratulate you on the agreeable face cast on our affairs by the equitable treaty of amity and commerce with France, which gives general satisfaction, and was received here with a *feu de joie*. Our troops are in high spirits after the distressing sufferings of the winter, which nothing could equal but the unparalleled patience with which they were endured. The noble commander-in-chief, whose heart ached to see it, says they deserve every thing from their country. I wish their merit might be rewarded. It gives me pain to see the nakedness of many of the soldiery. The clothing is but little of it come in yet. Numbers of our brigade are destitute even of a shirt, and have nothing but the ragged remains of some loose garments as a partial covering.* But this is more tolerable now than when colder. We have no prospect of clothing for more than three regiments of the brigade, and I never expect to see the troops of our State furnished till there is an agent appointed for that purpose, as the other States have, to see it delivered to our men. I hear the town's clothing is on the way; so I hope the shame of our nakedness will not long appear. Great improvements are making in the discipline of the army—several hours every day being devoted to that purpose. Our strength increases faster in this way than by the addition of numbers. We lay very quiet in camp—very little skirmishing, of late, between parties. The enemy lately burnt two frigates up the river, and did some other mischief. 'Tis a disagreeable thought, that the price of necessaries in Massachusetts, where they abound, is much higher than in these [middle] States, for which they are greatly reflected on. Our living in camp is comfortable. My compliments to all friends. Please to accept, and divide with your lady, the sincerest regards

Of, sir, your most humble servant,

E. HITCHCOCK.

CAPT. BATCHELDER.

---

* In a letter from Quartermaster Jonathan Conant, dated at Valley Forge, Jan. 5th, 1778, he says, that nothing "except grace" is more wanting in the army than clothing; and adds, "I am sorry to say it, our regiment goes by the name of the ragged regiment."

CAMP GREENWICH, July 23, 1778.

DEAR SIR :—Your favor in answer to mine, I received some time since. I am happy to inform you that the state of the troops, as to clothing, is much better; their spirits, as usual, good. After a long and tedious march of more than two hundred and twenty miles, in the excessive heat of summer, the successful action of Monmouth rewards every toil. Mr. Conant and the other gentlemen will give you a particular account of matters. I must congratulate you on the present happy state of affairs, to which the friendly disposition of France, in part, contributes. Their powerful fleet you have doubtless a particular account of. I hope the happy period is approaching, when peace will smile upon us, though it may be at the expense of the peace of Europe, and we may be called to carry war into the extremes of the continent.

The court passed a resolve to present the officers with two shirts, shoes and stockings. 'T was to be supposed the things presented would be agreeable to the character of those to whom offered; but many of each have been sent, bearing no proportion, in quality, to the town's clothing to soldiers. I have mentioned these things from an earnest wish that all occasion of bickering between those gentlemen and their brethren may by some means be prevented. By being in the army, officers cultivate tender notions of honor; and this is highly necessary for the government and well-being of it.

I hope, if God please, to see you and my other friends, after having seen New York and a total demolition of the British army there. Wishing health and happiness to you and family, to whom present my regards, and to other friends, I am, with respect, sir,

Your friend and humble servant,

E. HITCHCOCK.

CAPT. BATCHELDER.

The following partakes of the gloom that hung over the prospects of the army at the time of its date :

WEST POINT, July 13, 1779.

DEAR SIR :—Your kind favor of June 25th came safely to hand by the last post. It was the more acceptable, as I feared you, among my other friends, had forgotten me.

As to the western expedition, it goes on well so far. Gen. Sullivan, with the middle division, was at Wyoming the last accounts we had, and Clinton with his brigade was crossing the country from Cherry Valley via lake Otsego, to join him. One hundred and twenty of the remnant of the Onandago tribe joined him on the way. The whole country, 'tis said, are greatly alarmed. The Seneca nation will be the first and principal object of their operations. The accounts of our success in the back parts of Virginia, you will have in the papers. They are at a great distance, and do not so immediately affect us, but are of great consequence to that State. The affairs of South Carolina are uncertain. Our success there, I believe, has not been equal to common report. Ignipotent Tryon, with a band of furies, makes shocking havoc on the Sound. New Haven is sacked, some of its inhabitants murdered, and a few houses burnt. Fairfield, the handsomest town in Connecticut, is in ashes, the people cruelly treated, and some of the fair sex, 'tis said, carried off. Yesterday, they landed an army of 4000 at Norwalk, marching from the main body, to unite and facilitate their operations. The militia flock in fast. Gen. Heath, with the two Connecticut brigades, marched from us last Lord's day, to operate with them against these enemies of God and goodness, yea, of humanity itself.

'Tis unhappy that Gen. Washington has not been enabled by the country to afford them more assistance from his little army. As one plan of the enemy is to draw him from protecting this post, he will be on his guard till it is rendered so strong in works, that a garrison will be sufficient to cover it with the aid of militia, on emergencies. A vast deal of work is necessary to put it in such a state. We never fail to pay dear for our supineness, dreaming of peace when there is no peace.

No period of the controversy has appeared to me more critical and alarming than the present. The country is asleep, to appearance totally inattentive to what ought to be their grand object—

24

defence.   The currency is on the eve of destruction.   The army
is groaning under an unjust and unsupportable proportion of the
burden, entirely neglected by their brethren in the country.   Officers are daily resigning, soldiers are frequently deserting, our
troops are falling sick faster than I ever knew them to do for want
of the means of health, their fatigue being very hard.   No vegetables, acids, or spirits, are to be had.   'Tis very little, except
beef, bread and water, that any of us can get to live on.   For
more than three months no stores from our State have been furnished us.   Every circumstance forbidding our continuance in the
service, that falls within the limits of imagination, takes place with
us.   'Tis the united voice of all our officers, whose circumstances
will permit them to tarry so long, to wade through the fatigues
and distresses of this campaign, and then retire from the service;
but it has been hard to prevail on many to tarry so long.   A number think they can't, and are now urging for resignations.

The above are no chimeras of my own brain, but facts of public
notoriety, which will soon be represented to Court in form, by the
officers of our line, who feel in the most poignant manner the evils
mentioned.   We are sensible many difficulties attend the movement of government, and that the depreciation of our medium has
had a great hand in embarrassing them; but that our friends at
home should abound in the comfortables and luxuries of life, and
we be wholly destitute, seems not to be equal; nor do we know
how to account for it, but by setting it to the score of inattention.
We conceive it would have been the easiest method government
could have taken, to make up, at least in part, the depreciation of
the currency to us, to afford ample supplies in the small-store way,
with which the country abounds, and of which we have been in
want most of the time since we came out.

I write with the more freedom, sir, as I address a public officer
whose well-known attachment to the rights of the army leads him
to wish for correct information of their state.   That which I here
give stands on the broad foundation of truth, is dictated by the
feelings of humanity for others, ardent wishes of safety to my
country, and sincere desires to experience, in common with my
brethren, that relief for which our situation loudly calls.

It gave me great pleasure to hear of your appointment to the
committee of supplies.   I trust your exertions will not be wanting

for us, and that all just grounds of complaint will be removed. It would be a great alleviation to the hardships of camp life, if we were furnished, according to stipulation, with the following articles:—tea, coffee, chocolate, sugar, pepper, ginger, mustard, vinegar, dry cheese, port wine, writing paper, ink-powder, wafers and wax, shoes, stockings, (a proportion of them fit for officers,) linen, thread, silk and trimmings of various kinds; soap much wanted, and rum, the least useful of all these articles. Many things have doubtless escaped my mind, which may be suggested to yours. The small quantity of those articles we are able to command in this vicinity, soon consumes our wages, and leaves us far from a supply.

I long to see my countrymen reanimated and inspired with that spirit of virtuous patriotism, which at first fired their breasts and invigorated every nerve in the common defence. Till then we look in vain for peace. Without this, we may expect desolation, like a flood! Wishing that the blessing of heaven may attend you and family,

I am, sir, your obedient servant,

ENOS HITCHCOCK.

The next letter is written under a brighter sky.

WEST POINT, Oct. 12, 1779.

DEAR SIR: My last contained many gloomy truths. We had for a long time been extremely destitute, which discouraged numbers; resignations therefore became frequent, and I am sorry to say, they are not quite out of fashion yet. Two captains in our brigade have resigned this week on receipt of intelligence of the disagreeable condition of their families at home. . . . . . Our small supplies have afforded great relief. The 27th August we received the first for the season, about ten loads. These furnished one pound of sugar and a quarter of a pound of tea to a ration. The 18th September we received half a pound of sugar and the same of coffee to a ration. We have received eighteen or twenty loads, and hear of more on the way.

There is a pleasing change on the face of affairs, not only abroad but at home. . . . . . We are big with expectation of some great event. By the brisk and rapid preparations now making, we apprehend a speedy and general movement of the army. I conclude it depends on Count D'Estang, who is hourly expected. A great many pilots are sent off to go on board his fleet, and a large number of flat-bottomed boats are building with all possible despatch, to carry troops. Our light infantry lay within a few miles of Stony Point, and I suppose will open batteries upon it soon. The season is so far advanced as, I fear, to interrupt if not prevent the Count's operations this way.

The affair of the Penobscot is only a little spot on the fair face of a successful campaign; and as an inquiry is making into it, when, I presume, truth will be brought to light, let a veil remain on it till judicially removed. It has been too common to prejudge, censure and condemn.

I sometimes indulge a thought that we may see New York this fall, but dare not harbor it. . . . . . Is it possible for me to return while these things are in agitation? I have seen my country, and the army in particular, in deep distress. I have suffered with them. Can I leave them when they hope to give a blow that will do honor to themselves, and render essential service to their country? But I must not anticipate too much. It depends on so many contingencies that the whole may fail. I expect to see home early in November if these operations do not take place; if they do, 'tis uncertain when.

You have, doubtless, heard of a second freight of Germans carried into Philadelphia. Our friends are all well in camp. Please give my regards to Mrs. Batchelder and such friends as think me worth inquiring after.

I am with respect and affection, sir,

Your obedient servant,

ENOS HITCHCOCK.

In 1780, Mr. Hitchcock was chaplain to Gen. Patterson's brigade. While connected with the army, he preached occasionally in Providence, R. I., where, after the army disbanded, he received a call to settle, and was installed Oct. 1, 1783. He died Feb. 27, 1803, in the 59th year of his age. He was a good preacher, a sensible and learned divine, a man of active benevolence, and took a deep interest in the education of youth and the establishment of free schools. He bequeathed $2500 at his decease, for the foundation of a ministerial fund in his society in Providence. He published a book of catechetical instruction and forms of devotion for children and youth—Charles Worthy, or the Memoirs of the Bloomsgrove family ; a work on education in two volumes, and a sermon at the dedication of his meeting-house.

From Mr. Hitchcock's dismission until 1787, the pulpit was supplied by Revs. Obediah Parsons, John Cleaveland and Daniel Story, when Mr. Daniel Oliver received and accepted a call to settle. His ordination took place Oct. 3. The council consisted of seventeen churches, viz : those under the pastoral care of Rev. Messrs. Wadsworth and Holt, of Danvers, Swain of Wenham, Parsons of Lynn, McKean of Beverly, Hopkins and Barnard of Salem, Frisby of Ipswich, French of Andover, Forbes of Gloucester, Morrill of Wilmington, Breck of Topsfield, Cleaveland of Chebacco, Robbins of Plymouth, Smith of Middleton, Dana of Ipswich, and Cutler of Hamilton. On the day of his ordination he was received to this church, by letters of dismission and recommendation from the second church in Boston. In *doctrine*, Mr. Oliver is understood to have agreed with Hopkins, and shortly after his ordination drew up a *new confession of faith*, which, by a vote of the church, was substituted for Mr. Chipman's platform, as already noticed.

In 1791, Mr. Oliver declined giving a receipt in full for his settlement and salary unless the parish would allow him interest upon the principal for the delay of payment of the principal beyond the period when it

24*

was contracted to be paid. This gave offence to
many, and laid the foundation of a series of difficulties, which ultimately resulted in his dismissal. In
1792, several of the disaffected persons seceded, and
joined the Baptist society in Danvers. This led to a
lawsuit, which put the parish to great expense. In
1794, at the request of the parish, Mr. Oliver relinquished £20 of his salary, being probably the proportion formerly paid by the seceders. The next year
his salary was voted in full. The difficulties just
alluded to, now assumed a more decided character.
March 29, 1796, the parish refused to vote Mr. Oliver
his salary, and instead thereof appointed a committee of eleven persons to request him to resign. Parish
and church meetings were frequently called, and
various methods suggested to accomplish a final ad-
justment of the difficulties, but without success, until
1797—when a council was convened, the complaints
and grievances of both parties were fully investigated
and discussed, and a final separation was effected
upon specified conditions. Mr. Oliver's salary was
continued to him up to August 5, 1797. The use of
the parsonage lands was continued to him for the
current year, and in 1798, $300, the award of the
referees, was paid him. He died at Roxbury, September 14, 1840, in the 89th year of his age.

After the dismission of Mr. Oliver, the pulpit was
supplied by Messrs. Story, Alden and Micah Stone,
the latter of whom was invited to settle, but declined.
October 13, 1800, the parish, in concurrence with the
church, invited Mr. Moses Dow, of Atkinson, N. H.,
to settle with them, at a salary of $500 per annum
for the first five years, $480 for the sixth, and *after*
that $400 per annum so long as he should continue

with them. This invitation was accepted, and the 18th of March, 1801, assigned for the ordination. The exercises of the occasion were as follows : introductory prayer by Rev. Mr. Adams, of Middleton ; sermon by Rev. Stephen Peabody, of Atkinson, N. H. ; consecrating prayer by Rev. Mr. Frisby, of Ipswich ; charge by Rev. Mr. French, of Andover; right hand of fellowship by Rev. Joseph M'Kean, of Beverly; concluding prayer by Rev. Mr. Webster, of Ipswich.

Mr. Dow continued in the pastoral office here until 1813, when his relations to the parish were dissolved by mutual council. Mr. Dow graduated at Dartmouth college in 1796, and died at Plaistow, N. H., 1837, aged 66. He was highly esteemed as a Christian, as a man of talents, and as a public speaker. The council for dismission, of which the late Rev. Dr. Abbot was scribe, in their result say, " We have long known him, we have long loved and esteemed him ; and we most heartily add our testimonial to this of the church. We believe him to be an able and faithful, a discreet and devoted minister of Jesus Christ ; and while we lament his removal as a great loss to ourselves and this vicinity, we affectionately recommend him to the churches, and devoutly hope that he may soon be placed in a situation where his talents and virtues, his gifts and graces, may be employed for the benefit of many." His publications were : a funeral sermon, 1807, a fast sermon, 1812, and farewell sermon, 1813.

From 1814, to Dec. 15, 1816, the pulpit was supplied by Rev. David Batcheller and others, when a call to settle was given to Mr. Luther Wright, which he declined. Sept. 15, 1818, Rev. Humphrey Clark Perley was invited to settle. He accepted the invitation, and was installed on the 2d Dec. 1818. Eight clergymen were on the council, viz: Rev. Dr. Cutler of Hamilton, Rev. Benj. Wadsworth of Danvers, Revs. Peter Eaton and Isaac Briggs, 1st and 2d parishes in Boxford, Rev. Bailey Loring, Andover, Rev. Abiel Abbot, Beverly, Rev. Mr. Thurston, Manchester, and Rev. Isaac Braman, Rowley. This connexion was dissolved by mutual consent June 13, 1821; and measures were taken to supply the desk during the remainder of the year. August 13, 1823, Mr. Ebenezer Poor received and accepted a call to the pastoral office, and was ordained Oct. 29, 1823. Rev. Mr. Dana of Marblehead, offered the introductory prayer; Rev. Mr. Walker of Danvers, preached the sermon; Rev. Dr. Abbot of the first parish in this town, offered the ordaining prayer; Rev. Dr. Wadsworth of Danvers, gave the charge; Rev. Mr. Oliphant of the third church in Beverly, gave the right hand of fellowship; and Rev. Mr. Sperry of Wenham, made the concluding prayer. The connexion was dissolved at Mr. P's request, in March, 1829. During this and the year following, the desk was supplied by various clergymen.

Mr. Poor was succeeded by Rev. Ebenezer Robinson, who was installed in Oct. 1830. The exercises of the occasion were as follows : introductory prayer by Rev. Mr. Sewall of Danvers; sermon by Rev. Mr. Bartlett of Marblehead; installing prayer by Rev. Mr. Loring of Andover; charge by the same; fellowship by Rev. Mr. Thayer of Beverly; and address to the people by Rev. Mr. Sewall. Jan. 27,

1833, Mr. Robinson requested a dismission, which was granted him. He was succeeded by the present incumbent, Edwin M. Stone.

In 1837, after several meetings for consultation, the parish adopted measures to re-model the meeting-house, which were immediately carried into execution. The original frame was retained, and removed about thirty feet north of its former site. The front is in the Grecian style, neat and tasteful, and shaded by a venerable elm. The interior aspect of the house is very pleasant. There are forty-two pews on the lower floor, and ten slips in the gallery, besides ample accommodations for the choir. The pulpit is of mahogany ; it is of the altar form, open and unique in design. The house is surmounted with a cupola and furnished with a bell.

The alterations were completed in about five months, and are highly creditable to the public spirit of the society. Feb. 1, 1838, the house was opened for public worship with appropriate solemnities, which were participated in by a very large and crowded audience. The prayer of dedication was offered by Rev. C. T. Thayer, of the first church, and the sermon, from Haggai ii. 9, was delivered by the pastor.

When the re-modelling of this house had been determined on, the committee of the fourth congregational society politely tendered the use of their house of worship to the second parish, which was gratefully accepted—the two congregations worshipping at different hours.

Between the first and second churches an uninterrupted and friendly communication has been maintained, from the organization of the latter to the present time ; and soon after the dedication just

mentioned, the first church presented to the second
a handsome silver communion-vessel, " as a token
of the christian harmony and fellowship which has
long existed, and which it is devoutly to be desired
may ever continue, between these ancient sister
churches." This beautiful and touching evidence
of kindly feeling was acknowledged in the following
resolutions :

" *Resolved*, That this church accept the ' token '
of sympathy and fellowship so appropriately offered,
and that we hereby express our grateful acknowledgments for a gift calculated to remind us of our
common sisterhood, covenants and worship.

" *Resolved*, That the cup, which to every follower
of our common Lord and Master is an emblem of
undivided love, union and fellowship, be applied to
the services connected with the most sacred of all
recollections—the blood that was shed and the body
that was broken; and that as often as we drink of
this cup, the spirit of this memorial will bind us together, in the unity of the spirit and the bonds of
peace."

THE FIRST BAPTIST CHURCH

Was constituted, March 25, 1801, of fourteen
members dismissed from the Baptist church in Danvers. The meeting-house, 48 by 45 feet, was erected the same year. In 1832 the house was enlarged
by adding 16½ feet to its length. The locality being
inconvenient for a majority of the society, it was
taken down in 1837, and reconstructed on a more
central site under the direction of Nehemiah Roundy,
Robert Curry, Edward Pousland, John Pickett, Sam-

uel Smith, Benjamin Pierce, Francis Lamson, Andrew W. Standley, John P. Webber and John Meacom.

The house is 62½ feet long and 45 feet wide, and presents a handsome front, ornamented with pilasters. The tower contains a bell weighing about 1300 pounds. The pulpit is of mahogany, and the interior aspect of the house is chaste. The cost of re-construction exceeded $7000.

In September, 1801, the church was admitted to the fellowship of the Warren Association. The first minister was Rev. Joshua Young, who supplied the pulpit from May 7th, 1801, to Dec. 1802, but was not installed. He was succeeded June 15th, 1803, by Rev. Elisha Williams, a graduate of Yale College, whose pastoral relations were dissolved at his own request, Oct. 9th, 1812. An invitation was then given to Rev. Herry Jenks of Hudson, N. Y. and accepted. His settlement was prevented by his sudden decease.

August 14, 1816, Mr. Nathaniel West Williams, of Salem, was ordained, and continued in the office of pastor till Nov. 7, 1821, when, at his own request, he was dismissed. The successor of Mr. Williams was Mr. Francis G. Macomber, a graduate of Waterville College. His health failed soon after his ordination, and at the suggestion of several friends, of whom the late Dr. Abbot was one, he was induced to try the temperature of a southern winter for its recovery. He sailed for Charleston, S. C., where he spent several months, and died of fever July 3, 1827, soon after his return. The late Rev. Joseph Grafton, of Newton, who preached at his ordination, was also called to discharge the melancholy duty of pronouncing his funeral discourse. Mr. Macomber's remains were interred in the first parish burial-ground, near the common, beside those of Rev. Samuel Ingersoll. He possessed an ardent and devout mind. He loved his profession as a high and holy calling, and gave earnest of extended usefulness. He was universally beloved, and his memory is still fondly cherished by many. In the course of his short ministry, forty-two members were added to the church.

Feb. 1st, 1829, Rev. Richmond Taggart, from the State of New York, was chosen pastor, and continued till December following, but was not installed.

June 30th, 1830, Rev. Jonathan Aldrich, a graduate of Brown University, was installed pastor; and, at his own request, was dismissed May 24, 1833.

September 10th, 1834, Mr. John Jennings, from the theological institution at Newton, was ordained pastor. He continued until June, 1836, and was then dismissed at his own request. In the month of August following, Rev. N. W. Williams was requested to return and resume the pastorship, with which he complied; and in March, 1840, at his own request, he was dismissed. November 11, 1842, Mr. Charles W. Flanders, a graduate of Brown University, was ordained pastor. The exercises of the occasion were as follows : introductory prayer and reading the scriptures, by Rev. P. P. Sanderson; sermon and charge, by Rev. Mr. Wayland, of Salem; ordaining prayer, by Rev. Lemuel Porter; right hand of fellowship, by Rev. Mr. Banvard, of Salem; address to the society, by Rev. L. Porter; concluding prayer, by Rev. Joseph Abbot; benediction, by the pastor elect. Several members of this church have been dismissed, to constitute churches in Salem, Gloucester and Wenham.

DANE-STREET CHURCH.

The Dane-street Church was organized November 9th, 1802. The society obtained an act of incorporation March 7th, 1803, under the name of the Third Congregational Society, which name was changed in 1837 to the "Dane-street Society in Beverly." The meeting house was raised in September, 1802, and finished in December, 1803, at an expense of between $6000 and $7000. The dedication sermon was preached by Rev. Samuel Worcester, D. D., of Salem. The house was 64 feet long and 50 feet wide, with a porch at each end, from which were entrances to the floor and flights of stairs to the gallery. There was also an entrance to the body of the house from the south side. At the western end, a tower rose about twenty feet above the main building, in which, about 1815, a bell was placed weighing 1143 pounds.

In the winter and spring of 1831, to accommodate an increasing congregation, some important alterations and improvements were made, which rendered the house much more convenient. On Saturday night, Dec. 8th, 1832, between 10 and 11 o'clock, a fire was discovered on the lower floor, near the entry, and in the balcony. The firemen and other citizens, with engines and fire apparatus, proceeded immediately to the scene of conflagration, but their efforts were unavailing, and the edifice was entirely destroyed. A reward of $500 was offered by the parish committee, but nothing conclusive, as to the origin of the fire, was ever elicited. As no meeting had been held, and there had been no occasion for a fire during the week, it was suspected to be the work of an incendiary.

In 1833 a new house was erected, by shareholders, on the same site, 73 feet long and 63 feet wide. The architecture is a mixture of Gothic and Ionic. It is a convenient edifice, and its frontal view, with pillars, presents an imposing appearance. The house, including a fine-toned bell weighing 1600 lbs., cost about $10,000.

The first minister of this church and society was Rev. Joseph Emerson.

Mr. Emerson, the son of Daniel and Ama Emerson, was born in Hollis, N. H., October 13th, 1777, and at his birth was devoted in heart by his father to the ministry. Of this he was early informed, and the impression no doubt had some influence in forming his character. His constitution was greatly impaired by a complicated disease with which he was attacked when about six months old, and which lasted more than a year. In childhood he was distinguished for vivacity, regard for truth, and frankness in expressing his opinions. A vein of pleasantry ran through his whole life, but well subdued and modified in maturer years. In person he was tall and slender; complexion dark, eyes hazel, and expression mild. His motions were quick, but not strong; and in the latter part of his life he was bowed and emaciated by disease.

Mr. Emerson pursued his preparatory studies at the academy in New Ipswich, N. H., under the direction of Mr. Hubbard; and in 1794, in the seventeenth year of his age, entered Harvard University; and though, during the period of his college life, he was subjected to much severe illness, he graduated with a good character for scholarship. While at

Cambridge, his mind received strong religious impressions, and in 1797 he made a public profession of religion, by uniting with the church in his native town.

After leaving college, Mr. Emerson took charge of the academy in Framingham, where he continued about a year, and then removed to Franklin to pursue the study of divinity under the direction of Dr. Emmons. In 1800 he returned to Cambridge, with the intention of remaining six months as resident graduate of the college. While residing with Dr. Emmons he received, through President Willard, the offer of a tutorship, which he at first declined, but at length accepted. Having been approbated, he preached in various places, though still pursuing his professional studies. In March, 1803, he was engaged for six weeks in this town, and in June following received a call to the pastoral care of the third congregational society, which, after prayerful consideration, and counselling with christian friends, he accepted. His ordination took place on the 21st September. The exercises were introduced by a pertinent and solemn address to the crowded assembly, from Rev. Mr. Hopkins; Introductory prayer, by Rev. Mr. Kellog; sermon, by Rev. Dr. Emmons, from Eph. iii. 10; consecrating prayer, by Rev. Mr. Spring; charge, by Rev. Dr. Dana; fellowship of the churches, by Rev. Mr. Worcester; concluding prayer, by Rev. Mr. Bailey.

Soon after his ordination, Mr. Emerson was married to Miss Nancy Eaton, of Framingham, a former pupil and friend, who, by education and temperament, appeared singularly qualified to promote his literary and religious plans, as also to ensure domestic enjoyment. But this " treasure in an earthen vessel" he was not permitted long to possess, as, in less than a year from the consummation of their union, Mrs. Emerson died, having just entered her 26th year.

In the summer of 1805, Mr. Emerson was again married to Miss Eleanor Read, of Northbridge, who was distinguished for energy of character and superior conversational powers. By this marriage he had one child, a daughter, who was early called to mourn a mother's loss. She died at Leicester, Nov. 7th, 1808, where she had gone for the improvement of her health. This affliction was severely felt by Mr. Emerson, but in the religion he professed he found a present and efficient support. His third wife was Miss Rebecca Hasseltine, of Bradford, Mass. to whom he was married in 1810, and by whom he had several children.

Mr. Emerson's ministry in this town was active and successful. Beside his ordinary pastoral duties, and the labor incurred in carrying out various plans for promoting the good of his charge, he devoted much attention to the subject of education, in which he felt an enthusiastic interest, and also prepared for the press the Memoir and Writings of Miss Fanny Woodberry, the Evangelical Primer, and several other works.

In 1811, Mr. Emerson's right wrist was affected by a disease that disabled him from using his pen. It settled afterwards in the left wrist, and finally in both ancles, so that it became necessary for him to sit while performing the duties of the pulpit; and the state of his health, in 1816, was such as to require, in his judgment, a release, for a time at least, from professional labor. On the 21st September, just thirteen years from the day of his ordination, his pastoral relation was dissolved by mutual council.

" This crisis was doubtless extremely trying both for him and for his affectionate people. It was sundering the bonds of first love on both sides, as he was their first minister and they his only people. Still, the severity of the shock was much broken by a long and gradually increasing anticipation of its necessity."

After the dissolution of this connexion, Mr. Emerson sailed for the south, where he passed the winter, with the hope of improving his health. In Wilmington, N. C. he became a member of the masonic fraternity, and, on the 1st Jan. delivered an occasional sermon before the freemasons in that place. He also preached on several other occasions, and received numerous tokens of affection and regard. In Charleston, S. C. the following June, he delivered a course of lectures on the Millennium, which was published.

After his return from the south, Mr. Emerson established a literary seminary at Byfield, and, in the ensuing winter, delivered a course of astronomical lectures to a popular audience in Boston. From Byfield he removed to Saugus, where he continued his school. In the autumn of 1823, the state of his health requiring another voyage to the south, he sailed for Charleston, where he passed the winter in the society of kind friends, "forming plans and projects" for the future. On returning to Saugus, he continued his seminary through the summer, but his feeble state compelling him to relinquish it, he removed to Weathersfield, Con. In 1829, he visited his friends in Beverly, and delivered a course of lectures on history. The winter of 1830 he spent in Charleston, S. C. and repeated his historical lectures. On his re-

25*

turn, he again visited Beverly, and gave a course of
familiar lectures on Pollock's Course of Time. His
literary labors were continued till near the close of
his life, which terminated at Weathersfield, about
midnight, May 13, 1833, in the 56th year of his age.
He died without a struggle, and "peace—more than
peace." were among the last words he was heard to
utter.

Mr. Emerson is remembered by his numerous friends
with a more than ordinary depth of friendship. On
some occasions he was inclined to reserve, but generally the natural enthusiasm of his nature imparted
a peculiar charm to his conversation, and made him
a most welcome guest and desirable companion. As
a student, he was diligent almost beyond the bounds
of prudence, and the rapidity with which he multiplied plans for the moral and intellectual improvement of mankind is a sufficient evidence of the activity of his mind. As a teacher of youth, he was
original, practical and successful, and deeply interested in the moral culture of his pupils. As a man,
"he knew not how to dissemble nor to wear a
mask.   As a Christian, he was characterized for the
habitual fervor of his devotional feelings, an earnest
love of truth, a deep-wrought humility, and a warm
and expanded benevolence." *

Mr. Emerson was succeeded in the pastoral office
in this place, by Rev. David Oliphant. The services
of installation took place Feb. 18th, 1818, in the following order : Introductory prayer by Rev. Mr. Dana ; sermon by Rev. Dr. Porter ; consecrating prayer
by Rev. Mr. Thurston ; charge by Rev. Mr. Worces-

* See Life of Rev Joseph Emerson, by Prof. Ralph Emerson.

ter ; right hand of fellowship by Rev. Mr. Emerson; concluding prayer by Rev. Mr. Edwards. Mr. Oliphant was dissmissed, agreeably to the result of a mutual council, in 1833, and Oct. 13th, 1834, Mr. Joseph Abbot was ordained pastor of the church and society, at which time the present meeting-house was also dedicated. The exercises of the occasion were as follows : Introductory prayer by Rev. Dr. Dana, of Newburyport; reading selections from the Scriptures by Rev. M. March, of Newbury; prayer of dedication by Rev. Leonard Withington, of Newbury; sermon by Rev. Professor Ralph Emerson, of Andover Theological Seminary, from John iii. 29 ; ordaining prayer by Rev. Mr. Dana, of Marblehead ; charge by Rev. Dr. Dana, of Newburyport; right hand of fellowship by Rev. Mr. Ober, of Newbury ; address to the church and society by Rev. Brown Emerson, of Salem ; concluding prayer by Rev. Mr. Emerson, of Manchester ; benediction by the pastor elect.

FARMS CHURCH.

THE Farms Church was organized in 1829, for the better accommodation of the families residing in that part of the town, who were living from four to five miles distant from the meeting-houses in Beverly ; and September 23d, Mr. Benjamin Knight was ordained as their pastor, in the meeting-house of the first parish. The introductory prayer was offered by Rev. Mr. Robinson, of Rowley ; sermon by Rev. Mr. Millard, from the State of New York ; ordaining prayer, by Rev. Mr. Kilton, of Salem ; right hand of fellowship, by Rev. Mr. Pierce, of Essex. The name assumed by the church, was *Christian.* In January, 1830, their meeting-house was dedicated to the public worship of God. This house is of brick, about forty feet square, and contains forty-four pews on the ground floor, besides six in the gallery. The cost was about $1600. August 4, 1831, the first church presented this church a silver tankard, with the following inscription : " The gift of the First Church in Beverly to the Church at Beverly Farms." The present was suitably acknowledged in a letter from the pastor. Mr. Knight afterwards united with the Baptist denomination, with which the church is now in fellowship, and in 1834 or '35, his pastoral relation was dissolved. His successors have been Rev. Mr. Gilbert, Rev. P. P. Sanderson and Rev. Sumner Hale.

FOURTH CONGREGATIONAL CHURCH.

The Fourth Congregational Church was organized September 1, 1834, and the society December 11th following. The corner-stone of a new meeting-house was laid, and the frame erected, September 6th, 1836, on which occasion a prayer was offered by the pastor, Rev. John Foote. The house was consecrated December 29th, the same year. The services on the occasion, besides appropriate music, were as follows : Introductory prayer and reading select portions of the Scriptures, by Rev. E. P. Sperry, of Wenham ; prayer of dedication, by Rev. Joseph Abbot, of Beverly ; sermon, from Psalm lxxxiv. 2, 3, by Rev. Brown Emerson, D.D. of Salem; concluding prayer, by Rev. John Foote. The exercises were interesting and appropriate, and were participated in by a large assembly.

The meeting-house, which presents a neat appearance, is located opposite the house formerly the residence of Rev. John Chipman. It was erected by Mr. Jacob Dodge, of Wenham, under the superintendence of Messrs. Benjamin Woodberry 2d, Peter Shaw, Samuel Lummus, Francis Woodberry and Charles Moulton. The house is fifty-one feet long, thirty-seven feet wide, and is surmounted by a cupola with pinnacles. It is entered by two doors, and contains forty-six pews, besides six slips for the choir. The whole cost, including the site, was about $2,500.

WASHINGTON-STREET SOCIETY.

THE Washington-street Society was formed in 1836. The meeting-house was raised September 5th of the same year, on which occasion religious services were performed by Rev. David Oliphant, formerly pastor of the Dane-street church. This house was built by William Webber and Benjamin P. Kimball, under the superintendence of Jonathan Batchelder, Philip English and Ezra Ellingwood. It is 77 feet long and 52 feet wide. The pulpit is of mahogany, and the whole interior arrangements are neat and convenient. A handsome Grecian portico ornaments the front, and the cupola contains a bell weighing 1738 pounds. The whole cost was $9387 33. The house is eligibly situated on Washington-street, the appearance of which it greatly improves.

The church was constituted February 8th, 1837. and March 29th following, the meeting-house was dedicated to the service of God,—on which occasion an appropriate discourse was delivered by Rev. Worthington Smith, of St. Albans, Vt. from Gen. xxviii. 17. On the 3d of January, 1838, Rev. William Bushnell was installed pastor of the church and congregation. The interesting solemnities were as follows : Introductory prayer by Rev. Mr. McEwin. of Topsfield; sermon by Rev. William Williams, of Salem; installing prayer by Rev. Brown Emerson, of Salem; charge by Rev. Robert Crowell, of Essex : right hand of fellowship by Rev. Joseph Abbot, of Beverly; address to the people by Rev. Milton P. Bramin, of Danvers; concluding prayer by Rev. Samuel Worcester, of Salem. May 9th, 1842, Rev. Mr. Bushnell, at his own request, and by advice of a mutual council, was dismissed from his pastoral relations, having previously received an invitation to become pastor of the first church and society in Newton.

Mr. Bushnell was succeeded by Mr. George T. Dole, whose ordination took place Oct. 6, 1842. The introductory prayer was offered by Rev. Mr. Foote. of Beverly ; sermon by Rev. Mr. Blanchard, of Lowell, from Rom. x. 4; ordaining prayer by Rev. Mr. Mann, of Salem ; charge by Rev. Dr. Emerson, of Salem ; fellowship of the churches by Rev. Mr. Taylor, of Manchester ; address to the church and society by Rev. Mr. Worcester, of Salem ; concluding prayer by Rev. Mr. Sessions, of Salem ; benediction by the pastor elect.

A UNIVERSALIST SOCIETY was organized in 1839, and meetings are occasionally held in the town-hall.

SABBATH SCHOOLS.

FROM the establishment of the first church in this town, the religious education of the young was made a part of ministerial duty. The parish minister visited the families of his charge at least once in each year, or gathered the children at some convenient place for catechetical instruction. About the commencement of the present century this practice, owing probably to a diversity of views concerning the manuals used, fell into disuse, and nearly the whole responsibility devolved on parents and guardians. The devout and conscientious among them faithfully executed their trust; but still many youth were found to be growing up under no other religious influence than that resulting from public worship on the sabbath, which, as it was not always seconded by moral precept through the week, often failed to produce its legitimate and happiest effect. The evil resulting to society from the neglect of domestic religious instruction, was felt and acknowledged throughout the country. As the interest deepened for the moral improvement of the rising generation, various plans were suggested and temporarily adopted. The sabbath-school system originated by Robert Raikes in England, for the benefit of the neglected children of his neighborhood, now began to attract public notice, and one of the earliest trials of it in New England was made in this town. In 1810, two ladies of the

first church (Miss Joanna Prince, now Mrs. Ebenezer
Everett, of Brunswick, Me., and Miss Hannah Hill,)
collected a number of children and commenced a
Sunday-school. Their efforts were crowned with
entire success, and they before long enjoyed the pleasure of witnessing the establishment of similar institutions in each of the religious societies in town.
The number of pupils and teachers connected with all
the schools, is between eleven and twelve hundred,
and the catalogues of the different libraries present an
aggregate of nearly 2000 volumes.

The importance of Sunday-schools is a point too
well established and too universally admitted, to
require argument or illustration. As related to the
future, their value is incalculable. The field they
open for moral culture is all the most devoted friends
of religious progress can desire. They constitute at
once the fountain of the church and the nursery of
public morals. Among the pleasing incidents in their
history here, is a Union celebration of the Fourth of
July, 1842.

At eight o'clock, A. M., according to previous arrangement, the sabbath-schools connected with the
seven churches, accompanied by their teachers and
respective pastors, entered the public square on the
southerly side of the town-hall, where a stage had
been prepared for the performance of the services of
the occasion, which were participated in by Rev.
Messrs. Thayer, Abbot, Stone and Flanders. After
the singing of a hymn by a large volunteer choir,
an appropriate and impressive prayer was offered by
Rev. Mr. Thayer of the first church. This was succeeded by a temperance hymn, sung to the inspiring
strain of "Scots wha hae." Robert Rantoul, jr. Esq.,

then addressed the teachers and pupils, amounting to between eleven and twelve hundred, and the crowd of spectators, amounting probably to as many more. His subject was the effects of the declaration of independence on us, and its probable effects on our children. He contrasted the present with former methods of celebrating the nation's birth. Formerly our rejoicings were for victories bought with blood—now we triumph in moral victories. He spoke also of the temperance movements as a sign of good, and of the influence of sabbath-schools on the present and future condition of our country. Much, he said, of the present happy condition of this nation was owing to institutions like those assembled around him. Another hymn was then sung, and the services closed with a benediction by Rev. Mr. Flanders.

The scene was one of intense interest. The happy countenances of so many youth hemming the verdant lawn, and the eager gaze of the multitude surrounding the square and thronging the windows of the adjacent houses, formed a picture of surpassing beauty; and as a thousand voices swelled upon the air with melodious sounds, the mind leaped forward with the swiftness of thought to the glorious consummation of prophecy, when the united and innumerable assembly of the redeemed will fill the eternal temple with songs of everlasting praise.

After the exercises on the square were closed, the schools formed in procession, and marching through several streets entered the town-hall, where an elegant collation had been provided, on which a blessing was craved by Rev. Mr. Foote. Here the scene was more animating, if possible, than that just described. The tables were tastefully decorated with flowers,

26

and profusely provided with cake and fruits. The pupils were seated, and served by their teachers, and for an hour or more, a rational and orderly hilarity was indulged, with no other stimulant than cold water. It was truly a spectacle for gratulation and hope, and the enchanting display might incline an imaginative spectator to the suspicion that the " modest inquiry into the nature of witchcraft " put forth by the pious pastor of the first church in 1692, had failed to answer its design, and that the necromantic art still prevailed. It was evident, however, that if such were the fact, the character of enchantresses had radically changed. They were no longer like the " weird sisters " of Avon's bard, performing their orgies in lonely glens and gloomy caverns, or " flying over steeples, towers and turrets," as wayward dispositions prompted. Nor did they resemble those of Salem Village memory, who were said to appear in hideous forms, and torment good people " before their time." Beyond a doubt, the fair enchantresses of the day were of the good genii order, and the exercise of their art to gratify was entirely successful. They had here called up a beautiful reality, the delightful impressions of which time will only serve to deepen. The christian and social sympathies awakened by the occasion will not pass away with the hour that gave them birth. We rejoice to believe that they will have a permanent existence, and produce extensive good.

CONCLUSION.

The changes wrought in two hundred years have not been dissimilar here to those which have marked the progress of civilization elsewhere. The sturdy forests have become fruitful fields. The footpaths of the aboriginal owners have been supplanted by numerous and well-constructed highways; the rude "log cabins" of the early settlers have given place to neat and commodious dwellings; and nothing in its aspect remains to testify that, two centuries ago, the town was a howling wilderness! The habits of the first settlers, if tradition may be relied upon, were simple, and in harmony with the rudeness of their habitations. The conveniences of life were few—its luxuries less. The table presented little that was tempting to an epicurean palate, yet a long and vigorous life and "a short doctor's bill" were doubtless satisfactory equivalents for the "delicate morsels" so indispensable to a modern gourmand. More of the farinaceous and less of the animal entered into the composition of their food. Knives and forks were in limited use, but spoons were in universal requisition. The joint of meat seldom exhaled its savory odour to quicken a sluggish appetite; but the huge pot might be daily seen suspended by "the long trammel" over an ample fire, fulfilling its destiny in blending, with mysterious simmerings, the ingredients which composed the standard dishes of the age—black broth and bean porridge. The popular esculent of the Emerald Isle was but little cultivated, and as little used ; but the emblem of Dutch obesity, commonly known as the Dutch turnip, was a universal favorite both in the field and on the table. Six bushels of potatoes were a sufficient winter's supply for a neighborhood, but fifty bushels of turnips were necessary to the comfort of a single family.

Among the articles not indispensable, that early found grace in the eyes of the provident housewife, the " wooden trencher " holds a conspicuous place. Its neatly sunken interior surface rendered it a convenient substitute for delf or finer potter's ware, and when scoured to almost linen whiteness, and placed before the " good-man " at the hour of repast, it is not surprising that his eyes twinkled with satisfaction. It was not an every-day luxury, enjoyed by the mass, and happy the favored household in humble life who could substitute an article so well contrived, for the square bit of board that served the purpose of a plate. But short-lived was the trencher's triumph. The " good-wife " grew weary of her rustic ware, and soon the ample " dresser " displayed its rows of shining pewter, from the " great platter " down by regular gradation to the little " porringer " with its broad lattice-work handle, combining show with economy, and displacing forever its unpretending predecessor, while the angular shelves of the " bowfat " in the corner of the " clock-room," were graced by a " tea-set " of more brittle ware, used only " for company " or on holiday occasions. These, too, had their day, and a glorious one it was in the house of thrift. But its sun has set. Piece by piece, the pride of the kitchen has sunk into that "receptacle for things lost," the Yankee pedler's wagon, and the workmanship of Liverpool "reigns in their stead."

The sanded floor, so curiously drawn in figures, is no longer the theatre of the house-maid's skill. Paint has usurped her vocation, while a "Wilton," or the manufacture of Brussels, adorns the "best room," with their accompaniments of stuffed chairs, ottomans and sofas. The capacious "settle," too, the birth-place of many a winter evening's tale, is gone. The mammoth fire-place, on whose ample hearth once blazed huge logs and crackling faggots, and within whose deep jambs the youthful household speculated on the distance of the stars that met their upward gaze, has been supplanted by the economical and unsocial stove. The "good-wife" and modest maiden no longer mount the tastefully trimmed pillion, as, at the church bell's bidding, "goodman" and "intended" convey them to the sanctuary. The jolting chair has yielded precedence to the chaise and carriage. The flowing wig and venerable cocked hat, so cherished by ministers, deacons and all high in office, are among the things that were. The huckster's stand, and the portable "bar" emitting its alcoholic fumes, have ceased to collect a motley group of patrons at the church door on ordination days, blending as it were, pandemonium with paradise. Hoops and pattens, silk clocks and topknots, tunics and scarlet riding cloaks, sacks and ruffle cuffs, smallclothes and silver buckles, embroidered vests and neck-ties, powdered hair and

26*

cues, have all mirrored the fashion of their time, and given place to the less stately, but perhaps not less graceful, costume of the present.

To the legendary there are few points of interest in this town, and but little to gratify lovers of the marvellous. It is true, the accusation of witchcraft reached several of its inhabitants and procured their condemnation during the prevalence of that popular frenzy ; but neither of them was executed here or elsewhere, nor is it known or suspected that Kidd or any other bucaniers ever buried any of their ill-gotten booty in the sands of this harbor. Here are neither gloomy caverns nor murderous-looking glens, with which are associated tales of terror and woe. No fortune-teller has ever had habitation here, to give eclat to the annals of mystery, neither has the appearance of a veritable ghost ever been authenticated. In these, and many similar particulars, Beverly must relinquish the palm to other towns. And though it may dissipate the illusion of a well-told story, and take somewhat from the capital of succeeding writers of fiction, as well as lose to the town a certain description of notoriety, regard for truth compels the affirmation that *Gallows Bridge* is a corruption of *Sallows*, (the name of a family early settled in that neighborhood,) and that no execution ever took place in this town.

The inhabitants of this town are characterized for industry, prudence, sobriety and love of order. That they possess a commendable public spirit, the improvement of their streets, churches, and other public buildings, affords sufficient evidence. They have never been eager to engage in extravagant speculations, by which many make unsuccessful "haste to be rich," but have been contented with a safe and sure business, affording moderate and uniform profits. Hence, they have experienced few of those embarrassments by which the prosperity of many places have been seriously affected, while they have built up for themselves a sound and honorable credit. There is nothing peculiar in the address or habits of the present generation, by which they are distinguished from other towns in the county. The anecdote related, of the vessel sailing from this port making signal of distress, when within three days of her destination, in consequence of having but three barrels of beans on board, though plentifully supplied with other provisions, was doubtless intended as a pleasantry upon the supposed unusual consumption of that article here; but, like many other fictions, has not the merit of a fact to give it point.

Instances of litigation in this town have been few. The late Nathan Dane, who for many years had the entire business, observed some time before his decease, that his receipts for practice as a lawyer, in Beverly, had never been sufficient to pay his annual bill for fuel. So reluctant have the citizens generally been to adjust their difficulties by legal process, that no member of the profession has ever obtained a livelihood here from his fees alone. Criminal prosecutions have also been rare; and it was recently remarked, by a distinguished member of the Essex bar, as a singular fact in his experience, that during a practice in the courts of nearly forty years, he had never known a native of Beverly convicted of any heinous crime.

The clerical profession has ever sustained here a high character for talents, piety and patriotism. The

records of the town, and of the parishes, show that
the clergymen took enlarged views of their duties
and responsibilities as pastors and citizens; and that,
besides the labor they devoted to the cause of education, their services were frequently required by the
town in the transaction of important public affairs.

It is pleasant and instructive to contemplate the
character of the generations who have lived here
before us. For the most part, they were a pious
people, and mingled the religious sentiment with all
their acts. Their numerous fasts declare with what
constancy they relied on an interposing providence
in every scene of trial and hour of calamity. They
loved the house of God, as the place in which they
might feel the divine presence, and improve their
hearts, refresh their spirits, and be disburdened of
their sorrows. To them and their household, the
sabbath was a day of sacred rest. Before sunset on
Saturday, the toils of the week were closed. The
meat and vegetables were brought from the cellar
and prepared, as far as possible, for the Sunday dinner; and when the sabbath sun arose, the stillness of
the day was not permitted to be disturbed by unne-
cessary noise. No member of the family was excused from "meeting," except for sickness; the bible
and religious books engaged the attention of each between the seasons of worship; rambling in the fields,
riding for pleasure, and visits, were prohibited; the
children were "catechised," and questioned concerning the sermon; and at an early hour retired to repose. They were a prayerful people, and there were
but few dwellings in which a family altar was not to
be found. They sincerely desired to train their families in the nurture and admonition of the Lord; and

though some may think the means employed were not always the best adapted to accomplish the end, or may smile at their "puritan strictness," it is a point worth considering, how much is likely to be gained to morals by a less scrupulous sanctification of holy time.

The religious character of preceding generations has doubtless contributed essentially to the soundness of moral sentiment at the present day. The direct influence of Christianity on the habits of the inhabitants of this town, is visible and general. The number who habitually absent themselves from public worship, is comparatively small; and the institutions of religion are, for the most part, liberally sustained.

To the young, the pages of the Past are replete with practical suggestions. In the integrity, patriotism, reverence for constitutional law, and piety, of their ancestors, they may perceive the index that points their own course to usefulness, respectability and happiness.

NOTES.

A.—PAGE 27.

" THE battle of Bloody Brook, that fierce onslaught, of which the old record says, with a native poetry, ' Never had this country seen such a bloody hour,' " has been celebrated by one of our native poets (George Lunt) in a ballad, from which are subjoined the closing stanzas :

> " Ah, gallant few ! No generous foe
>   Had met them by that crimsoned tide ;
> Vain even despair's resistless blow,—
>   As brave men do and die,—they died !
> Yet not in vain,—a cry that shook
>   The inmost forest's desert glooms,
> Swelled o'er their graves, until it broke
>   In storm around the red man's homes !

> " But beating hearts, far, far away,
>   Broke at their story's fearful truth,
> And maidens sweet, for many a day
>   Wept o'er the vanished dreams of youth ;
> By the blue distant ocean-tide,
>   Wept years, long years, to hear them tell
> How by the wild wood's lonely side
>   The FLOWER OF ESSEX fell !

> " And that sweet nameless stream, whose flood
>   Grew dark with battle's ruddy stain,
> Threw off the tinge of murder's blood,
>   And flowed as bright and pure again ;
> But that wild day,—its hour of fame,—
>   Stamped deep its history's crimson tears,
> Till BLOODY BROOK became a name
>   To stir the hearts of after years ! "

B.—page 120.

During the revolutionary war, the vessel on board of which a part of the library of the celebrated Dr. Richard Kirwan was shipped for transportation across the Irish channel, was captured by an American privateer. These books were brought into Beverly and sold. A company of gentlemen, consisting of Rev. J. Willard and Dr. Joshua Fisher, of Beverly, Rev. S. Barnard, Rev. J. Prince, Dr. E. A. Holyoke and Dr. J. Orne, of Salem, and Rev. M. Cutler, of Hamilton, became the purchasers; and thus was laid the foundation of the Salem Philosophical Library (probably in the spring of 1781). The Philosophical Library and the Social Library, formed in 1760, were united in 1810, under the name of the Salem Athenæum.

C.—page 156.

Henry Hale, the second son of Robert Hale, sen. was born in Beverly, Dec. 19, 1712. At the age of seven, his father died, and the responsibility of his preparatory studies and collegiate education devolved on his brother, to whom he was tenderly attached. He graduated at Harvard College in 1731, at the age of 19, and was master of the grammar-school in this town one or more years. August 25th, 1735, he was married to Anna, daughter of Benjamin Ober. The time of his death is not known; but his wife was a widow in 1740, in which year she sold an estate to William Bartlett, of Marblehead, for £300. Henry Hale owned a lot of land "at upper side" (probably second parish), and a "right in Gilmantown." In an account current, his brother credits his estate with £7.10 for "his part of the land of Nod, sold to John How." The only remains of Henry, are a few letters written to Col. Robert Hale, while in college.

D.

PROVINCE TAX.—The following table exhibits the amount of the Province tax assessed in various years from 1670 to 1751, with the proportion paid by the county of Essex and by this town:

Years.	Tax Assessed.	Paid by County.	Paid by Beverly.
1670	£1,205 13 0		£14 10 0
1674	1,299 9 2		15 13 0
1675	unknown.		16 0 0
1675–6	1,280 9 11		16 0 8
1692	30,000 0 0	*£4,851 11 6	*297 15 11
1696	9,619 10 0	2,403 0 0	120 0 0
1698	8,168 5 0	1,916 5 0	100 0 0
1702	6,063 14 6	1,400 2 0	68 2 0
1705	22,422 10 0	5,272 10 0	261 0 0
1709	22,778 7 3	5,320 4 2	261 0 0
1710	about same.	about same.	about same.
1711	"	"	"
1712	"	"	"
1713	"	"	"
1714	"	"	125 9 0
1715	11,000 0 0	2,556 14 2	unknown.
1721	6,000 0 0	not complete.	60 18 9
1726	20,000 0 0	4,118 8 8	199 7 0
1730	10,591 18 0	2,063 19 5	97 13 0
1737	48,920 9 3	9,855 13 6	392 4 3
1741	†18,000 0 0	1,823 18 6	70 6 3
1746	3,169 1 3	6,034 2 0	236 11 9
1751	35,685 0 0	6,513 7 0	237 1 0

* Paid on two parts.   † "Present tenor."

E.—PAGE 174.

The following persons belonging to Beverly were committed to Mill Prison, England, during the revolutionary war:—

Michael Down, of brig Rambler, taken Oct. 21, 1779; committed Feb. 16, 1780.

Benjamin Chipman, of schooner Warren, taken Dec. 27, 1777, and committed June 4, 1778.*

Joseph Leach was taken and committed to Pembroke Prison, in 1779, and re-committed to Mill Prison, Oct. 14, 1780.†

Joseph Perkins, Levi Woodbury,‡ Robert Raymond, Matthew Chambers, and Andrew Peabody, of ship Essex, taken June 10, 1781; committed July 21, 1781. James Lovett and Benjamin Sprague, of same ship, committed Aug. 25, 1781.

William Haskell, of the brig Eagle, taken June 21, 1780; committed July 25, 1781. Alexander Carrico and George Groce, of same brig, committed Feb. 6, 1782.

John Baker, of brig Black Princess, taken Oct. 11, 1781; committed Oct. 20, 1781.

John Tuck, Thomas Hadden, Josiah Foster, Hezekiah Thissell, Nathaniel Woodbury and Zebulon Obear, of Snow Diana, taken June 15, 1781, and committed Jan. 23, 1782.

F.—PAGE 41.

Letter from Col. Robert Hale to Gov. Belcher.

May it please your Excellency:

It is not a contempt of the authority of your Excellency and his Majesty's Council, but a hearty desire to the interest of my country, that inclines me steadily to pursue the affair of the Manufactory scheme, in which I am engaged; and as, by your Excellency's proclamation of the 5th instant, *that* is made incompatible with my holding a commission under the government, I do now most readily and cheerfully resign the trust of a Justice of the

* Run-away.
† Entered a man-of-war, with fifteen others, June 5, 1781.
‡ Died, probably in prison.

Peace, which I received by your Excellency's favor, and always endeavored to execute to the honor of his Majesty and the good of his subjects, so far as concerned me.

I am your Excellency's most obedient and

Most dutiful humble serv't,

ROBERT HALE.

To his Excellency Governor Belcher.
Boston, Nov. 10th, 1740.

G.—PAGE 44.

William Shirley, Esq. Captain General and Governor in Chief in and over his Majesty's Province of the Massachusetts Bay, in New England.

[SEAL.]   To ROBERT HALE, Esq.   Greeting.

Whereas the Council and House of Representatives of the Province aforesaid, did, by public resolve or vote, on the 15th day of this month, February, declare their sense of the importance and necessity of an expedition for erecting a strong fortress upon his Majesty's lands near the French fort, at Crown Point, and did likewise, in the same vote, desire me to apply to divers others of his Majesty's governments, and to urge them in such manner as I should think most effectual to join their forces with the forces of this government in such an expedition :—I do therefore, reposing special trust and confidence in your known loyalty, integrity and ability, constitute and empower you, the said Robert Hale, in the name and behalf of this his Majesty's Province, to make application to the government of New Hampshire to solicit the said government to a compliance with the proposals made by the Council and House of Representatives of this Province, and to such other measures for promoting such an expedition as shall appear to you for his Majesty's service, and shall be agreeable to the instructions you may receive from me for your conduct in this affair.

In testimony whereof, I have caused the public seal of the Province of Massachusetts Bay aforesaid to be hereunto affixed. Dated at Boston, the 22d day of February, 1755, in the 28th year of his Majesty's reign.   W. SHIRLEY.

By his Excellency's command:
    J. WILLARD, *Sec'ry.*

CHRONOLOGICAL APPENDIX.

1638. Jan. 22. John Winthrop, jr. had liberty from his father, Gov. Winthrop, to set up salt-works at Rialside, and to have wood enough for carrying on the works, and pasture for two cows.

1655. Jeffrey's Creek is called Manchester.

1667. Nov. 6. The town agreed to lay out the ways, from the meeting-house to the mill.

—— Dec. 10. The church held a fast by order of the General Court, " for the trouble of God's people in England and elsewhere abroad—for the tokens of God's displeasure in this land, in the loss of divers of the vessels by sea, and divers sins abounding; in which day we made it one special part of the work to seek the Lord's favor to look upon the church, to direct and prosper the small beginnings, and continue his presence and mercy with us."

1668. Mar. 26. A general fast observed, "appointed by the council of magistrates, to mourn for profaneness, superstition and popery increasing—prayers for the king and parliament," &c.

1669. Aug. 4. " Fast by the congregation because of immoderate rains, blasting mildew, cold and storms, to find out the cause and desire the removal of God's frown."

—— Aug. 16. " By unanimous consent of the whole congregation, a fast appointed for great sins abounding and breaking forth scandalously in this country— deaths of five ministers in about half a year," &c.

—— Nov. 17. Public thanksgiving to bless the Lord for staying the immoderate rains which threatened to destroy the whole harvest of corn and fresh hay, and for the harvest the Lord hath given.

1670. Apr. 7. " A day of fasting kept by the congregation under a sense of God's frowning dispensations, in taking from this jurisdiction six ministers away from his church by death, in the last year, and permitting those divisions and breaches, which are already begun in sundry churches and feared of more ; and continuing the snow so long on the earth, and the frost in the ground, hindering seed-time, and pinching cattle for want of food ; that the Lord may reform us of the sins we have provoked him by, and return unto our churches in mercy, and reserve for us the appointed weeks of seed-time and harvest, and prevent blighting and mildew this summer, so far as may be for his glory and our good."

—— June 16. A day of fasting appointed by the General Court, observed, on account of prevailing sins.

—— Sept. 22. A fast appointed by the council of magistrates, observed, " because of the low estate of the churches of God all over the world, and the increase of sin and evil among ourselves, and God's hand following us for the same."

—— Nov. 24. A public thanksgiving appointed by the General Court, " for our peace and liberty continued, and the last year crowned with God's goodness in answer of prayer."

1672. Feb. 14. The town contributed £13 towards the funds of Harvard College.

—— Mar. 18. Bounds between Beverly and Manchester settled by agreement.

—— May 15. The General Court granted the town one barrel of powder. John Stone, by vote of the town, desired to keep an ordinary or tavern, one year.

1675. June 29. A fast held by order of the council, upon the rising of Indians about Swansey.

1676. Dec. 5. The town chose two constables, " by reason of the difficulties of the times on account of the Indian war."

1678. John Edwards was allowed £3 for killing three wolves.

1679. Feb. 13. Andrew Elliot and Nehemiah Grover had liberty to cut two loads of timber on the town's common, to be used in building a ketch.

—— Mar. 29. John West presented a flagon to the church, "as a token of his love."

1684. Dec. 4. "John Batchelder and his wife being deceased, gave good hope of their being in the faith, and if they had lived longer, purposed to join in communion with this church, but being prevented by death, their children are subjects of baptism." In 1676, the children of John Dixey, deceased, were baptized on similar grounds.

The town this year voted to purchase land to enlarge the common.

1685. Measures were adopted for laying out the road from the second parish meeting-house to Topsfield.

1690. The selectmen afforded relief to Lawrence Dennis and family, who were sick with smallpox. The town borrowed £48 10s. "to buy great guns and ammunition," and to build a fort for defence.

1695–6. The road between the first parish meeting-house and Manchester laid out two rods wide.

1696. Dec. 22. The town allowed Isaac Woodberry to cut timber for the masts and yards of a vessel he was then building.

1697. Money in the hands of Deacon Hill, contributed to redeem some person from Turkish captivity, not being improved, was devoted to the relief of the poor.

1700. May 2. A storm of rain and hail commenced which continued three days. Many cattle were lost.

—— Sept. 22. Miss Emma Leach, aged 52, and only 25 inches in height, visited Salem and excited much curiosity.

1706. Standard weights and measures provided by the town.

1710. The town paid 3s. 6d. for "treating" the jury and attornies who attended court in a suit with Salem.

1711. Mihil Sallows and Joseph Gray killed by Indians at Winter harbor. Snow fell this winter eight feet on a level.

27*

1712-13.   The town granted a lot of land to the people at the Farms, on which to set a schoolhouse.

1714-15.   Benjamin Dike killed by Indians at Cape Sable.

1715-16.   At a town meeting it was " voted, that votes sealed up and orderly sent into this meeting by persons qualified for voting in said meeting, that cannot attend either by sickness or being removed out of town about their lawful business, be allowed to pass with the other votes of the same nature."

1722.   John Ober chosen town clerk.   He remained in office till 1733, and was again chosen in 1735.

1733-4.   Bartlett-street laid out to the sea at Tuck's Point.

1742.   A person chosen constable was excused from serving, not being able to write or read.   Voted to repair Thissle's bridge.

1746.   Selectmen received £40, old tenor, for the relief of Jane Bartlett, whose husband was in the army at Cape Breton.

1748.   The town voted a bounty of 20s. for old foxes and 10s. for young.

1751.   Mill Lane laid out.

1753.   The town voted a bounty of 2s. on every dog's head brought to the town treasurer.

1754.   Selectmen directed to take measures for the destruction of wolves.   Assessors chosen this year distinct from the selectmen.

1755.   The town having grown more sympathetic towards the canine tribe, a bounty of 5s. " to encourage the keeping of dogs," was severally paid to eighty-eight persons, amounting to £22 lawful money.

1757.   The selectmen licensed a slaughter-house belonging to Benjamin Raymond.   The town hired part of a house for the use of two families of French neutrals.

1765.   Widow Priscilla Trask appointed pound-keeper.

1766.   The selectmen were authorized to purchase a gravel-pit of John Dodge.

1767.   A powder-house built on the south side of the common.

1769. Feb. 11. Harbor frozen over down to Baker's Island.

1775.

Capt. Hugh Hill took and brought into Beverly, schooner Industry, Capt. Francis Butler. The cargo was sold in conformity to existing rules, and the vessel delivered to the order of General Washington for the public service. Robert Haskell, a native of this town, obtained permission of the General Court to return to Yarmouth, N. S., where he resided. The General Court ordered two half-barrels powder to be delivered to Josiah Batchelder, jr. to replace so much loaned the province by the town. The selectmen of Watertown delivered 2½ barrels to Col. Henry Herrick for the use of the town. The town paid for 47 gallons of rum used in building the breastwork at Woodberry's head.

About the last of November, this year, Capt. Manly, in the Lee privateer, captured and brought into Cape Ann harbor the British brig Nancy, bound from London to Boston, laden with warlike stores, among which were 2000 muskets, 2 six-pounder cannon, 3000 twelve-pound shot, 20,000 one-pound do., and a 13-inch brass mortar. The cargo was conveyed to Cambridge for the use of the army, to which it proved a valuable and timely acquisition. The mortar was named the Congress, and was "pronounced to be the noblest piece of ordnance ever landed in America."

1777.

The town voted to give £14 to each non-commissioned officer and private who would enlist in the continental army for three years, or during the war ; and £4 additional to such as had been in the army and would re-enlist. Provision was made for barracks to accommodate the seacoast men stationed at Woodberry's point. £300 were voted to supply the families of the non-commissioned officers and privates belonging to this town, enlisted in the continental army. The next year £200 were appropriated to the same purpose.

—— April 1. The General Court refused the petition of the committee of inspection for leave to sell the coffee that had a long time been stored according to the rule adopted in such cases. Thomas Woodberry and others petitioned the General Court and obtained liberty to send the schooner Swallow to the West Indies with lumber and fish to exchange for molasses, cotton and salt, which were much wanted in town.

1778. Price of labor on the highways fixed at 18s. pr day.

1779. This year forty men from this town were lost at sea, for which reason the town petitioned the General Court to be released from its obligation to furnish the quota required for the army. A sum not exceeding £12000 was voted for procuring men for the army. In succeeding years, sums varying from £5000 to £50,000, were provided for the same purpose. Labor on the highways fixed at 30s. per day.

1780. The selectmen were directed to purchase five horses for the public service. To encourage enlistment, the town offered a bounty of 100 lbs. sugar, 100 lbs. coffee, 10 bushels corn, 100 lbs. beef and 50 lbs. cotton, or £1370 in money ; but this not proving a sufficient inducement, 67 lbs. of coffee were afterwards added, and the bounty in money increased to £1611 4s. Price of labor on the highways fixed at £12 per day. Salt sold for £50 per bushel.

1781. Sept. 15. The selectmen petitioned the General Court to decide whether Beverly or Rowley should have the service of William Campbell, a soldier, who after being hired by Beverly, let himself to Rowley. The constables were directed to receive one silver dollar instead of $75 of the old continental paper, and $1 of the new emission instead of $40 of the old.

1783. French troops passed the night in the second parish, on their way to Portsmouth to embark for France.

1784. Price of labor on the highways fixed at 5s. per day. A building on Woodberry's Point belonging to the town, given to Wm. Woodberry in full consideration for the use of his land, &c.

1785. Four shillings and half a pint of rum allowed by the town for a day's labor on the highways.

1786. Two collectors of taxes chosen. Previously to this, the taxes had been collected by constables.

1787. Bonfires prohibited under penalty of 10s. Selectmen fixed the price of bread at 3 cents and 7 mills per lb. First firewards chosen, viz: Joseph Lee, Moses Brown, Joseph Wood, Andrew and George Cabot.

1790. Town divided into six school districts. Enginemen were excused from serving in town offices. Snow fell this year, Nov. 27, and laid till April 15th following.

1792. Capt. Gideon Rea returned from a fishing voyage in the Bay of St. Lawrence after five months absence, with 122,222 fish, making about 1200 quintals. Mrs. Judith, "the amiable and virtuous consort of the late Col. Ebenezer Francis, died very much lamented," aged 43.

1794. The selectmen were authorized to sell the old schoolhouse in Bass river district. Elias Smith, jr. died in the West Indies, "suffering under British spoliations." Israel Dodge fell dead while driving a team, aged 21.

1795. Jan. 20. William Bartlett, A. B. died, aged 30. Capt. Robert H. Ives died at Lisbon.

1798. The second parish granted a part of the parsonage for a gravel-pit.

1799. The second parish granted the Bass river school district a site for a schoolhouse.

1801. Dodge's Row school district formed. Hon. Israel Thorndike presented the second parish $100.

1802. The town, for the first time, voted to assess the highway tax in connexion with the town tax for general purposes. Farms school district divided.

1803. Washington street laid out.

1806. Widening of the Chebacco road through Dodge's Row begun.

1807. The present mode of warning town meetings by posting notices at each of the meeting-houses, adopted.

1808.   New powder-house built. April 16th, the snow three or four feet deep in many places.

1809. Apr. 17. An infant tied up in a pillow-case found in the river near the bridge.

1811.   The road from Grove's hollow through Rial-side to Frost fish brook, laid out.

1812.   Henry Fornis, his mother and sister, died at the hospital of small pox.

1816.   Juno Larcom, "a half Indian and half negro woman," died, aged 92.

—— July 19. John Joseph, a son of Rev. Dr. Abbot, drowned, aged 4 years and 5 months.

1817. Feb. 14 and 15. Thermometer at 18 deg. below zero.

1823.   Town voted a bounty of 12½ cents per head for all crows killed.

—— Aug. 4. Deborah Larrico killed by lightning.

1828.   The road leading from the main street by Pyam Lovett's house, accepted by the town.

1829. Jan. 12. Mrs. Dr. Fisher died, aged 71.

1834. Dec. 10. Robert Thorndike, a native of Beverly, died at Camden, Me., aged 100 years and 5 months.

1835. Jan. 4. Thermometer before sunrise 18 deg. below zero.

—— Jan. 31. Thermometer before sunrise 58 deg. above zero— sharp lightning and much rain.

1836. Jan. 19. Jonathan Smith died aged 68. He was appointed Justice of the Peace in 1807, and was for many years surveyor of the customs and post-master.

1837. July 6. Barn of Elliot Woodberry burnt, supposed by lightning.

—— Aug. 15. John Huddle killed by the explosion of a rock while in the act of charging.

1838.   Dec. 9, Wm. Leach, grandson of John Leach, died aged 80.

—— Mar. 16. Hannah Hill died.

1841. Aug. 20. Hale Hilton died, aged 81. He was a fifer in Capt. Low's company.

1842. Apr. 25. Joseph Woodberry, a descendant of the earliest settlers of that name, dropped down dead in his yard, aged 75.

—— Aug. Samuel Cole, a revolutionary pensioner, died aged 90 years.

INDEX.

324 INDEX.

Milton Keynes UK
Ingram Content Group UK Ltd.
UKHW012151270324
440282UK00003B/28